A fresh mount—with Erwin E. Smith up. Mr. Smith, who roamed the ranges of the west with a camera in the early days—to win fame for himself as the greatest cowboy photographer of all time furnished many of the pictures which appear in this book.

# CATTLE KINGS
# of TEXAS

*By*

C. L. DOUGLAS

STATE HOUSE PRESS

Austin ★ Texas

1989

Library of Congress Cataloging-in-Publication Data

Douglas, C. L. (Claude Leroy), 1901-
    Cattle kings of Texas / by C. L. Douglas : with a foreword by Lionel Chambers.
        p.    cm.
    Reprint, with new introd. Originally published: Dallas, Tex. : C. Baugh, c1939.


    1. Ranch life—Texas—History. 2. Ranchers—Texas—Biography. 3.
Cowboys—Texas—Biography. 4. Cattle trade—Texas—History. 5. Cattle
breeders—Texas—Biography. 6. Frontier and pioneer life—Texas. 7. Texas—
Social life and customs. 8. Texas—Biography.
I. Title.
F391.D714 1989
976.4'06'0922—dc20                                                          89-21772
[B]                                                                              CIP

Manufactured in the United States of America

State House Press
P.O. Box 15247
Austin, Texas 78761

*Dedicated to*

TAD MOSES AND HENRY BELL

# ACKNOWLEDGMENTS

With the presentation of this book I wish to acknowledge the invaluable assistance given me in its compilation by the following:

The Cattleman Magazine, official publication of the Texas and Southwestern Cattle Raisers Association, for the encouragement and technical advice offered by its editor, Mr. Tad Moses, Secretary Henry Bell, and Mr. Bell's predecessor, the late Berkeley Spiller.

J. Frank Dobie, for his interest and assistance with material relating to Shanghai Pierce and other Coastal Cattle Kings.

John Mackenzie, manager of the Matador Land and Cattle Company, for helping with material otherwise unavailable. Likewise Phil Maverick, John Hendrix, J. Frank Norfleet, W. D. Smithers and Erwin E. Smith.

Miss Harriet Smithers, archivist in the state capitol building, for assistance in research.

And, in particular, those last connecting links with pioneer cattle days who had a tale to tell and gave me opportunity to hear it—Ab Blocker of Big Wells, Col. R. P. Smythe of Plainview, the late Mrs. George Reynolds of Fort Worth, the late Ike Pryor of San Antonio, the late A. P. Borden of Mackey, Jake Rains of the SMS, Willie Le Bauve, and others.

C. L. DOUGLAS

# NEW FOREWORD

In the October 1935 issue of *The Cattleman* magazine, editor Tad Moses wrote:

> *The Cattleman* is embarking on a hitherto untried and pretentious field in beginning in this issue a series of articles on the "Cattle Kings of Texas" by C. L. Douglas of Fort Worth. This work is to be published in each issue of *The Cattleman* beginning October 1935 and ending in August or September 1937. The sum total will be a thick, book length novel of from 100,000 to 115,000 words.
>
> Mr. Douglas' work represents two years of painstaking effort, countless interviews and the ceaseless poring over of old documents, records and scrap books. He has gone to all sections of the state in an effort to unfold the lives and interests of those people who made the name Texas synonymous with the cattle business, Texas' first major industry. His product is highly interesting and to the best of our knowledge an authentic portrayal of the lives of Texas cattlemen represented. Each chapter has been checked and rechecked by various individuals, often relatives and associates of the subject.

Then in the July 1968 issue of *The Cattleman*, editor Paul Horn wrote :

> The late C. L. Douglas, long a contributor to *The Cattleman*, wrote a book *Cattle Kings of Texas* which was published about 30 years ago. The book was dedicated

to Tad Moses, then editor of *The Cattleman*, and Henry Bell, then secretary of the Texas and Southwestern Cattle Raisers Association. It is through the courtesy of Mr. Douglas' widow that *The Cattleman* is reprinting this book in serial form.

It goes without saying that readers of *The Cattleman* admired and respected Mr. Douglas' work. And now in 1989, after reading these chapters once again, I still marvel at what type of special people were these men and women that God designated to build the cattle industry in Texas. The years of working in this business also leads me to marvel at what a powerful writer C. L. Douglas was . . . I wish I could have known him.

Lionel Chambers
Editor
*The Cattleman*

# FOREWORD

In the subconscious thought of the world Texas typifies the cowboy—the last *cavalier*. At the very base of the tap root of Texas' weal is the cow. As has been said

> "Other states were carved or born,
> Texas grew from hide and horn."

When Austin's colonists turned to cattle raising they found, between the Rio Grande and the Red, the greatest cow-pasture known to man. Nature understands no blackouts; heifer calves became cows, they had calves and their calves produced and reproduced, wild and free and highly prolific in the prelude to the most romantic era of American history—the decades of the trail drives.

Of the South, overwhelmed by superior force and greater means but not ravished by civil war, bankrupt but bulging with cattle valueless at home for want of a market but worth a score and ten in the North, Texans drove their only asset to the rail heads of Kansas and to the empty prairies of the West. Hills that for centuries had known only the bellow of the buffalo and the yell of the redman became the sounding board for the *moo* of the Texas cow—the only tide of our civilization that flowed from South to North.

Trail herds went North and cow-dollars came South to build the Texas we now know. Foreign money begged for a taker and the boom was on. Sod-busters, barbed wire and the windmill underwrote the doom of the open range. Out went glamour but in came better beef sires, greater range utilization and efficiency in operation. The old Texas cowman measured his kingdom in size; his 20th Century counterpart in vaulation—he sought to improve what his fences enclosed.

By and large, Texas is a land of powerful contrasts. She sprawls over ten degrees of latitute and there is an average temperature difference of 20 degrees F. from north to south. Rainfall varies from more than 50 inches on the east to less than 10 on the west. Of her landed area of 262,398 square miles, economists estimate that 70 per cent is devoted to grazing, and for all time to come over 50 per cent will nurture the best all-around and cheapest beef producer—grass.

Texas was the natural theatre of existence for the old "cattle king."

> "The King is dead
> Long live the King!"
>
> TAD MOSES
> Editor, The Cattleman Magazine

# CONTENTS

*Changing range—as in the days when Lot took the Jordan Valley and big Abe the Canaan prairies*

Photograph by W. D. Smithers

# Panorama

ABRAHAM AND LOT SPLIT THE RANGE

LONGHORN

● The First Beef Barons
Roamed the Banks of
the Jordan

THERE had been trouble on the Jordan range. Bad blood had arisen between the punchers of the Lazy A and the boys of the LOT, and something had to be done about it if the country west of the river was to escape one of those bloody cattle wars which inevitably send prices tumbling to hide and tallow levels.

The feud had been long smouldering, its historical origin

1

lost even to the memory of the oldest line-riders, but in recent weeks the situation had gone steadily from bad to worse.
Pasture was plentiful and the water good; the steers were fat
and the ponies sleek; but in all this broad and smiling land
there could be no peace while the hands of the two top outfits
were at each other's throats like hungry wolves. The range
just wasn't big enough for both . . .

Big Abram, boss of the Lazy A, realized this as he jogged
over to the headquarters of the LOT. The old man was sick
and tired of the whole belligerent business. He had tried,
time and again, to patch up differences, and so had the boss
of the other herd, but in vain—for cowboys will be cowboys.

Big Abram muttered beneath his breath. He wasn't one
to let a passel of brawling *vaqueros* wreck a well-established
business, and this time he would thresh it out with Old Man
Lot once and for all—yes, by ganny, if he had to split the
range to do it! He, Big Abram, would show them who was
law and order west of the Jordan!

"Lissen here, Jim," he said, as he reined in at the corral
of the rival camp, "th' boys have been scrappin' again and
something's gotta be done. Why, only yesterday down in that
back pasture . . . "

"Git down, Abe, and rest your saddle," said Old Man Lot
by way of greeting. "Git down an' we'll talk things over.
I been figurin' some myself. Been sorta thinkin' about driving down t'wards Sodom."

Throughout the hot summer afternoon they sat in the shade
of the corral, fanned flies, and talked; and, after weighing
each problem carefully, came at last to an agreement with
Lot taking the Jordan Valley and Big Abe the Canaan prairies.

And thus, in the days of Genesis, the first cattle range was
split and the first of the cattle kings made their appearance
. . . beef barons whose work would be to fill the mouths of

a world just learning the taste of a sirloin steak; men whose herds, in later years, would cause the psalming David to sing of "the cattle upon a thousand hills."

But compared with those to come in centuries yet unborn these early ranching kings were pikers. For, as the map of the world spread in fanciful whorls toward the west, the live-stock industry kept pace through an evolutionary process which as a matter of course was to mark it among the greater pursuits of man . . . because where man went the herds came close behind.

Centuries passed, with the hoof marks of shaggy beasts following down the trail of human migration into Eastern Europe, following across the Mediterranean nations and into the mountains of Andalusia until the great Western Ocean, still mysterious and uncharted, blocked the course of further progress. But only for a time. Columbus conquered the Atlantic and in the wake of his caravels followed the first of the *conquistadores*—to settle in Paraguay and Peru, in the West Indies and Mexico; and to found the *ranchos* which ultimately became the forerunners for cattle baronies larger than entire kingdoms in the Old World from which they came.

**The Brand—the cowman's coat-of-arms—was first fashioned by Hernando Cortes**

Among the cattle kings Don Hernando Cortes was one of the first. In the process of beating down the Plumed Serpent of Montezuma's Aztecs to establish the rule of the Spaniard in Mexico, that dour invader took time from the sterner duties of conquest to import from Andalusia a dozen cows and a few choice bulls with which to stock the first of New World *haciendas*. Wisely, he chose for his purpose a hardy breed, identical with the cattle bred on Moorish and Castilian plains, and they thrived . . . increased in number and spread so rapidly through the country, especially with new importations, that Don Hernando began casting about for some means of distinguishing between stock of his own and cattle held by neighbors. Consequently, he fashioned a metal device bearing a marking of his own—a sort of coat of arms— and thus it came to pass that a branding iron was hung for the first time on an owner's door. At least that is the story. Others, like Governor-General Vilalobos, who imported some of the first cattle in 1521, followed suit; and the cow business took on impetus in Mexico.

And then, following the course of Spanish exploration and expansion, the ever-growing herds trailed up the Valley of Mexico toward the plains of Texas-Coahuila on the north; for the wanderers, like the stay-at-homes, liked beef. Not that there was any lack of meat in this new land; there wasn't. The shaggy "hump-backed cows" described by Hakluyt in his *Voyages* were plentiful on the prairies, but somehow buffalo did not please the Spanish palate.

Cattle plodded after Francisco Coronado when, in 1542, he trekked across Southwestern America in quest of Cibola's seven golden cities; they followed on the trail of Onate when he crossed the Rio Grande in 1601; and St. Denis found them when he came in 1716 ... wild Spanish longhorns left to their own resources when the missions of East Texas had been abandoned a few years before. The first settlers from the south also brought herds of their own—small, but quite large enough for personal needs. Gil Ybarho brought a few when he came to settle Nacogdoches; and so did Martin de Leon, who founded the city of Victoria. And there were others— men like Don Jose de la Garza, who established the *rancho* of *Gertrudis*.

Then, with the turn of the 19th century, arrived still other settlers ... the *Americanos*, bringing with them from the east cattle that descended from Mayflower stock from cows transported from the south of England to the settlement of Jamestown, and from Louisiana breeds of French origin. The grass was good and the water plentiful in what is now the south of Texas and here the varied types, with the Spanish predominating, intermingled to create one of the most hardy breeds in livestock—the Texas longhorn steer.

Peculiar to this area alone, he wasn't much to look at, this great beast of the prairies. He was lanky, tough and wiry, with a slender, rangy body and a hammer head surmounted by a set of enormous horns which sometimes attained a spread of six to eight feet; but with all his unsightly appearance he was beefsteak—an animal which was to become the central figure in an industry that would produce more "kings" than all the states of Europe, and which in time would prove the economic salvation of its native Texas.

In the formation of the world's greatest cattle country geography, of course, was a large contributing factor. The range was practically limitless and climactic conditions favorable, but there was also something else—the productivity of the longhorn itself; and the end of the Texas war for independence from Mexico found the range of the border country stocked with hundreds of thousands of cattle, some carrying the burn of the owner's brand, but just as many unmarked "slicks" running free and wild in the open country.

And so arrived in Texas one of the first of those eras in which the extent of a man's poverty was estimated by the size of his cattle herd. The small droves, brought in by the settlers for personal consumption, had developed into something of an economic Frankenstein. Here in a far and remote corner of the world, was enough beef on the hoof to supply a nation, but there was no market. The settlers couldn't sell it and, quite obviously, they couldn't eat it. The situation was puzzling.

The first solution of the problem came with the Gold Rush for California in 1849. James Ellison, who lived in what

is now Gonzales County, bethought himself that the hard-
working miners of the west coastal area might be hungering
for the taste of prime rib roast.  Accordingly he made up a
large herd in the south of Texas and took the trail with two
partners, one McKinley and one Erskine.

Photograph by Erwin E. Smith

*"The Pitchfork Kid"—day herding*

And that was a drive! Across the plains, through the mountains, into the desert nothingness of sand and cacti . . . months
in the saddle behind slow moving longhorns . . . long days
of thirst and heat and danger . . . sleepless nights as Apache
raiders menaced the ambling, shifting herd . . . eternal watch-
fulness when the wolf packs swept out of the darkness to slash
down steers that straggled from the line.

But the firm of Ellison, Erskine and McKinley made it—

and added another kaleidoscopic scene to the panorama of the cattle industry; and even though Indians, wolves and thirst took heavy toll in stock, the owners found good compensation at the end of the trail cut by the wagon wheels of the '49'ers. The miners of Red Gulch, Poker Flat and Frisco really did hunger for beef and to get it they were willing to pay almost fabulous prices.

But few others ever drove the long and weary trail to California, for by the time the pioneering trio reached home a new and easier market had opened, one James Foster having conceived the plan of shipping to New Orleans by boat, with Indianola on the south coast as the Texas terminus. A ship was chartered and the first consignees—Foster, Thomas O'Connor and Captain Abner Kuykendall—realized $10 a head in the Louisiana metropolis; a great price, or so it seemed to the Texans, who were little short of amazed a few months later when buyers paid a top of $16.

### Trail to West and Boat to New Orleans proved that markets could be found

This bonanza, however, was not long lasting; for after a time the New Orleans buyers, with an eye to business, began taking only prime beef and no she stock, a move creating an unhealthy condition. Naturally the culls were left in Texas. The she stock produced, and although the herds began to increase rapidly the quality fell behind the quantity, and prices sagged.

But the trail to California and the boat to New Orleans already had proved one thing—that markets could be found—and the dwellers in the south of Texas began measuring distances to the great overland rail route of the north, the Union Pacific. At the same time the ranch country began extending itself toward the north and west, and the lure of the new industry, which promised large returns to those hardy enough to withstand the ordeal of thousands of miles on the trail, became infectious. Men scrambled to muster herds for the free and open range—the unfenced grazing paradise which belonged to any who cared to take it.

A new panorama was about to open—the greatest and broadest cow country in the history of the world, a vast area covered with individual kingdoms which would in time make the Jordan Valley holdings of Lot and Abram appear, by comparison, as a mere back pasture milking lot. A new empire was in its beginning and the greatest of the "cattle kings," mounted and ready to ride, were in the making.

No man ever has placed on paper the complete and detailed story of the cattle industry; no man ever shall, or can—because the work, if it dealt merely with Texas alone, would be too far-reaching and stupendous for human mind and hand, but in the lives of those who pioneered the business may be found some appreciable estimate of hardships endured, trails conquered, and dangers braved that the steak of the steer might find its place upon the platters of the world.

Texas alone has produced a hundred or more men whose names might be set down as cattle kings, but for the limited purpose of this series only a comparative few will be dealt with; these, however, are representative of the regal circle.

He preferred to be called just "cow man," the early "cattle king." There was something about the latter term he didn't like, but just the same that's what he was—a king as surely as any monarch who ever ruled a nation.

His authority was his word; his sceptre the red hot branding iron; his subjects the cowboy and the longhorn steer; his throne the saddle on which he sat; his kingdom his ranch or range ... often larger than an entire eastern state.

He was, in truth, a king ... and beside him Old Man Lot and Big Abram of the Lazy A were pikers.

# Don Martin
# de Leon

SPANISH DON

BRAND
DON MARTIN DE LEON

BRAND
DON FERNANDO DE LEON

● **Spanish Rancheros cleared way for American Stockmen**

**H**IS MAJESTY, the King of Spain, was a good and gracious monarch, and he was generous.

It was no little thing that he, by the grace of God, ruler of Spain and all her dominions overseas, should be called

9

"the empire builder"—and he was well pleased with himself as he sank into the plush of his Madrid throne.

Like his father and his grandfather before him, he was carrying on the tradition of national expansion, sharing with his true and faithful subjects that portion of his land he could not use.

Could he be blamed if those lands, which his *conquistadores* had wrested from the heathen, lay far byond the Western Sea?  Could he help it if those subjects bold enough to take the royal bounty should be forced to spend half their days in fighting hostile Indians from their flocks and herds ... and scheming schemes to keep their scalps upon their heads?

No ... the King of Spain could well afford to be generous with his lands.  He did not have to live in Texas-Coahuila.

And now let us leave the monarch on his Madrid throne and shift the scene to a spot on the Aransas River near the present South Texas town of San Patricio.  There, perhaps, may be found one reason why His Catholic Majesty was called "the empire builder."

Don Martin de Leon was starting on a journey, and mighty were his preparations.

Early on that bright spring morning in 1806 he had called a servant, a *vaquero* he had brought from Mexico, and had told him to saddle two of the best horses, catch one of the best and strongest mules, and then bring out the cannon.

Those devils, the Comanches, again had been in among the cattle, and had driven away some of the best beeves.  The dark eyes of the Spaniard flashed as he watched his helper put on the saddles and tighten the *latigos*.  Knowing as he did the location of every Comanche village for many leagues around, he anticipated little difficulty in finding the stolen stock, but this time he intended teaching the *ladrones* a swift and lasting lesson.

At last, when the saddles were on and the horses stood waiting, the *vaquero* went into the 'dobe ranch house and brought forth the artillery—a small, portable cannon of ancient manufacture, but still serviceable. It was a piece Don Martin had brought from Mexico, and already it had justified itself to the owner.

The rancher lost no time. Like one who knew his business, he called for the powder cask, poured an extra heavy charge into the muzzle, tamped it down, and dumped in a double handful of scrap metal.

### Don Martin used his mule as carriage for his 'thunder gun' artillery

Dona Patricia, a half-smile on her face, watched her husband from the doorway, the while attempting to explain to the four wide-eyed children—Fernando, Candelaria, Silvestre and Guadalupe— what papa was about. Of course, little Fernando, eldest son, wanted to go along. He was eight years old, he reminded his mother . . . and if papa was planning to shoot some Indians with the thunder gun he wanted to see the fun.

But Dona Patricia merely laughed and patted the boy on the head as Don Martin and the *vaquero* lifted the cannon to the mule's back and cinched it on, its iron muzzle pointing over the animal's hind quarters.

She explained to little Fernando that he need not worry his head about it; that the cannon probably would not be used because the Comanches were afraid of it. She remembered all too well the day the Carancahuas, daubed with red war paint and apparently bent on mischief, had visited the *rancho*.

On that occasion, while her husband and two servants had armed themselves with muskets to stand off the threatening attack, she herself had stood with a lighted fuse beside the cannon, which Don Martin had mounted in the doorway at the first sign of trouble. That time the Indians, having previously heard the gun belch thunder from its nose, had gone away in peace—after Don Martin had presented beef and a few blankets.

Dona Patricia thought of that day as she watched her husband and the *vaquero* mount and ride away . . . but despite her prediction to the contrary the cannon was about to see action.

Don Martin told her about it when he returned home in the evening . . . minus the mule which acted as gun carriage.

He and the servant, he explained, had not ridden ten miles when, as luck would have it, they came suddenly upon a Comanche scouting party. The surprised and excited *vaquero* had forgotten himself and had applied the fuse without removing the cannon from the mule's back. The resultant roar had frightened away the savages—

"But the poor mule," said Don Martin, sadly, "its back was broken by the recoil."

—And so ended one day's work in the life of a south country cattleman in the days when Spain owned Texas.

Don Martin de Leon was only one among the early Texas "cattle kings," but he was typical. These first Spanish settlers were not, in the same sense that the term "cattle king" later was used, really large stockmen. The Indians wouldn't give them peace enough to build enormous herds, but they were the greatest that the day and time afforded . . . the men who cleared the way for the greater Anglo-Saxon "cattle kings" to come.

Felipe Partilleas, Jose Casiano, Jose de la Garza, Erasmo Seguin, Jesus Cantu, Francisco de Arocha, Don José Perres Rey . . . all these and many another Spanish gentlemen left marks upon the South Texas ranges, but the de Leons were typical.

Don Martin de Leon came of an old aristocratic family.

His father, Bernardo de Leon, and his mother, both natives of the Burgos district in Spain, had come out to Mexico when Jose de Escandon had settled the province of Nuevo Santander, now the state of Tamaulipas.

Don Bernardo had hoped that his son would attend school in Monterrey after elementary training by a tutor in Burgos, but the age of eighteen found Martin with other ideas in his head.

In the mining district of Real de San Nicholas, profit was to be made in furnishing supplies, and Martin acquired a string of pack mules and went into business. He prospered—

Photograph by Erwin E. Smith
*Cowboy on guard*

to the extent that in 1795, when he married Patricia de la Garza at *Soto la Marina,* he had amassed quite a comfortable fortune, at least for those times.

Then it was that he first began considering a move to Texas, but it was not until after the birth of the fourth child that he decided to drift across the *Rio Bravo del Norte* for a glimpse of that land which the Spanish king was so generously parceling out to faithful subjects.

In 1805 he visited La Bahia, now Goliad, and then San Antonio. Around the latter place he found many occupying grants—the families of Padron, Delgado, De Armas, Goras, Curbelo, Leal, Santos, De Niz, Rodriguez, Cabrera, Melano, Provayna, Arocha and Perez—descendents of a group of Canary Islanders who came over in 1730 as colonists. They seemed to be doing quite well on the grants issued by the Spanish governor, and so De Leon decided to try his fortune in the new country.

Photograph by Erwin E. Smith

*Roping a mount*

Accordingly, he moved his family (and his cannon) into that section of the San Patricio country which lies back of Nueces Bay between the Aransas River and Chillipin Creek. Here, without the formality of taking a grant, he established a *rancho* for the purpose of corraling and breaking wild mustangs. He reasoned that he could test the country and then, if he cared to stay, apply for a grant.

The work of domesticating the mustangs was not child's play, for the animals—descendents of the horses brought into Mexico by the armies of Cortes—were as wild as the brush country deer. But Don Martin persevered. He enclosed with brush fence a pasture of several leagues, built corrals, trapped a few animals, and looked forward to the time when he would be selling horses in New Orleans and the north of Mexico. The venture, however, did not meet with signal success and by 1807 De Leon had decided on cattle rather than horses.

By this time he had come to consider the San Patricio country home, and he petitioned Governor Salcedo in San Antonio for grants taking in the pastures surrounding his rancho, but since governmental troubles were brewing in Mexico and since erroneous rumors had gone about that the De Leons were not fully loyal to Spain, Salcedo ignored the petition. He did say that he would have an investigation made into the charges of disloyalty . . . as though De Leon, in his sequestered corner of the world, could have been in contact with revolutionaries!

**Changing political events in Mexico kept Texas Spaniards in hot water**

Two years passed, and the De Leon household had been blessed with two more children—Felix and Agapito. Don Martin sent another petition to the governor, but like the first, nothing came of it. The family continued to live on the Aransas, but not for long.

The Indian raiders were becoming bolder—so bold, indeed, that they even lost their fear for the little cannon. The six-foot, fair-faced Don was forced to sit in his saddle every day, riding herd on the rapidly diminishing stock of cattle. Had he been a less pious and God fearing man De Leon might have broken under the strain, but he held faith that all would come out well in the end.

He was disappointed. Rebellion in Mexico caused withdrawal of Spanish troops from the province of Texas, and with this restraining influence gone the Indians became bolder than ever before. The De Leons feared for their lives. They gathered up what property they could transport and moved

Photograph by Erwin E. Smith
*Range Riders*

to San Antonio, where they listened with increasing interest to reports coming from below the Rio Grande.

Events were stirring in Mexico. In September of 1810, in the town of Dolores, Miguel Hidalgo y Costilla, the fighting priest, had raised the first defiant cry for independence from the "bonnet-wearers" of Spain—"Death to the *gachupines!*" Revolt swept the land, the Spaniards were swept from power, and Texas fell under the rule of a new government, the Republic of Mexico.

De Leon, when at last he felt conditions favorable for a return to San Patricio, went back to his ranch wondering over the turn of events. Since the Spanish government, in refusing a grant, had accused him of sympathy for the Mexican revolutionaries, surely the new government would not hesitate to act favorably on his petition.

But, alas for high hopes! When the Mexicans received his request, they remembered that Don Martin was a Spaniard. Could he, then, be loyal to the new government? An investigation must be made—with the result that two more years elapsed before De Leon was notified of a decision in his favor.

Then fortune smiled. The Mexicans not only issued the requested grant—they made Don Martin an *empresario* with authority to settle forty-one families on land in what is now Victoria county. His own share was to be five leagues and five labors, about 25,000 acres.

When news of this good fortune came from Saltillo, the city from which land grants were issued, Don Martin was overjoyed. The year 1824 found him on the way to Victoria with the 41 families, the cattle herd of the Aransas trailing along.

The *empresario* and his son, Fernando, put their ornate Spanish brands on thousands of calves during the next few years, finding a market in San Antonio de Bexar, or selling to an occasional buyer from Louisiana. Although their herds never reached the enormous proportions of those to appear at a later date in the plains country, the De Leons, and others like them, were the true cattle kings of their day.

Eventually, Don Fernando took over management of the Mexican longhorns, almost exclusively. His father had other irons in the fire. He was, for one thing, looking after 150 new families he had brought into the settlement. The 1830's arrived. Some of the children—there were now ten—were in Europe attending school, and being entertained in royal courts. One of the sons, Silvestre, was magistrate of the town of Guadalupe Victoria. And Don Martin, now sixty-nine years old, was dreaming one of his greatest dreams, which had nothing to do with raising cattle and horses for the markets.

He would use a part of the family fortune in the erection
of a huge cathedral, patterned after the great churches of
Mexico.  It would be the most magnificent place of worship
in all Texas, outrivaling even the missions of Bexar.  Already
he was completing plans to bring masons and the architects
from Mexico, and then —

In 1833 a scourge of cholera swept through the southern
country, and Don Martin de Leon was among the first to die.

His son Fernando kept the family branding irons in the
fire for the next two years.  He liked the cattle business and
had it not been for the Texas Revolution he might have become one of the industry's leaders in later years.  The revolution ruined Fernando financially, although he was as loyal
as any American among the Texans in the cause of freedom
from the tyranny of Mexico.

The fall of the Alamo marked the beginning of his reverses.  Shortly after the butchering of San Antonio's garrison by the troops of Santa Anna the Texan army entered
Victoria and one of their first acts after occupation was to bring
about the arrest of Fernando de Leon, at that time commissioner of the colony.

Don Fernando protested that he was a Spaniard, that his
sympathies were known to be with the Texas cause.  He reminded them that in 1834 he and his brother-in-law, José
Carvajal, had purchased arms and ammunition in New Orleans for the use of Texas colonists against the government
of Santa Anna.  He reviewed the history of that affair—how
the boat they had used had been overtaken on the Matagorda
coast by the Mexican gunboat *Montezuma*; how he and Carvajal had been taken as prisoners to Matamoras; how they had
escaped jail and returned to Victoria.  Wasn't that proof
enough of loyalty?

It was not.  Don Fernando was arrested and placed under

guard, just because Spanish chanced to be his mother tongue. Once during his detainment he almost lost his life while bathing, under guard, in the San Antonio River—being wounded by a bullet fired for no apparent reason by a roistering Texas soldier.

Finally he was released, but he faced continued persecution and so the De Leons fled to New Orleans, taking with them only their clothing and family jewels. Their cattle, numbering several thousand head, were left to roam at will. The family remained in New Orleans three years, then moved to Mexico, but in 1844 Don Fernando felt that he must see once more the city his father had founded. Accompanied by his immediate family, he returned to find the unjust animosities of the Revolution forgotten.

**The Dons were the cattle empire builders and also the martyrs**

His land, however, had been taken up by others, and because of his long absence and the fact that the grants were Mexican in origin he had no recourse by law. He did manage to salvage a small portion—the *Rancho Escondida*, on the bank of the Guadalupe River a few miles north of Victoria. Here he attempted a new start. The De Leon branding iron went into the fire and onto the hides again, but at the time of his death at *Escondida* in 1853 he possessed but a few hundred head of stock—a sorry lot compared with the herd which one time carried his brand, and that of the *empresario*.

He never knew the fate of those longhorned thousands. Perhaps many of them were taken up by the Americans; perhaps many of them became wild cattle, ranging the unfenced brush country as free and unfettered as the deer and the buffalo ... so many of these early Spanish longhorns did.

The fate of Don Fernando ... and his unwilling contribution to the latter-day cattle industry ... was that of many another of his race.

Don Felipe Partilleas, for instance, established a ranch in the late '20's on the San Marcos River above Gonzales, but he never succeeded in getting together more than a few hundred head. He, like Martin de Leon, found himself occupied more with Indian fighting than with animal husbandry—and finally he, too, was forced to abandon his stock and make fast tracks for San Antonio. Don José Domingo de la Garza of the *Gertrudis,* Don José Perres Rey were others . . . their names were legion.

They might be called, in a sense, the "martyr kings" of the Texas cattle ranges. They fought against terrific odds—the Indians, changing governments, Nature herself—to build in the wilderness private empires of their own. And, except in rare cases, they failed . . . leaving to the *Americanos* who followed close behind a heritage of error and experience through which they might profit in the building of the greater kingdoms.

They left something else, too—the wild Spanish longhorns which only a hunter could touch . . . animals which were to be crossed, eventually, with the more domesticated breeds the Americans brought to the Matagorda, the Trespalacios and the Nueces countries.

Thus the Texas Longhorn came into his own, and a great industry was born.

The Anglo-Saxons were close behind the *dons,* and the first of the so-called *Americano* ranches was established in what is now Chambers county in the spring of 1819 by James Taylor White, a young Louisianian who moved into the wild country with his bride and a small herd of longhorns.

He built a one-room log cabin about ten miles east of the present site of Liberty and in the years that followed added a room as each of his fourteen children arrived.

James Taylor White lived on his land and watched his herds multiply until, by the time the battle of San Jacinto freed Texas from Mexican rule in 1836, he could count his longhorns in the thousands ... Many of these he drove overland to the New Orleans market, and many he sold at the meatpacking plant which Jones and Company, an English firm, established at Liberty Landing in 1840.

Photograph by W. D. Smithers
*Brewster County Cowboy*

This enterprise, which shipped salted beef to London in iron containers, probably was the first packery in the state of Texas.

The White ranch, in the old open range days, covered all of

*Where Texas melts away into the Rio Grande—*

Photograph by W. D. Smithers

what is now Chambers county and parts of Jefferson, Liberty and Polk, but after the founder's death in 1845, and the arrival of many other Anglo-Saxons in the area, the scope of the layout narrowed. His son, another James Taylor, succeeded him, and after him there was still another James Taylor. It has been that way throughout the one hundred and twenty years that the Whites have been on the south-eastern coast . . . a James Taylor White from one generation to the next. There's one there today . . . on the 26,000 acres which make up the last remnant of the first Anglo-Saxon ranch in Texas, land which has known but one ownership under four flags, those of Mexico, the Texas Republic, the Confederacy, and the Stars and Stripes.

The Whites were the forerunners of such colorful *Americano* cattlemen as Grimes of the Trespalacios and the inimitable Shanghai Pierce.

*Catch 'im, Cowboy! Swinging a loop in the Texas Highlands*

Photograph, by W. D. Smither

# Grimes

# and the

# Trespalacios

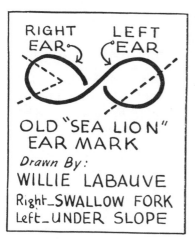

RIGHT EAR
LEFT EAR

OLD "SEA LION"
EAR MARK
*Drawn By:*
WILLIE LABAUVE
Right_SWALLOW FORK
Left_UNDER SLOPE

● Texas Coastal Plains cradled the Cattle Industry

**T**HE WORLD is wide, and its variety great, but few spots compare in geographical beauty with that flat stretch of coastal plain which sweeps gently upward from Matagorda Bay to lose itself in the rolling country of the north.

A land of deep grass and Siberian clover; its liveoaks

draped with bearded Spanish moss; its acres touched by the sun and the caress of winds from the Mexican gulf; it is paradise within itself . . . but there are few who call it by that name. Those who live in the land are well content with the two general appellations first given by the Spanish fathers in the days of old—the *Matagorda* and the *Trespalacios*.

Stripped by islands and peninsulas, and cut by the blue waters of placid bays—the La Vaca, the San Antonio, the Trespalacios, the Espiriti Santa, and the greater Matagorda—it is an alluring coast of romance and adventure.

Fact is hand-maiden to fancy on those shores. The ghost of Alvar Nunez Cabeza de Vaca still walks the sands where first he placed his foot on Texas soil in 1528; and sheltered in the land-locked bay which bears the Spaniard's name, the phantom frigate *Belle* swings idly at her chains as Rene Robert de la Salle raises the *Fleur-de-lis* of France over the log ramparts of St. Louis, the fortress builded for his king.

These things the traveler might imagine as he wanders through the ancient land. More too—for when the wild West Indian hurricanes roar across the finger of Matagorda Peninsula from the waste of white-capped waters on the south, the wailing wind may seem to carry the eerie note of a savage Carancahua yell, remindful of the day when those cannibalistic tribesmen roamed that section of the coast.

Or yet again . . . it may be only Captain Jean Lafitte and his buccaneers of the good brig *Pride*, rolling in from seaward to seek a haven from the storm, and stay out its time of fury with a round of roistering on the beach.

A brave, green land; a detached corner of a perilous paradise—what better place to cradle the great Texas cattle industry? Perhaps it is significant that even the term La Vaca means "the cow" . . .

The Matagorda still was wild when Captain Richard Grimes arrived in 1840 from the more peaceful precincts of Connecticut.  He settled with his family on a farm at Palacios Point (not to be confused with the present town of that name) and bought a few cattle, just enough to fill the family needs.  Because no outside markets were available he had no thought of raising cattle as a means of livelihood, for under the circumstances ownership of a sizeable herd was considered more of a burden than an asset.

The captain, however, did not find himself alone in the Matagorda and the Trespalacios.  Others . . . tillers of the soil and boatmen of the bays, had come before him—men who would become, in later years, pioneers just as great as he in the formation of the South Texas cattle industry—but the captain typified this pioneering breed.

### The 'Days of Richard Grimes' still a time marker in the Matagorda

It is not for this reason alone, however, that he takes his place among the principals in this narrative . . . for his advent into the livestock business a few years later began the forging of an eventful chain of circumstances which originated one of the greater kingdoms of the south, and which even now causes patriarchs of the Matagorda to hearken back to "the days of Richard Grimes."

It might just as well be "the days of Samuel Robbins," or any other neighbor, but Fate failed to see it quite that way.  That erratic old harridan knew exactly what she wanted— an ultimate history of the Matagorda cattle country which would revolve about one central and outstanding figure;  and although she selected neither Grimes nor Robbins for the place, she used them indirectly for her purpose.

When Captain Grimes arrived Samuel Robbins, having been a resident of Texas since the year before the Revolution, already had a thriving business, a productive farm supplemented by a small but seaworthy boat which he used to carry provisions along the jagged coastline.

Like his neighbors, he had few cattle; for he was another who could see no future in the business—and so they were among the first of his possessions offered for sale when in 1848 he decided to close out partially his Texas affairs and return to his old home at Petersburg, Virginia.

He had made quite enough money to retire in modest comfort, and he parceled out his belongings in small lots, gathered up the remainder, and loaded the boat which was to carry him back to old Virginia. The craft lay at anchor in a Matagorda cove, but on the very night he planned to hoist sail and take to sea a party of renegade whites came aboard, shot Robbins to death in the pilot house, looted the boat, and then departed—after throwing their victim into the bay.

A searching party of friends, including Captain Grimes, found the body and took it from the water several days later. Weeks passed, and then news of the tragedy reached a son in Petersburg ... Chester Hamlin Robbins. He immediately quit his job in the general store of Abel Head, said goodbye to his young friend, Abel Head Pierce, nephew of the merchant, and departed for Texas to look after any property his father might have left. He liked the country and he stayed, to become a neighbor of Captain Grimes.

The murder of the elder Robbins had left the captain the principal livestock owner in the region, but he really did not begin to call himself a cattleman until the early '50's, after his home on the Point had been swept away by one of the great hurricanes which periodically lash that coast.

The big storms from the Gulf did seem to be more or less periodical then. At least the oldest local inhabitant, old Bill Dunbar of the town of Matagorda, will tell you so.

"Dam'me, sir, I've seen some blows!" says he, as he looks out toward the Peninsula from the window in the loft of the old barn he calls his home. "I've been here since '53, and in the early days we used to look for 'em in September ...

every September, reg'lar as the calendar ... but now it's hell knows when one'll come roaring across th' bay with another chasin' at its tail. But we had some holy howlers, we did ... back in the days of Grimes."

Anyhow, whatever the tempo and character of West Indian disturbances during his era, Captain Grimes learned with his first blow what every succeeding Matagordian has learned with bitterness—that the hurricane is the one great serpent in that paradise, and that the wise man puts a few miles between his place of habitation and the shore.

Accordingly, Grimes and his son Bradford gathered up what fragments of the family property they could find and moved to a more inland spot on Trespalacios Creek; and now, since William Foster and others in the vicinity had opened by boat what promised to be a good market in New Orleans, he went into the cattle business with his son.

The first stock, descendants largely of the small herds left behind by the mission-building Spaniards, were plentiful and cheap, but the Grimeses bought carefully. Even the New Orleans market could be glutted, and it was this very fear, perhaps, which prompted the son to give thought to a new experiment. Why not eliminate the middle man and the commission broker? Why not send the meat of the steer direct to consumer from producer?

Down on Trespalacios Creek, in a few sheds equipped with huge stew kettles, the young man opened a "packery"—one of the first in Texas.

But Bradford Grimes was not destined to become either an Ogden Armour or a Louis Swift. With rare exception the weather which cloaks the Trespalacios is warm, and much to the chagrin of the experimenter the stew kettles in the sheds along the creek produced more potential ptomaine than protein. Quick to learn his lesson, Grimes gave up in disgust.

He looked again toward the New Orleans markets, as his longhorn herds increased.

It was about this time that Neighbor Chester Robbins went back to Virginia for a visit, and when he returned again he brought a wife. But Robbins, on that trip to Petersburg, did something besides marry, something which later would change the entire complexion of South Texas ranching history.

He talked; told glowing tales of the new country in the Southwest, and the youthful store-clerk of Merchant Abel Head listened, and dreamed dreams.

**Too many big doses of sanctimony brought a future cow-man to Texas**

Abel Pierce was eighteen. Born at Little Compton, Rhode Island, the son of Jonathan Pierce, a blacksmith, he had been sent, at the age of thirteen, to serve an apprenticeship with his uncle. He had found Uncle Abel an intensely religious man who made no secret of his determination to instill in his namesake a certain amount of spiritual education—all of which was received with much less grace than it was offered.

Young Pierce had fallen prey to restlessness, and under the spell of Robbins' stories of the West he thrilled as any other Down-East boy might be expected to do. A quarrel with his uncle—"too many big doses of sanctimony," he used to say—resulted in the boy's departure for New York, where he prowled the docks until he was fortunate enough to sign on with the crew of a schooner bound for Texas. The boat sailed on Abel's nineteenth birthday, June 29, 1853.

Nearly four months later a tall, gangling youth, whose trousers were a bit too short for his long legs and a bit too tight for his exceptionally large frame, walked down the gang-plank at Port La Vaca, then one of the principal seaports on the Matagordian coast.

Brusque in manner, and possessed of a booming fog-horn voice . . . which he always used at that tempo, regardless of surroundings . . . he was a young Goliath. His remarkable physique attracted attention even in a country where strong men were the rule rather than the exception; but not one of his roustabout companions guessed, as they unloaded the vessel's assorted cargo and refilled the hold with cotton, that the loud-mouthed Yankee was on his way to becoming the peer of coastal cattle barons.

With the schooner ready for sea again, the maritime career of Abel Pierce came to an end, and he began looking for employment. The chances at first appeared rather discouraging, the town having been visited by an epidemic of yellow fever, but fortune smiled and put young Pierce in the path of Captain Richard Grimes.

The captain couldn't use him, his son having become the leading light in the family cattle enterprises, but the captain would see what he could do . . . making good his promise by taking Pierce down to Bradford's home on Matagorda Bay.

"Wonder if I've got a horse he won't break down?" thought the younger Grimes, as he surveyed the giant for the first time. He was dubious of a tenderfoot, especially if the tenderfoot chanced to be a Northerner. He might have been even more dubious had he been allowed a glimpse into the future, but he gave the former store clerk a job . . . and smiled to himself as young Pierce asked if he could take his first year's pay, two hundred dollars, in cows and calves.

Grimes was a hard taskmaster. He first put his new employe to wood chopping, and then found a place for him among the riders on the range, at that time open and unfenced from the Gulf to the Arctic Pole. Thus began the evolution of a cowboy, but it was not until the end of the first year's service that Abel found himself completely initiated.

When that day of reckoning came Grimes, according to agreement, paid off the two hundred dollars at the rate of fourteen dollars for cow with calf. This was all very well, except for two things—the price rate was much too high and the cows too old . . . ancient she-stuff which Grimes couldn't dispose of elsewhere.   Most of the cows died soon after calving.

Pierce bore his misfortune with Spartan courage, but he shelved the incident in his memory for future consideration. It was his initiation into the cow business but the time would come when, as one contemporary put it, "he was to have the pleasure of initiating his old boss into the Royal Arch degree of the same order."

Photograph by Erwin E. Smith

*The Buster—*

But even the lad from the East could see one thing . . . he was learning his lessons well.   Under the tutelage of Grimes, who seemed to take a peculiar delight in passing out the toughest assignments he could lay thought to, he was becoming a real cowboy . . . a real, rip-snortin' top-hand whose skill on the hurricane deck of a bronc already was beginning to attract wide attention.

Grimes was a slave holder and several of his dark-skinned boys also excelled in this line of endeavor, but the boss was a man who believed in playing safe.

"Put Pierce on the bad-un," he used to say at horse-breaking time. "Don't risk the niggers . . . they cost a thousand dollars apiece."

None, however, enjoyed the joke more than the tall, gangling youth himself. But with all the hardboiled treatment accorded Abel Pierce, the boss evidently had some liking for the lad, or at least respected his ability to adapt himself to the rough-and-tumble customs of the country.

Anyhow, when Grimes began shipping in earnest to the New Orleans market in 1855, Pierce held the job of boss driver . . . his monthly salary of $22.50 included the responsibility of buying, shaping up, and then getting the beasts to the coast for shipment.

Thereafter he progressed, both in salary and enthusiasm, and by 1860 he had succeeded in inducing his brother Jonathan to come out from Connecticut and try his hand in the new country. Jonathan, with approximately one hundred dollars in the pocket of his jeans, stepped off the schooner *A. C. Leverette* at Indianola in December of that year, and he arrived just as much a tenderfoot as brother Abel, proving it on his first horseback ride by dismounting on the right side . . . which, of course, is the wrong side.

Despite this grievous error, however, Grimes took him on as clerk, for the cattle business was showing a steady improvement and Grimes could afford that sort of secretary.

**The Yankee cowhand takes a name destined to stick—
'Shanghai'**

Jonathan Pierce, in many ways, was quite different from his brother. He preferred the plow to the back of a bronc;

he was less noisy, and he was a great deal shorter and a great deal stouter than Abel. It was this variance in physical appearance, perhaps, which helped Abel acquire that almost legendary title which fitted him as hand to glove—"Shanghai Pierce."

Perhaps he did resemble in some ways the tall, long-legged "shanghai" rooster, but there are versions other than the foregoing, given by his grand-daughter, Mrs. Clive Runnels of Chicago.

Willie LaBauve, the diminutive Louisianian who in later years became Shanghai's range boss, believes that Pierce took the name for himself; and that LaBauve's own cousin Gilbert was present at the "christening."

"I've heard Gilbert tell about it more than once," says little Willie, whose handle-bar mustachios recall the days when he rode the trail to Kansas with herds of South Coast steers. "It was just before the war, while Shang was working for Grimes."

Gilbert LaBauve (said Willie) met Pierce one morning over on East Carancahua Creek. They never had crossed paths before and since they were of similar age, Gilbert was rather surprised to hear the cowboy address him with:

"Good morning, young man"—a peculiar habit Pierce had of addressing most everybody, regardless of age, as "young man." He asked Gilbert's name and LaBauve told him.

"And what's yours?" Gilbert wanted to know, as the two lolled in their saddles, each surveying the other.

"Pierce . . . Shanghai Pierce, by God!" bawled the young giant. "Just call me Shanghai."

Willie LaBauve says that Pierce himself told the story that night at the cow camp; and that cousin Gilbert later remarked to various acquaintances that he had met up with a man who called himself "Shanghai." That is one story, but whatever its origin the name stuck, and it remains to this day one of the greatest in that section of the state.

Even at that time ... the early days of 1860 ... Pierce had won more than passing attention in the camps, and although he was little more than a penniless *vaquero* working for hire, his name was more or less familiar to cattlemen all the way from Matagorda to the *Brasada*—the brush country along the Nueces.

Photograph by Erwin E. Smith
*Chuck wagon—getting ready to put it on*

A Grimes top-hand naturally would be known—and men marveled at his patience in remaining so long with an employer who obviously and openly foisted upon him all the disagreeable tasks possible. But Grimes knew a real cowpuncher when he saw one, and he recognized the fact that Shanghai, for all his Eastern breeding, might have been born to the business. No man in the country could throw a better rope at branding time. No man could trim down an unruly bronc in quicker time. No man was better acquainted with the whims and instincts of the cow brute. Pierce had caught on from the very first, and that's why Grimes, in 1860, was paying him one hundred dollars a month—for which princely sum a man could afford, in those days, to put up with a great deal.

It was the War Between the States that brought the first break between Pierce and Grimes—or "Bing", as Shanghai sometimes called him. When the South first raised the Stars and Bars and the Texans began rallying beneath it, Shanghai hesitated. Naturally enough, he was reluctant to fight against his recent neighbors in the North—and then, too, there was that one hundred dollars a month—but finally he went to Grimes and told him he was through; that he was enlisting in Captain J. C. Borden's troop of the First Texas Cavalry.

"Now about that five hundred dollars you owe me," Shang said to his employer, "I wish you'd keep it for me until I come back. This war can't last long and I'll need the cash when I get home."

Grimes, so the story goes, said he would be glad to play the role of banker; that he would guard the fund carefully until it should be called for—and Pierce rode away to the wars.

In the First Texas Cavalry an important post was awaiting the big cowboy from the Matagorda. Captain Borden, knowing the recruit's qualifications as a cattleman, saw to that. He gave Pierce an appointment—as regimental butcher.

An acquaintance who came in contact with him quite often about that time recalls Shanghai in these words: "A giant in size, he looked like his shoes were running over with feet, and when he was mounted his saddle seemed to disappear. His eyes had a half-closed, sleepy appearance, but you can bet he wasn't asleep."

Of his military career Pierce himself often said: "I was of the same rank as a major-general; always in the rear when the regiment advanced, always in the lead on a retreat."

He did not participate in much of the fighting, but he and his staff kept the regimental meat box well supplied . . . helping the Texas Cavalry march in the best of Napoleonic traditions, on its stomach.

**Into the saddle and away once more for the coastal plains**

The war lasted much longer than Shanghai had anticipated and so, when the last shot was fired, he was more than eager to beat his butcher knife into a branding iron.  Homesick for the Matagorda and the Trespalacios, he lifted his six-feet-four, two hundred and thirty pound bulk into the saddle and streaked for the cow camps on the coast.  He went first, of course, to his old employer.

Bradford Grimes hadn't changed much.  He was, in fact, the same old Grimes, but he was cordial.  He even shook Shang's hand and said he was glad to see him, and then, after the usual exchange of pleasantries, the two got around to the matter of money.  It was Pierce who broached the subject. He hoped that Grimes hadn't forgotten.

"Oh, no, . . . not at all," W. B. assured him.  "A little account of five hundred dollars, wasn't it?"

"To the dollar," said Pierce, "and I can use the money now."

Grimes was solemn as an owl, except for the peculiar little grin which played over his face for a moment.

"Let me see, now," he mused, "as I rec'lect that was for pay due in the first year of the war . . . the first year of the Confederacy."

With narrowed, puzzled eyes Shanghai gazed at his old boss.

"What's that got to do with it", he demanded.

"Nothing," said Grimes, calmly, "except that it seems to me that since the work was done under the Confederacy you should be willing to take Confederate money.  There's a whole barrel of it in the next room.  Help yourself, Shang . . . and take some for interest.

He moved a step nearer the door, lest the big cowpuncher should suddenly explode. But Shang didn't—though he knew the money wasn't worth the ink on the signature of Jefferson Davis. Instead, he choked back his rising anger, looked Grimes squarely in the eyes, and in his deep, rumbling voice uttered the threat which was to become ... almost ... a prophecy. "By God, Bing," he said, "I'll put you on the Black Hills for this. I'll make you wish, damn you, that you could eat your no 'count money, barrel and all!"

And Grimes, surprised by what he had heard, wondered ... then laughed loud and long.

# King
## of the
## Sea Lions

SHANGHAI PIERCE

BULLDOGGING

● Shanghai Pierce—
"as uncouth as the
cattle he drove, but
at heart, one of the
best men in this or
any other land."

T HE INCIDENT of the
Confederate money barrel did more than mark an important
turning point in the career of Shanghai Pierce; it signaled,
too, the beginning of a new era in the South Texas cattle
industry.

39

When Abel Pierce stalked out of the Grimes headquarters down on Matagorda Bay he boiled with the rage of righteous indignation.   He knew that behind it all was something deeper than a mere quarrel over money.

Immediately he began devoting himself to the fulfillment of his threat to put his old boss "on the Black Hills"—which in those days meant driving a man from his chosen range and attempting to push him so far north that his final destination would be the Bad Lands of the Dakotas, a place in the cattleman's geography comparable to hell itself.

Other than a sullen determination, Shanghai didn't have much to start on, but as a first step in his contemplated program he called on a friend, J. M. Foster, who was handling cattle over on the Trespalacios.   Foster agreed to give him a certain amount of backing—enough to buy a herd, shape it up, and drive to New Orleans.   He bought his stock from John Woods of St. Mary's, and returning from the Louisiana port with a profit of fourteen hundred dollars, he formed a partnership with Foster and the Collins brothers, James and Joseph, and together they bought in the Matagorda and sold in New Orleans.

Soon the big cattleman had enough cash to go into business for himself.   He bought a few steers, adopted the BU as his brand, but at this juncture—just as he was getting his feet settled in the stirrups—came the great break in the Louisiana market, at that time practically the only outlet for South Texas cattle.

This distressing situation was brought on by the war for Southern Independence—because, while the conflict raged between the states, cattlemen not only in the Matagorda but all over Texas, rushed away to join the colors, leaving their herds free to roam the range at will.   Many cows had calved during the years of warfare, with the result that thousands of neglected, unbranded yearlings and two-year-olds were prowling the country, fair game for any man who cared to heat an iron.

And with every other discharged soldier temporarily cutting in on the industry, the meat surplus soon made itself evident in the market. Prices fell.

Shang's brother likewise had been caught. Jonathan Pierce also had served in the Southern army, but before the end of the war he had used what Confederate money he possessed to purchase cattle from Tom Kuykendall, a small herd which he branded with the Ace of Clubs.

The brothers met and discussed the situation, with the result that they entered that phase of the business which within a year or two would help to restore the shattered industry to a semblance of normalcy.

They established headquarters on the Trespalacios and began buying herds—to slaughter for hides and tallow. Tallow at that time was selling at ten and one-eighth cents a pound, two or three times what the larger steers would bring on the hoof, and the Pierces killed thousands of head. They fed the meat to the hogs.

Since many others in the Matagorda were engaged in a like manner it wasn't long until the range surplus began to dwindle, bringing a better tone to the New Orleans market. This return to better times found Shanghai prepared. He had not only made money in hides and tallow, but he had built up a good-sized herd during the big kill—for in the stock he bought at that time were many young cattle and calves which would have meant dead loss had they been butchered. These Shanghai branded and turned on the range, and they multiplied so rapidly that with the return of better prices he found himself in a comfortable position.

About this time he took a wife—Miss Fanny Lacy, the daughter of a neighbor—but even his marriage did not cause him to forget his quarrel with Grimes. That little score remained listed under the heading of unfinished business, which he intended to settle in his own way . . . when he had money enough to do the job properly.

"Shang fought with money," explains Willie LaBauve. "Regardless of his size he didn't take much to scrappin', and I've heard him say more than once 'Just give me thirty minutes and I can talk any man out of a fight.' Not that he was afraid . . . he wasn't . . . it was just his way of doin'."

A partnership formed at this time with Allen and Pool, a Galveston firm, helped him get a little more of the cash he needed.  A wharf was built out into Matagorda Bay, contracts were obtained in New Orleans, Havana and Pensacola, and the partners began shipping at the rate of about twenty-five thousand head a year.

Shanghai did the buying and the shaping, and of his operations in those days the late George W. Saunders of Fort Worth, who lived in the Matagorda then, leaves this description:

"He was a large portly man; always rode a fine horse, and would be accompanied by a negro, Neptune, who led a pack horse loaded with gold and silver which, when he reached our camp, was dumped on the ground and remained there until the cattle were classed and counted out.  Then he would empty the money on a blanket, and pay it out to the different stockmen from whom he purchased.  He would generally buy two or three hundred head at a time . . . we all looked upon him as a redeemer, as money was scarce in those Reconstruction days before the northern trail started."

### Shanghai Pierce's Sea Lions were fast-going critters

After the trail did start to Kansas in 1867 Shanghai became one of the greatest drivers in the south, every year sending up big herds of Matagordian steers, a breed which became familiarly and jocularly known in Abilene and Dodge City as "Shanghai Pierce's sea lions."

They were, in truth, little different from the general run of Texas "moss horns," except that they appeared a bit more rangy after the long drive from the coast, and for some unexplainable reason a little more wild. We have Pierce's own word for it that the "sea lions" were fast on their feet, for he used to say:

"It took two men to see them—one to say here he comes, and one to say there he goes."

Charlie Siringo, who was one of the *vaqueros* at Pierce's *Rancho Grande,* has intimated in some of his reminisences that certain of the animals were a great deal tougher than sea lions.

One of the contracts with the Cuban government, Siringo said, called for one hundred thousand head of bulls to be used as army ration. Siringo himself helped load some of these beasts for Havana, but only a comparatively small portion of the order was shipped. He assumed that the Cuban army rebelled at being fed such bully beef.

The Galveston company went on the rocks in 1871, but Shang had quite a nice personal nest egg put away and, his wife having died, he sold out his Texas holdings and went to Kansas City to live.

James Cox, an historian of that day, gives a very tactful but mysterious explanation of our hero's sudden hankering for a change of climate and environment.

"He had been having sundry troubles and was not perfectly in accord with the state administration in matters of politics and religion," says this chronicler, "and so he went to Kansas City to enjoy a little well-earned rest and the pleasures of society. The Kansas City air seemed purer to him at that time than that which he had been accustomed to breathe, and his appreciation of the change induced him to remain in the land of blizzards and grasshoppers for four delightful years.

"In the meantime, he had made some money and lost more, but eventually tiring of his new surroundings, and finding that

Photograph by Erwin E. Smith

the air of Texas had become somewhat purer, and the society improved to a noticeable degree, he returned to his old range."

Not a very lucid statement, but down in the Matagorda today the old-timers will tell you—quietly and very casually —that there were extenuating circumstances ... that just before Shang's departure for the north five or six young men, who had been caught stealing and skinning cattle, had been hanged to a liveoak tree.

Pierce, according to the popular theory, feared that he might be credited with having a part in the affair ... particularly since several hundred of the recovered hides carried the burn of his brand. Anyhow, he "high-tailed" for Kansas City.

During his exile there the cattleman engineered one of the most clever financial coups ... or "re-coups" ... in the annals of that midwestern metropolis. When he first breezed in from Texas his cash assets amounted to about one hundred thousand dollars, and of course he was eager to invest in some worthy enterprise.

Finally he went into the banking business, but unfortunately the two gentlemen with whom he became associated were not quite as honest as they might have been, and before long it became apparent to Shanghai that the gilt edge on his one hundred thousand in stock somehow lacked the proper lustre. He tried, unsuccessfully, to secure statements, and then hit upon a plan which still is regarded in Kansas City cattle circles as a master stroke of financial dealing.

One day he went before his partners with the glowing tale of two gigantic herds  coming up the trail ... herds which would bring big money to the men lucky enough to buy them. He proposed that the banking firm pluck the plum, that he go to meet the drive farther south and make all the arrangements.

"But," he added, "it will take about one hundred thousand to swing the deal."

The two greedy bankers were more than willing to furnish the stake (if Shang advised it), and within a few days Pierce was boarding a train to ride south. His valise packed with currency, he stood on the rear platform of the train to wave goodbye to his associates, and it was not until then that they realized that they had been handed the double-cross.

"Good-bye, damn you!" shouted Pierce, as the train chugged out of the station. "We're even now. I'm out of the banking business and I'm goin' back to Texas!"

Home on his old range, his thoughts turned once more to Bradford Grimes and the barrel of Confederate money . . .

The atmosphere had cleared somewhat during his four years of absence, but otherwise he found that life in the Matagorda had changed but little. Grimes still was the leading cattleman in that section, and regularly was trailing herds to the Kansas terminals of Newton and Wichita. The country remained open range, the various cowmen buying and branding and turning loose on the almost limitless pasture, and in this situation Pierce saw his opportunity to put his old enemy "on the Black Hills."

Assets were counted then in cattle and not in land, and many ranchmen, though they owned thousands of steers, boasted just enough acreage to establish a place of residence. At one time the Pierce brothers themselves owned more than fifty thousand head and only eleven acres of ground. In fact, few of the operators wanted real estate, and in this connection Shang remembered having heard Grimes say he had rather leave the country than buy a chunk of it. Those who had taken up state land held large tracts, and Grimes, or anyone else, could lease what he had to lease for practically nothing.

What more simple then, reasoned Pierce, than to buy the earth from under the hoofs of the Grimes steers? He could purchase all the land he wanted at five to ten cents an acre, and he told himself that the plan, in time, might turn out to be a good investment.  He began seeking additional money to finance the project.

Taking the cash he had brought home from Kansas City he threw in with Dan Sullivan, and later with his brother Jonathan.  They began buying and selling and in a short time their cow camps were dotting the length and breadth of the Matagorda and Trespalacios—one of the largest outfits on the coastal slope, larger even than that of Bradford Grimes.

### Willie LaBauve made five trips up the trail to Kansas

With his pockets again well-lined with money Pierce took a second wife in 1875—Miss Hattie James of Galveston— and he began forming new partnerships for the purpose of land buying.  With Sullivan, Bill Kyle, B. Q. Ward and Jonathan Pierce as allies, Shang started his purchases and before anyone realized what was in the air he held an interest in nearly all the large tracts lying between the Trespalacios and the Colorado River.

The "sea lions" continued to plod up the trail to Kansas, furnishing added resources for the enterprise.  Shanghai himself rode with many of the herds, to become a familiar figure in Dodge City and in Wichita.

"Every Spring the big herds would go up," recalls LaBauve, who was one of the foremen in those days.  "We would shape up early and usually leave about the last week in April, arriving in Kansas in June or July."

LaBauve, who was twelve years old when he first began working with Pierce, and who rode the trail five times behind the "sea lions", emphatically denies that the boss was a roistering leader of wild Texans—as some sensational writers have depicted him in connection with his visits to the Kansas cow towns.

"I don't think I ever saw old Shang take a drink," says La-Bauve.  "It was his size and his roarin' voice which misled the North Texans who met him in Dodge. But with all that he was just a little shy. He seldom went armed, for as I have said, he fought his fights with money."

When Pierce and his associates at last had gained control of much of the land upon which the Grimes cattle grazed, Grimes and several other large cowmen were ordered to gather up and move.

Bradford, however, wasn't disposed to be rushed, and he continued the even tenor of his way as though nothing at all had occurred. Shang gave him ample time and then went to court for an injunction to force the removal. Grimes and the others likewise ignored the court order—until the judge appointed a man to turn them out.

The gentleman assigned to this task was Tom Nye, lately a foreman for Shang, and he used the cattle king's own *vaqueros* to make the roundup and carry out the removal.

"In the fall of that year, 1878, we put out eleven thousand head," said LaBauve, who at the time was foreman for the Pierces and B. Q. Ward, "and we had no trouble at all."

Then Shanghai and his partners fenced in from the coast to the Navidad River, and for a second time a turnout was effected over a thirty-mile area, only a few of the smaller cattlemen escaping the comb out. Grimes now was a bit nearer to those Black Hills . . .

Encouraged by his success in the first ventures, Pierce then began negotiations with the owners of a two hundred thousand acre tract near El Campo, still farther north. He also struck up a deal with Koontz Brothers of New York to go in with him on a fencing project which would move all the remaining big stockmen out of the lower country—specifically John Stafford and Grimes, whose holdings were based on the remnants of the old Allen and Pool herd.

The fence was built, according to Willie LaBauve, by his brother, O. J. LaBauve. After four strands of wire had been stretched along many miles of cypress posts near the Southern Pacific railway branch recently built through that section, Willie and the *vaqueros* again began a collection of alien brands.

They put the Grimes and Stafford cattle above the Southern Pacific and in the move these owners lost many head of stock. Of course, they were not at all pleased with the trend of events, but what could they do? Shang now controlled the range, and he had developed into the greatest beefsteak baron in all the south country. There was nothing to do but admit defeat.

Photograph by Erwin E. Smith
*Scouting Party*

Shanghai, to all intents and purposes, already had his old boss "on the Black Hills," and he was willing to call a halt on his program of vengeance. He remembered those ancient cows which Grimes had given him in lieu of salary in the

early days.   He remembered the incident of the Confederate
money.   He wondered if Grimes remembered, too . . .

Grimes kept the remnant of his cattle business in Texas,
although he moved to Kansas City to engage in the wholesale
dry goods trade.   In the '80's he formed a partnership with
Andrew Drumm and ran cattle in the Cherokee Strip of the
Indian Territory, but until his death a few years later he
remained an exile from the Matagorda and the Trespalacios.

The climax of the great "putout" explains the "Royal Arch
degree" which the contemporary biographer, Cox, hints at so
vaguely in telling the story of those ancient cows Grimes gave
the tenderfoot Shang for his first year's work.   The only
comment of Mr. Cox was:

"It was a sharp transaction on the part of Mr. Grimes, and
he probably congratulated himself on his adeptness in giving
a novice his 'first degree' in the cattle business, but having
since initiated his old employer in the mysteries of the 'Royal
Arch degree' of the same trade, Mr. Pierce is willing to consider all accounts squared, and can honestly say, 'peace to his
ashes.' "

Thereafter, Shanghai Pierce was the undisputed king of the
coasters in that section.   In the early '80's he established headquarters at what is now the little town of Pierce, on the Southern Pacific in Wharton County.   He and his brother Jonathan owned most of the country between that point and Matagorda Bay and they made a division, Shang taking the upper
country and Jonathan the lower.

### How Shanghai and his brother named two railway stations

When the railroad built a station near his place Shanghai
furnished the material, and as the building was nearing completion and a painter was blocking out the letters *Pierce* on
the station sign, the king of the coasters happened along.   He

studied the painter's handiwork for a moment and then bawled out an order.

"I bought the lumber for this depot," he shouted, "and the building's mine ... put that other letter on there!"

The workman obeyed, and the station became *Pierce's.*

*With the corn-belt buyer and sale by weight came the demand for hornless cattle, necessitating the chute and squeezer. This scene was photographed while dehorning was in process.*

When the railroad erected a depot down the line near Jonathan's place he was given the right to choose the name. He was so pleased at getting a station that he wanted *Thank God* painted on its side, but he finally compromised on *Blessing,* present headquarters for his son Abel, who was named for his uncle.

Purchase of the range from under the feet of Grimes proved a fortunate financial move for the Pierces, and by the arrival of the 1890's Shanghai had under his control more than a million and a half acres. He had shortened the horns and otherwise improved his stock with Durham blood. The old "sea lions" of trail days began disappearing from his pastures, and with the railroad now at his own front gate, he sold at home.

He remained not only the greatest cattleman in that area, but one of the largest farmers. He held, under a state law which permitted that sort of thing, a contract calling on the state prison system to furnish seventy-five field laborers each year. In his herds at this time he ran a variety of brands— the BU, the Half Moon, and the D, the latter being the most prominent.

All this vast empire he ruled from his headquarters of *Rancho Grande*, and old-timers in that part of the world still recall how he sometimes stood on the second floor gallery of the ranch house giving orders in his booming voice—in tones distinct enough to be heard a mile away.

"Once you heard it you never forgot it," says Fred Montier of Port LaVaca. "It was like the bellow of a bull . . . "

"Or the roar of a hurricane," in the opinion of old Bill Dunbar of Matagorda town.

Even Shang himself took great pride in that voice. He often said he had "a national reputation as a loud talker," and he liked to tell the story of how, when people would go to Dan Sullivan's home in Indianola to ask if Shanghai was in town, Sullivan would go to the door, cup a hand to one ear, listen a moment, and then say:

"No, Shang's not in town; if he was I could hear him."

Along with his loud voice he also could "cuss" as well as

any man in the country, his accomplishments along those lines being noted even by the court records. This is clearly brought out in litigation which followed dissolution of the Pierce-Sullivan Pasture and Cattle Company, a partnership in which Shang and his brother Jonathan joined with Dan Sullivan, the banker, in running cattle on a fifty-thousand acre ranch in Matagorda and Wharton counties—a partnership which ended after a personal disagreement between Shanghai and Sullivan.

In one of the suits involving land and cattle, lawyers in the case had this to say in a brief which still may be found in the court files at Galveston:

"That the court may at the inception get a fair idea of the parties to this litigation and their character, it can be truthfully said that it can not be proven that either the complainant or the defendent is a saint. If the principals in this case were characters as fit to run an Epworth League or manage a Sunday School, then that party would fail upon whom rested the burden of proof."

At the very start of the Pierce-Sullivan partnership Shanghai had found cause to look with disfavor on the banker's contribution to the enterprise—which was one-fourth of the cattle stocked on the range. There are some in the Matagorda who still remember the story of Shang's first view of some of the Sullivan cattle. He was riding the range with McCrosky, one of the foremen, when they came upon some especially scrawny cattle in one section of the pasture.

"Where in th' hell did you get all those sow-yearlings?" roared Shanghai. "Of all the rag-tags and bob-tails!"

Mr. McCrosky explained that they had been sent in by Sullivan.

"The scum of creation!" exclaimed the Goliath. "Look at those horns . . . little like your fingers! Dan probably took 'em in on debts, but there's no use cuttin' up about it, I guess."

And so he merely contented himself, as he put it in his own language, with giving McCrosky "plenty of hell."

Legion—and in many cases legendary, perhaps—are the stories which have grown up around Shanghai Pierce and his career.

In the '90's he took a vacation in Europe, visiting the British Isles, Holland, Austria, Germany, Italy, France and incidentally, the Pope. Unfortunately he neglected to make an appointment with His Holiness and when he walked unannounced into the Vatican he was turned back by the halberds of the Swiss Guards.

"When I saw those men come at me with their bayonets," he later told LaBauve, his old range boss, "I just threw up my hands western style and backed out."

Then there was that memorable cattlemen's convention in Austin where Shang is reputed to have dived through the window of the banquet hall to escape the wrath of Ben Thompson, the fancy gun handler, and city marshal.

The story goes that the range brethren, having sat down to a festive repast, laid aside their feeding tools long enough to throw into the street an inoffensive little attorney who had wandered into the hotel to see what the merriment was about. The man of law, however, chanced to be on friendly terms with the notorious Ben and he immediately sought out the gunman to complain about the rough play of the cattlemen.

Shortly after the ejection incident Shanghai, sitting at the head of the table, called upon friends at the opposite end of the board to pass the turkey, but finding his request ignored, remarked to a neighbor:

"I'll show you how to get that bird."

Reaching down, he slipped off his boots and climbed onto the table. He was just starting down the festive board in his sock feet, stepping gingerly around the potatoes and the peas, when Ben Thompson, a Colt in each hand, appeared in the room.

"Who th' hell says my friend can't come in here?" he demanded.

Shang, so the story goes, dived through a convenient window to escape the fireworks, which didn't come off. It was not a very dignified exit for the man who liked to proclaim himself to strangers as "the Webster of the cattle business, by God" . . . but the fact remains that Ben Thompson was not noted as a shrinking violet.

### How a feed of flapjacks put through a $90,000 loan

Whatever may be said of Shanghai Pierce he never forgot a friend. Once he even loaned a man an extra twenty thousand dollars because that man's mother was a good flap-jack maker.

This story comes from F. C. Proctor who, while practicing law at Victoria, represented Tom O'Connor, Ben Q. Ward, Pierce and other big cowmen at various times.

Ben Ward had moved to Houston, speculated in real estate, and had become so financially involved that finally his whole estate, including the Matagorda county ranch where for years he had been a neighbor of Pierce, was in jeopardy.

In 1900 he applied to Shanghai for a loan and Pierce instructed Proctor to look into Ward's affairs and see if a loan were warranted. Proctor made the examination and when Ward arrived to learn the decision the lawyer said that only $70,000 could be allowed on the property.

"But I need $90,000," declared Ward. "Just $70,000 won't save me. It won't do me any good."

"Well," replied Proctor, "I have followed Mr. Pierce's instructions. I am his advisor, you will understand, and $70,-000 is all your property is worth as collateral."

"Do you mind if I see Shanghai myself?" asked Ward,

who seemed to have some sort of idea that Proctor was acting as watchdog over the big cattleman.

"Why, of course not. I have nothing to do with Shanghai's decisions. He makes them himself. I act only under instructions."

Ward left. A day or so later he was back in Proctor's office. He told the lawyer that he had seen Pierce.

"And he's going to let me have the $90,000," he added. "Said he would wire you."

True to the promise, a telegram from Shanghai arrived a short time later. It read:

"Let Uncle Ben have the $90,000. His mother used to let me have flapjacks."

Proctor made out the papers, Uncle Ben Ward got the $90,000, but the next time the lawyer saw Shanghai he said to him: "What on earth did you mean about those flapjacks?"

Shanghai laughed long and hard, then told Proctor the following story:

"I was born in Rhode Island, you know, and it got too little for me. When I lay down, my head would like as not be in the lap of somebody in Massachusetts and my feet bothering somebody else in Connecticut. I just got too big for the state, so I thought Texas would be big enough for me, and came here.

"The first thing I did was to hire to W. B. Grimes at fifty cents a day. Directly I was breaking horses at that price. It happened this way ... One morning a prize buck nigger was ridin' a wild horse out in the pen close to the house. That horse was a terror. He was a-squallin' and the nigger was a-hollerin', and the other niggers joinin' in. Well, Mrs. Grimes came out, saw what was happening, and she gave old Bing (W. B. Grimes) a going over. 'Don't you know,' says she, 'that that horse is liable to kill that nigger—and he's worth a thousand dollars. What do you mean by letting him ride pitching horses when you've got a Yankee here working for four bits a day that could take the risk just as well?"

"Bing saw the point," continued Shanghai, "and from then on I took the risks. I was too poor to buy decent clothes, and the family didn't allow me to come into the polite part of the house. I ate in the kitchen and slept out in a shed. The Wards lived over on the creek, where Uncle Ben still has the ranch, and once in awhile while riding the range I'd get over there. When I did they'd treat me like sure enough white folks.

"Old Lady Ward knew I could eat more than a whole livery stable, and she'd just pile the flapjacks up to my chin and I have never been able to forget them and the good kind woman who made them. Now you know why I let Uncle Ben have the $90,000 against your advice."

Yet Shanghai was a business man. When he came to write his will he asked Proctor how much he was going to charge, and the lawyer placed his fee at $2,500.

The cattleman fussed and fumed. He went outside, kicked a dog, cussed a nigger, and finally re-entered the house.

"All right," he said, "it's agreed . . . but I was expecting you to charge me about $5,000."

Proctor is another who can attest to the volume of Shanghai's voice.

"He could sit in one end of a railroad coach and in a normal voice hold conversation with some other man in the far end of the coach," said the lawyer. "The other fellow, of course, had to yell. Being in the most conspicuous part of a Barnum and Bailey circus would be no more conspicuous than being in the company of Shanghai Pierce."

On the ranch, when the cold northers howled and the night herders were hard put to hold cattle just gathered in, old Shang often rode out to help the boys lull the restless herd with song. He felt more at home on the back of a horse than anywhere else.

### One of the best men in this or any other land—

Mrs. May Cleveland of Bay City, who roped and handled her own herd of cross-bred Brahmas at the age of seventy-three—the last year of her life—enjoyed telling how the aging Shanghai sometimes came to her home for dinner. She used to carry out a chair and help him mount his horse, and Shang—who once could stand flat-footed and vault into the saddle—would laugh and say: "Imagine me usin' a chair to get onto a horse!" But even then he could ride almost as well as ever . . . once in the saddle.

The South Coaster king died in December of 1900, leaving his vast estate to his grandchildren; to be administered by A. P. Borden, a nephew, and Mrs. H. M. Withers, a daughter of his first marriage. Both are dead now and the property is administered by J. F. Hutchins under the direction of the Pierce heirs.

The great Shanghai lies buried in Hawley cemetery, fifteen miles west of Bay City near Deming's Bridge, and today the passerby may see above his grave the monument which the cattle king built to himself—a large marble statue of "Shang" Pierce.

He stood in plaster of paris in New York to make the model for that shaft, and at the time he warned the sculptor that he would not pay for the work until a qualified judge could pass upon the likeness. When completed the statue was shipped to Texas and Shang called in an old negro employe, Jesse Duncan, to pass judgment. The resemblance, said Jesse, was remarkable—and the artist received his check.

Shanghai Pierce's best epitaph, perhaps, is not one written on his tomb, but one which comes from his old neighbor, Mrs. Cleveland:

"He was as uncouth as the cattle he drove," she used to say, "but with all his blustering ways there was no harm in him. He was, at heart, one of the best men in this or any other land."

BRAND
SHANGHAI PIERCE

Photograph by W. D. Smithers

*A good calf roping horse keeps the rope taut while the cowboy ties the animal.*

# The
# Mavericks
# of
# Matagorda

SAMUEL MAVERICK

● *"... MAV'ER-ICK, n. (Said to be from Samuel Maverick, a cattle owner in Texas who did not brand his cattle, his ranch being on an island). Cattle raising. An unbranded animal, esp. a motherless calf, formerly customarily claimed by the first one branding it. Western U. S."*
—Webster's Dictionary.

● How the term 'maverick' originated

T HE LONG roll of the drum rumbled and reverberated through the *Presidio de San Antonio de Bexar.*

Alternately a crescendo and then a dying murmur, it came from the Military Plaza; and as its sinister echo swept down

61

the narrow streets of Soledad and Acequia, citizens halted their
accustomed tasks and came scurrying to the square, eager to
witness whatever unusual event might be scheduled for the
day . . . for in that troubled time, October of 1835, anything
might come to pass in the Mexican state of Texas-Coahuila.

The Plaza soon filled with a curious throng, each man asking his neighbor the reason for the rolling drum, but even
the youngest among the spectators needed no second guess to
sense that this was an affair of more than usual importance.
Otherwise why should *El Coronel*, Domingo Ugartechea, be
abroad so early in the morning?

More than that, the commander of the post of San Antonio
actually appeared in high spirits as he stood on the square
twirling his mustachios under the admiring gaze of his dragoons, who were drawn up in company front, their muskets at
rest.  But more eyes were on the Colonel.  A bold figure in
his blue coat and gold braid, this dashing *caballero* from the
South . . .

And then the long roll sounded again as from one of the
avenues leading into the plaza  emerged another squad of
dragoons,  bringing with them three prisoners whose white
faces were touched with a certain paleness.

The populace gaped.  So that was it . . . the three *Americanos* were about to die!  A new ripple of interest ran through
the crowd, for these were the men Ugartechea had caused to
be arrested for plotting rebellion—for communicating with the
army of rebel Texans, even then threatening to march upon
the city.  They were spies, and was it not just that they should
die?

A silence, punctuated by an order from the Colonel, fell
over the Plaza.  The drum ceased its rolling tattoo, the line
of dragoons stiffened, their musket butts clanked against the
flag-stones,  as the three prisoners were  marched  to  their

places and faced about, their backs against a wall. The commandant of San Antonio smiled.

"Senors," he said, facing the trio, "it is useless to review the charges; it is best to proceed at once, but if you have anything to say I shall be pleased to hear. Senor Smith? ... Senor Cocke? ... Senor Maverick? ...

None responded. The men merely shook their heads, gazed sullen-eyed at the facade of the building across the way, and waited. There was little left to say.

The drum rolled once more, the Colonel stepped aside to draw his saber, the dragoons raised their rifles to the ready—and then from out the press of the crowd, came the shrill note of a woman's voice. She broke through the first line of spectators and before any could forestall her, ran to Ugartechea's side, and threw herself at his feet.

"Have mercy!" she cried, encircling the Mexican's boots with her arms. "Spare them ... Give them a chance to prove their innocence. They must not die!"

Ugartechea frowned, for he had not counted on such an impasse.

"But Senora Smith," he protested, "in these bad times we cannot countenance espionage; and your husband and his friends have been convicted ... sentenced by the court ... "

"Only on suspicion," replied the woman, looking up at the officer with tearful eyes. "It is injustice, and you are a just man. Investigate again ... I beg of you!"

The sobs of the woman filled the now tense Plaza and Ugartechea, gazing first at the waiting crowd and then at the prisoners, wavered. He could well afford to be generous; it would give him prestige in the eyes of the populace—but what would General Santa Anna say? That was something else, and a troubled expression came into the brown eyes of the Colonel as he thought of his master, the cold-hearted little man whose word was law over all the land that stretched between Mexico City and the Presidio of San Antonio. But already Ugartechea had weakened. He clicked the saber into the scabbard, waved a hand.

"Take them away," he ordered.

The muskets of the guard clattered again on the flags; the dragoons fell in, marched away with their prisoners; the crowd in the Plaza dispersed; and the lives of three men had been saved—through a woman's tears and a soldier's generosity.

### How a new and colorful cattle term was given to the world

And still something more had been saved—one of the most colorful stories in all the history of the cattle industry—for among the three who stood before that firing squad was one whose name was destined to become a household word, not only in Texas, but through every cattle country in the world. He was to be, first of all, an empire builder; never calling himself a cattleman; never owning, at any time in his career, more than a few hundred head of steers; but in the end it would be his destiny to give to the wild, unbranded cow-brute of the open range a designation that would live forever—and for that reason he takes his proper place in this narrative...

The name was Maverick.

Samuel Augustus Maverick was born at Pendleton, South Carolina, on July 28, 1803. He came of a prosperous family... his father, likewise Samuel, being a prominent merchant of Charleston and reputedly the first to ship a bale of American cotton to London.

The father had sent his son to Yale hoping that upon graduation in 1825 he would return to Carolina and take, through the legal profession, a leading part in community life. And Samuel Augustus did return home, and did take out a license to practice law, but his political ideas differed with those of his neighbors and, after wounding an opponent in a duel over the subject, he nursed his victim back to health and then departed for Alabama to manage the plantation of a widowed sister.

The sister, however, remarried, leaving Samuel free to drift. He went first to New York and then to New Orleans, where in 1834 he heard from a land agent the first of the tales which were to lure him into Texas. He took passage in the early summer of 1835, and the schooner dropped him on the shores of Matagorda Bay ... at a place called Cox's Point, just a dot upon the sprawling Texas coastline.

It was with a definite feeling of doubt that he made his first appraisal of the country, but he really hadn't expected much. He had come to Texas fully aware that this new land was a savage frontier stretching many wild miles into a hinterland where death and danger lurked at every turning. Tales of adventure heard in New Orleans still were vivid in his mind—tales of Indian raiders who swept down from the north on dark and bloody missions; stories of wild cattle roaming over boundless plains. He had heard, too, the first distant rumblings of the storm which even then was about to break over the virgin state of Texas-Coahuila, a gathering hurricane of hate and war and death which was to wrest the province finally from the power of the Dons who ruled in Mexico.

Attacked with a fever, he had lain ill for a time at the inland town of Brazoria, and then, with recovery on the way, had mounted horse to ride with a chance companion over the long westward road which led to the Presidio of San Antonio. It was on this journey that he first realized the possibilities presented by the infant empire of the west; that he first saw the vision which some day would make him foremost among the landholders of the country.

But that day was still far away. He found San Antonio in a state of unrest. The new Texas Republic, although still unborn, already had been conceived; and already a pitifully small force of Americans, under command of Stephen F. Austin, Colonel J. W. Fannin and old Ben Milam, were encamped north of the city in preparation for the blow which was to test the cause of Texas liberty.

The Mexican commandant at the Presidio, Ugartechea, hitherto scornful of the hated *Americanos* and their talk of rebellion, lately had been making a revision of his point of view. Aware of the plot to capture the city, he had become suspicious of the few Anglo-Saxons who remained in town ... and under the circumstances anything might happen.

This information Maverick received from Mr. and Mrs. John W. Smith in whose home he had taken lodgings upon his arrival September 8, 1835, and as a newcomer he was advised by Smith and a fellow-roomer, P. B. Cocke, to watch the trend of events carefully before considering any venture into the land and cattle business. The American families, he was told, were remaining close indoors, the Smith household being no exception.

Thus the weeks passed and the tension of the calm before the storm increased. The flame that Austin had lighted in the north was growing brighter and the Americans, sick of the autocratic intolerance of the Mexican militarists, were rallying ... while lines of worry were etching themselves deeper and deeper in the brow of Commandant Ugartechea.

His troubles were increasing. On October 2, 1835, he had sent a detachment to Gonzales to seize a cannon the rebels had secretly obtained, and though he had looked for easy victory his troopers had been forced to retreat and leave the old brass piece—which the Texans had used to fire the first shot of the Revolution!

And then something else of startling nature had occurred. The rebels, heartened by victory and by new recruits, had chosen Stephen Austin commander-in-chief, and on the ninth had surprised the Mexican garrison at Goliad, capturing a store of military supplies. Ugartechea, with reports on these maneuvers before him, now had little reason to doubt that he was faced with the real thing and since his military reputation was at stake, it follows as a matter of course that he should check on the Americans remaining in San Antonio. The arrest of Smith, Cocke and Maverick as spies, and the resultant fiasco in Military Plaza, followed.

But the arrest and escape from the firing squad was not the end of the trouble, though the incident did furnish one amusing element of irony—the three men, hitherto mere spectators in the political drama, now becoming spies in fact!

Angered over their treatment by the military, they contacted a small boy of the town, one known to be trustworthy, and for days sent secret messages to the Texans ... contributing in part to the victory that the rebels, 100 strong, scored over 400 Mexicans at *Mission Concepción* on October 28, 1835.

### Maverick is caught in the vortex of frontier politics

They continued this secret communication until a change in Mexican administration at the Presidio—Santa Anna having sent General Martin Perfecto Cos to supplant Ugartechea—brought a relaxation of vigilance at the Smith home long enough for the occupants to elude the posted guard and escape under cover of darkness on the night of December 3, 1835. They encountered the rebel forces at the sugar mill a mile north.

Thus Maverick found himself, only a few months after his arrival, caught in the swirling vortex of frontier politics. Small wonder then that he found no time to analyze the resources of the country and map the course of his future career. If Samuel Maverick could have looked into the future! His story, in the immediate years to follow, was to be the story of infant Texas itself.

Samuel Maverick acted as guide for Milam when, on December 5, 1835, the rebels swept in to storm Military Plaza;

and on the eighth, in the garden of the Veramendi Palace, when old Ben died with a sniper's ball through his head, it was Maverick who caught him as he fell. Then, on the tenth, when the white flag went up on Plaza House, he was present when General Cos handed over his sword and reluctantly agreed to retreat to the Rio Grande.

The early days of 1836 came on and still Samuel Maverick found no time to devote to his determined course in land speculation. The Texans were mustering for the grim and gallant effort for freedom, and already secret plans had been made for a Declaration of Independence, and a convention set for March 2, 1836, at the village of Washington-on-the-Brazos ... and already General Antonio Lopez de Santa Anna, with a strong army, was on the way from Mexico City to teach the Texans a little lesson.

Maverick, along with Don José Antonio Navarro, had been selected convention delegate from the Bexar district, and this appointment probably saved his life—for had he not been at Washington-on-the-Brazos in the early days of March he might have died with Davy Crockett, Colonel Travis and the others when Santa Anna stormed the Alamo and put the garrison to the knife on the sixth—but as it was he was saved to join Sam Houston and help strike the final blows of the revolution.

After that a farewell to arms—at least for awhile. The way now seemed open for the purchase of land, which was selling just then at prices ranging from five to fifteen cents an acre. The day of golden opportunity appeared to be at hand and with this in mind Maverick returned to South Carolina to visit his father and to dispose of property owned in the East. There had been, too, something infinitely more important—a girl he had met in Alabama, Miss Mary Adams, daughter of an old Virginia family—and when Maverick came back to San Antonio after little more than a year, he brought not only a wife, but an heir, likewise called Samuel.

The Charleston merchant at first had protested against the land venture; had sought to keep his son in South Carolina. He offered slaves and lands and money; he argued that the wild country was no place to take a woman and child, but no amount of pleading would turn the new-made Texan from his course. The lure of cheap land was too appealing and, as Maverick often said in later years:

"I had the Texas fever."

Immediately upon his return to San Antonio—it was in June of 1838—Maverick established his family in a house near Main Plaza and went to work on his land program while his young wife, thrilled and a little fearful, began taking stock of her new surroundings.

She found the city a dangerous, if an interesting place. She watched with alarmed fascination the raids of the Comanche Indians into the very outskirts of the town; and sometimes in the evening she sat in the parlor holding little Sam a bit closer to her breast as Captain Jack Hays and Capt. Juan Seguin of the Texas Rangers regaled the household with stories of Indian pursuits in the open country to the west. And at times these tales struck a bit nearer home . . . for often, after some particularly daring raid, her husband would join the dashing Hays on an expedition of vengeance.

Even these troubled days failed to shake Maverick's confidence in the new Republic, and though by this time he had definitely decided against any immediate venture into the cattle business—market facilities being too uncertain—he had committed himself wholeheartedly to the career in land speculation.

Well supplied with the proceeds from his eastern holdings, he bought one tract here, another there, and then he discovered a more rapid way to carry on his program of acquisition. At the close of the Revolution the Republic had been liberal with her soldiers, granting in reward for services rendered certain certificates for sizeable tracts of land, and many of the troopers were more than anxious to convert paper into cash. Maverick bought certificates; his holdings grew.

He was in his home examining surveys on one of these tracts on the morning of March 19, 1840, when the city was thrown into turmoil by the bloody Council House fight, which started when the Texans met representative chiefs of the Commanche nation to negotiate for the return of kidnaped white children and which ended with the slaughter of seven white men and thirty-five Indians in the blood-soaked hall.

Mrs. Mary Maverick, after her husband had gone to join in the battle, witnessed a part of the massacre from the window of her home, a scene which caused her to write in her journal: "What a day of horrors! And the night which followed was as bad!"

One incident of that evening was to remain forever stamped upon her memory. Late in the day she had gone to the home of her neighbors, Mr. and Mrs. Thomas Higginbotham, to wait with Mrs. Higginbotham and give assistance in event some of the wounded Americans needed treatment. About sunset they looked through the grilled front window of the house and saw the community physician, Dr. Weideman, approaching, carrying under one arm a misshapen object which could not be readily identified in the failing light. The good doctor bowed and addressed Mrs. Higginbotham.

"With your permission, madam," he said, depositing his burden on the window sill. Then he turned and hurried away in the dusk leaving the two women to stare—at the distorted features of a human head!

Within the hour the man of medicine was back, this time carrying the amputated head of a Comanche woman, for several women had been killed in the fight which followed disagreement over return of captives. The doctor placed this grim object on the sill beside its fellow, then bowed again.

"I have long been exceedingly anxious to secure such specimens for scientific purposes, and I have selected these two, male and female, for their skulls," he said. "And now ladies," he added, "I must hurry and get a cart to take them to my house."

#### A grim evening on the banks of the water ditch

A short time later the physician, a Russian who had been sent out by the Czar to study Texas, brought his cart and hauled away his gruesome prizes—and the women were glad to see him go.

But that wasn't the end of the matter. That night Weideman put the heads, together with two skeletons he had selected from the massacre heap, into a large soap boiler. Then he kindled a fire in the street before his home and cooked the flesh from the bones. His precious specimens secured, he dumped the water and flesh into a nearby ditch which, it so happened, furnished the drinking water for the town.

Next morning the dwellers along the ditch, soon after the first drink of the day, realized that something must be amiss, and the events which followed were both tragic and comic. According to the version left by Mrs. Maverick:

"There arose a great hue and cry, and all the people crowded to the mayor's office. The men talked in loud and excited tones. The women shrieked and cried, rolled up their eyes in horror, and vomited."

Dr. Weideman was, of course, arrested. He was tried and fined, but he only laughed . . . he had his skulls.

That was San Antonio in the '40's, but these Indian troubles gave but slight pause to Maverick's land program. By the early days of 1842 he was credited with holding more land than any other man in Texas. Although he had taken out a license to practice law, he spent more time with surveying parties than in court, and more than once he escaped death by narrow margins—once leaving his camp for San Antonio only a few hours before Comanches attacked and massacred the entire company of surveyors.

And then in February of 1842, a new blow. Mexico, still reluctant to surrender her new province of the north, had sent General Rafael Vasquez and an invading army across the Rio Grande. The Mavericks, like other residents of the city, fled San Antonio and reached Gonzales before the city fell, but during the occupation—before Jack Hays' Rangers routed the invaders—all their furniture and personal property was destroyed, forcing Mr. Maverick to journey again to South Carolina to replenish his finances.

He returned in September—in time to be caught in the invasion of San Antonio by 1,400 Mexicans under General Adrian Woll, French soldier of fortune. He was one of the 53 Americans, including officials of the district court, who were taken prisoner by Woll and marched to Mexico.

History already has dealt extensively with the tragedies of that affair—how Woll drove his captives, manacled and chained, toward the Castle of Perote, a thousand miles to the south; how he penned them like cattle in stockades at night; and how upon arrival at the military prison in the state of Vera Cruz, they were subjected to cruel and inhuman treatment, and put to the task of breaking rock.

In this labor, however, there was one "shirker"—for Samuel Maverick lost no time in showing his captors that he preferred death to the business of making little stones out of large ones, grimly demonstrating upon one occasion by suddenly looping his wrist chains about the neck of a particularly obnoxious guard and choking out his life before other Mexicans could interfere. (And those chains, if you should care to see them, may be found today in the archives of the University of Texas at Austin.)

In all his seven months of imprisonment Samuel Maverick never worked but once, and that once only out of pity when a fellow-prisoner, seriously ill, had been ordered to the rock heap. Maverick volunteered to take his place. In the face of his studied defiance during captivity the fact that he lived to tell the story of Perote remains one of the mysteries of the adventure—but he did. Destiny was not yet finished with him; Fate still needed him—to give to the cattle industry one of its most colorful stories.

General Waddy Thompson, United States Minister to Mexico and by marriage a kinsman to Mr. Maverick, took a hand —pleaded with Santa Anna for release of the prisoners, with the result that Mr. Maverick was among the first set free, in Mexico City on March 30, 1843.

He reached his family at LaGrange on May 4, but the happy reunion was somewhat marred by the fact that he found his wife and children (there were three now) in poor health; and so he moved his household immediately to Decrow's Point on the Matagorda Peninsula, that long finger of land which separates the bay of the same name from the waters of the Mexican Gulf. Then he assumed his place in the Eighth Texas Congress, to which he had been elected during imprisonment.

Fate works in many ways her miracles to perform, and now, after long delay, and after snatching from death a dozen times the object of her whims, she was ready to cast him in the role which was to preserve his name forever in the households of the cattle countries.

**They made a branding iron but the MK was little used**

It all came about because Maverick held a neighbor's note for $1,200, a debt of long standing which the neighbor said he couldn't pay—simply because he didn't have the money. Moreover, he saw no chance of getting anything that even closely resembled cash.

"But I do have 400 head of cattle," he told Maverick, "and I'll turn them over if you'll take them."

Maverick had protested. He didn't want cattle; he was certain about that. He had, he said, watched the trend of events in Texas long enough to conclude that little profit could be made in the business. He cited current prices— with steers selling for only what hides would bring in foreign markets. No...he preferred to deal in lands.

"In which case," sighed the neighbor, "we'll say no more about it. But I'll be honest...if you don't take the brutes I don't know how I'll ever pay."

Now $1,200 is an amount not to be dismissed carelessly and Maverick, realizing that it might be a matter of cattle or nothing, finally allowed delivery of the herd at his place on Matagorda Peninsula, whose tall grass and wild clover made the strip one of the best grazing pastures on the south coast.

Thus Maverick unwillingly entered the cattle business. But he displayed his lack of interest almost at once by placing the beasts under the care of his negro slaves, and when he and his family returned to the old home in San Antonio in 1847 he didn't even bother to give instructions for disposal of the animals. One is left to surmise that he was glad to forget the bellowing brutes.

But he wasn't allowed to forget. Under the management of the negroes, whose interest appeared quite on a par with that of "Mars" Maverick, the herd was left pretty much to its own resources. Contrary to the implication in Mr. Webster's International Dictionary, some of the employes did devise a branding iron...the MK...but it was allowed to grow cold and rusty, the excuse of the negroes being that they had heard "Mars" Maverick say on various occasions that he wasn't exactly in sympathy with the practice of burning a cow's ribs with a red hot iron.

Naturally the cattle multiplied as they fattened on the grass of the Peninsula, and as new calves came on and grew into yearlings and two-year-olds, many wandered to the mainland —wild, unrestrained bulls and calves that carried no man's brand. And so it came to pass that the ranchers of the coastal area, when they chanced to find a particlarly wild and unmarked animal on the open range, began to say:

"That's one of Maverick's."

Or—

"That's a *maverick*."

Photograph by Erwin E. Smith

*New Calves*

But did the neighbors respect these cattle as the rightful property of the man whose name they took? They did not . . . They caught the stray bulls and calves alike, heated their own irons and burned in their own brands; and thus the beasts, under the unwritten rules of the open range, no longer were Maverick's (or mavericks). But it did seem strange to behold one of the original and branded MK cows followed and sucked by a calf marked with another rancher's brand—a situation pointed out in the many letters of advice and warning received by Maverick in San Antonio. One anonymous note, still in possession of the family, had this to say:

"Send someone to look after your stock or cattle immediately or you will not have in 18 months from this time one yearling nor calf to 10 cows. It is said, and that by some of our most respectable citizens, that yearlings and calves may be seen by the dozens following and sucking your cows and branded in other people's brands."

And so, in 1853, Maverick sent a party of *vaqueros* down to Matagorda to round up the herd and move it to *Rancho Conquista,* a tract he had acquired on the San Antonio river about fifty miles from the city. The *vaqueros* found about 400 head, amounting to the original number, but they could make no guess as to how many had strayed away to be stolen.

Maverick, more disgusted than ever with the cattle business, took immediate steps to dispose of the herd. In the end, he struck up a deal with Monsieur A. Toutant Beauregard, brother of the general who was to distinguish himself a few years later as a leader of the Confederacy in the War between the States.

M. Beauregard agreed, after some bickering, to take the lot at six dollars a head "as they ran" and further agreed to conduct his own roundup of the animals unbranded. Needless to say, the *vaqueros* of Monsieur Beauregard earned their pay —for included in the transaction were a goodly number of Matagordian bulls that seemed determined never to hear the swish of a *riata* about their horns—and like a pack of wild lions the "mavericks of Matagorda" scattered over the plains of South Texas, adding wherever they appeared new flavor to the tradition of their name. The term caught on and spread beyond the borders of the state, and even unto this day the wild and untamed bovine, wherever he may be, is called a "maverick."

Samuel Maverick, who died in 1870, never claimed to be a cattleman.  He was, rather, one of the empire builders who led the way for the greater beefsteak kings, but he left his name upon the ranges of the world—a one-word monument that time itself has not been able to erase.

*Deep in the Brasada, on the great King ranch, the vaqueros and caporals pause at the conveniently camped chuck wagon for beef, bread, coffee, and a cigarette before entering the brush again.*

# The
# Santa
# Gertrudis
•
# King and Kenedy

CAPTAIN RICHARD KING

● **They created a buffer state between two nations**

MIFFLIN KENEDY

I T WASN'T Mexico! It
wasn't the States; and it wasn't exactly Texas. Rather, it
was a kingdom of its own, a sort of buffer state between two
nations.

79

It is a land of mesquite and sand; of prickly pear and chaparral; of clouds and sea and sky; of *vaqueros* and cattle. It was a range of giant herds, all burned with the brand of the Running W ... or, as the Mexicans chose to call it, "The Little Snake."

Washed on one side by the Gulf of Mexico, touched on the other by the half-desert of the brush country, this corner of the world—set in the southern tip of Texas—can hardly measure up to paradise, but just the same it has that subtle sort of lure which calls men back again.

And that is why, according to legend, that the good St. Peter keeps all *vaqueros* chained to posts in Heaven's pastures.

"I can't turn those boys loose," the old gentlemen once explained, "for if I did they'd high-tail it straight back to King Ranch."

And any old saddle-warmer among the coasters will tell you that the Keeper of the Gates is mighty well acquainted with his boys.

### Outsiders seldom reach heart of the great empire

Among the major ranches of the world the King has stood alone. The regular routes of highways west of Corpus Christi merely skirt its borders, and the casual tourist seldom sees more than the *Santa Gertrudis* headquarters near Kingsville, or the western boundary of the *Norias* division, which touches the Southern Pacific line extending south from Falfurrias toward San Juan on the border.

Few outsiders make their way, even by accident, to those divisions known as the *Sauz*, the *Laureles*, and the *San Antonio Viejo*. These romantically-named regions are swallowed up in the 1,250,000 acres of land which until recently made the King, with its 125,000 head of cattle, the greatest of all the ranches in the world.

There are 50,000 cows, as many steers, nearly half as many calves and 3,000 bulls of the Brahma, Shorthorn, Hereford, and Santa Gertrudis breeds, the latter type developed by the owners. There are 2,500 horses, and scores of Mexican *vaqueros* to ride them over a terrain which varies from loam to sand and clay ... over a territory whose corners are so remote that even the seasons vary. There are well-kept fences and trick Argentine chutes ... everything that might make up a cowman's fondest dream.

But was this giant enterprise, originally, a cowman's dream? It wasn't. The greatest of all the wide-world's *haciendas* really had its start because a small boy objected to looking after his employer's baby. One must turn back to 1833 to find that story ...

When the schooner *Desdemona* cleared the port of New York, outbound for Mobile, the captain had not the slightest suspicion that he carried a stowaway in his hold, for such a supercargo was rare in those days. Therefore, it is needless to recount that the skipper expressed some surprise and no little dismay when, four days out of New York, an eight-year-old boy appeared on deck to inform him that he had a new sailor.

The *Desdemona's* captain was not so sure about that, and he began plying the lad with questions. This much he learned —that his child guest's name was Richard King; that he had been born in Orange County, New York, on July 10, 1825; and that only a few weeks before he had been apprenticed to a jeweler for whom he had no liking.

"I didn't fancy the work, either ... 'specially minding the baby," said young Dick King. "When they asked me to do that ... well, I just ran away."

That, the captain informed him, was a bad thing to do— but he said it with a twinkle in his eyes, for he liked the lad from the moment of their first meeting. And then he added that since he had sailed without a cabin boy young Richard might as well have the job. The *Desdemona* plowed on toward Mobile Bay.

Before the boat came to anchorage on the Alabama coast the skipper had formed a decided attachment for the child, and while he unloaded cargo he began looking about for a proper guardian to take the stowaway when the *Desdemona* should return to sea. Richard made it quite plain he would not make the homeward voyage, and as a result he was put under the wing of Captain Hugh Monroe, a steamboater in the Alabama river trade.

A cabin boy's life on a packet was interesting, and Richard liked it. He worked a year or more with Monroe, and then took a job aboard the boat of Captain Joe Holland, who decided almost immediately that a little schoolin' wouldn't be wasted on his ward.

Some little persuasion was needed, however, to make Richard education conscious, but at last the skipper succeeded in packing him off to Connecticut. Eight months later the boy was back on the southern rivers. He preferred the steamboaters to the pedagogues, and those eight months in Connecticut gave him all the academic instruction he ever received. He took his lessons, instead, on the Alabama steamers.

He caught on rapidly, and in the immediate years which followed he qualified as a riverman in every degree from cabin boy to pilot. And then the glamour of military life gripped him.

Preparatory to acting out one of the blackest chapters in Indian history, the tragic story of Osceola, General William J. Worth was mustering troops for a drive against the Seminoles of Florida . . . and Richard King was at the romantic age of sixteen.

He joined the army, served under Captain Penny in the short-lived campaign, then returned to his beloved boats; and it was during this period that he met a kindred spirit—Mifflin

Kenedy, a young Pennsylvanian who had been plying the Apalachie and the Chattahoochie rivers of Florida as pilot aboard the steamer *Champion.*

They found a great deal in common, though Kenedy, who came of Quaker parentage, was older by seven years. He, too, had been cabin boy. After completing boarding school in 1834 he had shipped in that berth aboard the *Star of Philadelphia,* bound for Calcutta by way of the Madeira Islands. On the homeward voyage from India the *Star* had been caught by a typhoon in the Bay of Bengal and badly battered and leaking, had been forced to put in at Isle of France for repairs.

When seaworthy again the boat had touched St. Helena to fill the water casks, and had reached Philadelphia again in January of 1836. This long and hectic voyage had given young Mifflin quite enough of deep water for the time and next we find him in the role of school teacher, which job he kept until he listened to a friend's dramatic stories of steamboating on the Ohio. Thereupon, he chucked the master's ferrule, went at once to Pittsburgh, worked for awhile in a brickyard, and then hired out as a clerk on a river boat.

Both the Ohio and the Mississippi saw him during the next few years; and then, with pilot's papers in his pocket, he found a place on the *Champion,* which was plying the Alabama River between Mobile and Montgomery. The war took him to the Chattahoochie and to the meeting with King, now with pilot papers of his own.

### Toot of the King line boats whistled on the Rio Grande

Kenedy told King about the new project he had in hand. He was taking the *Champion* to New Orleans and thence to Pittsburgh to meet Major John Saunders of the Army Engineers.

"It's this way," he explained, "Zach Taylor will be needing boats down on the Rio Grande, and Major Saunders wants me to help pick 'em. We'll buy what we can in Pittsburgh, take 'em down to New Orleans and then on to Texas.   Maybe I'll go all the way."

The business had a romantic flavor, for events were stirring thick and fast on the Rio Grande at that time, the early months of 1846.   The war with Mexico was in the making.   General Zachary Taylor's army was preparing for the grand push on Monterrey, San Luis Potosi, and the City of Mexico.   Supplies were needed on the river, and the boats to do the hauling.

Kenedy had been so enthusiastic that King, after his friend's departure, had found it impossible to keep thoughts of Texas from his own mind.   His desire for a change of scenery became even more intense when he learned, later, that Kenedy really had helped purchase a fleet of steamers—including the *Corvette*, the *Colonel Cross*, and the *Whiteville*.   And Kenedy, as he had hoped to do, had gone with the armada down to New Orleans, where he had enlisted, signed on as master of the *Corvette*, and had been sent to the mouth of the Rio Grande.

This bit of news decided King at once upon a course, and he made the move which was to mark the great turning point of his life.   Still troubled with unsatisfied dreams of military adventure, he caught the first boat for the new theatre of action, and within a few weeks found himself on the deck of the *Corvette*, as pilot.

Busy days followed one after another.   There were troops to be taken to Matamoras, and food and guns and more men to Reynosa, Camargo and other points along the *Rio Bravo del Norte*; and upon one occasion they transported General Winfield Scott . . . "Old Fuss-and-Feathers" himself . . . down to Camargo.

Roma heard the toot of the *Corvette's* whistle, and so did Rio Grande City.   Men and guns and food and horses . . . regiment after regiment going south . . . and then a lull.   Days passed, then weeks and months.   News came back slowly.

Jack Hays and his Rangers had taken Monterrey. Taylor was driving on Saltillo. San Louis Potosi had fallen. The Stars and Stripes floated over Chapultepec Castle.

And then they all came back again . . . men and food and guns and horses, going north. When they had passed that small but important section of the naval service commanded by King and Kenedy, the latter two had little left to do.

In one way steamboaters are like cowboys. Ask the latter to leave his horse and plow an acre of ground and he will, as the saying goes, "hate your guts." Ask the steamboater to quit his deck and go ashore and he will feel the same lovely sentiment taking possession of his being.

King and Kenedy, however, had no intention of being left "afoot". They had saved a little money and they bought the *Colonel Cross*, entering it in the cargo business up the Rio Grande from Brownsville. The venture soon justified itself in a financial way, and by the early '50's they had a score of boats on the river and had taken in two partners, James O'Donnell and Charles Stillman.

About this time came the turn of fate which was to transform steamboater into steer man, and set the first stake for the largest cattle empire of all time—but some of the credit for that transformation must be given a young lieutenant of cavalry then stationed at Brownsville, an officer who had helped lead the charge which took Old Zack's men into Mexico City.

One day in 1852, while riding with this lieutenant across the mesquite flats between the Nueces and the Rio Grande, Captain King remarked on the physical aspects of the country —its almost limitless range, its warm climate, and its cheap cattle. He wondered what the future would be, and he asked the officer—whom he had come to regard as one of his best friends—what he thought about it.

"Well, it isn't like Virginia," replied the cavalryman, as

A three-crew branding outfit working in a brush corral. This type corral was usually made of cottonwood logs and brush dragged up from the creek bottoms by the saddle horn.

he watched the wind twist a sand dune into little whorls, "but it's a country with a future. Below the line cattle can be bought for practically nothing, the grass is good . . . in spots . . . and Mexican labor cheap."

"But the market . . . there isn't any," the steamboater reminded him. "You can't sell cows without a market."

"True enough, but all that will work itself out . . . and in time this will become one of the greatest cattle countries in the world."

Lieutenant Robert E. Lee was to be a prophet as well as a famous general . . .

Captain King did not forget that ride across the prairie, and in the months which followed he often discussed the matter with Mifflin Kenedy—casually at first, but more seriously as time wore on.

There was the *Santa Gertrudis,* a likely tract of about 75,-000 acres on the Nueces southwest of Corpus Christi, but its history wasn't all in its favor. The *Gertrudis,* originally, had been a grant from the Spanish crown to Don José Domingo de la Garza, but that gentleman, after repeated visits from hostile Indians, finally had been butchered in the ruins of the *hacienda* he had striven so hard to establish. The heirs had sold to Don José Perres Rey, who also had been pursued by ill fortune. The second Don José, however, did manage to escape with a whole skin. The tribesmen, raiding continually into his herds, had succeeded in making life so utterly miserable that he was glad, at last, to gather up what property he could find and take the trail for more civilized parts . . . as did most of his neighbors.

Despite all this, Captain King liked the *Gertrudis,* and he bought it—almost for a song. Kenedy still was doubtful, and he preferred to remain with the boats; but an arrangement was made whereby King, although he was going ashore, could keep his interest in the river enterprise. Money was being made in the cargo business, and Captain King knew he would need money for what he had in mind.

It did seem an almost hopeless task—the building of the *Santa Gertrudis,* and a less determined man than King might have met with swift and certain failure.

### Water was early problem on the Santa Gertrudis range

Señor Garza, during his stewardship over the place, had boasted but few cattle, for the simple reason that he lacked proper watering facilities. He had sunk a few wells, but since the water had to be drawn by bucket, naturally his operations were limited.

Captain King went to work with all the energy at his command. He improved the wells and then began stocking with Mexican cattle—rangy steers and hammer-headed cows of the longhorn variety—and below the line he purchased horses and brought in *vaqueros* to ride them.

The livestock market was small indeed, New Orleans and the South being the only outlet, but he refused to worry about that. He was certain that better days were ahead—so certain that in December of the following year, 1854, he went down to Brownsville and brought home a bride... Miss Henrietta Chamberlain, daughter of a Presbyterian minister who was doing missionary work among the Mexicans. Mifflin Kenedy also had found a bride, Mrs. Petra Vela de Vidal, of Mier, Mexico...

The *Gertrudis* now had a queen and the Captain proceeded with the building of his kingdom... At first what few cattle he sold were steers. He kept the cows and heifers, and with the natural increase in the herds acquisition of more property became a necessity. He bought new tracts and as his domain expanded the *Santa Gertrudis* began to assume the role of a buffer state between the two nations—protector for the smaller ranchmen against raiding Indians and marauding Mexicans from over the border.

By 1860 the ranch had become the major cattle enterprise on the coastal plains, and it was then that Mifflin Kenedy offered to buy a half interest.

Captain King was glad to take him in, and immediately they started building the *Gertrudis* on an even larger scale, just as they had built the boating business on the Rio Grande. They imported Durhams from Kentucky to mix with the Mexican stock, and within a few years a new and sturdier type of cow was making its appearance in the Nueces country. The neighboring ranchers, guessing at the cost, looked on with interest, but King and Kenedy called no halt.

They could well afford the experiment, for their boats were experiencing a sudden season of unexpected prosperity because of the War between the States.   True, the South Coast was blockaded by Yankee gunboats, but that did not prevent the river steamers from carrying cotton down to Brownsville and loading it on British merchantmen under the very eyes of the naval watchdogs.

The steamer profits helped, too, in the land purchasing program, and by the close of the Civil War the partners could count around 300,000 acres comprising three principal ranches, the *Santa Gertrudis*, the *Laureles*, and the *Agua Dulce*.   By this time the enterprise was a going concern in its own right. Steers were moving to the southern markets, more improvements were being made, more *vaqueros* were on the horses. The thing was getting just a little unwieldy.

It was then, in 1868, that the partners decided on a division, each to take share and share alike in acreage, cattle, horses and sheep.   The *Laureles* went to Kenedy—and now there were two kingdoms where one had been before.

And again the neighbors had cause to marvel at the daring of Richard King, for he began work on a strange and unheard of project—the fencing of the *Gertrudis*.   He was one of the first cattlemen to realize that the day of the open range was

La Parra, headquarters and home of John Kenedy, near Sarita, Texas. The Kenedy ranch was founded by his grandfather, Mifflin Kenedy, who came to South Texas with Captain Richard King to establish the vast King and Kenedy cattle empires.

limited, that the time was near at hand when all ranches would be enclosed, and he acted accordingly.

Since barbed wire had not yet been invented, he bought lumber from the sawmills in the hill country to the north, hauled it many weary miles, and fenced with boards.

But while this was taking place (the work was not completed until 1870) King allowed no grass to grow under his feet. He gained control of another ranch, the *San Juan Carricitos*, and additional pasturage in Cameron county, comprising in all more than 300,000 acres.

He did this in the face of the unfavorable market debacle caused by the Civil War, but during that time of great beef surplus he followed the example of all large cattlemen in establishing a rendering plant and killing for hides and tallow. Then the market in the north opened and the trail herds began ambling up across the Indian Territory to Kansas.

Naturally the Captain was pleased with this new outlet. Large herds have a way of growing unwieldy and more than once King was heard to voice that complaint familiar on the coastal plains:

"When there's grass there's no water; and when there's water there's no grass ... with the damn Mexicans always wanting higher pay."

So King steers went up the long stretch to Kansas, and the Captain became obsessed with the Great Idea, a permanent trail to the North—a sort of "neutral strip" through which ranchers could drive their cattle without interference with, or from, agriculture.

Realizing the lack of proper rail facilities in those days, and looking forward to the time when the farmers would begin fencing in earnest, Captain King believed that a fenced mile-wide "lane" to the North, extending from Brownsville to the Canadian line, was a virtual necessity. The new barbed wire (just invented by an Indiana eave-trough maker) would make the work easy.

King, in fact, was one of the leaders in a Texas delegation which championed the proposal before a cattlemen's convention held in St. Louis, but the passive attitude of the northern states killed the project in its formative stages.

The folly of the plan made itself evident in the coming of the railroads, an industry in which Captains King and Kenedy interested themselves in a large way. With Colonel Uriah Lott they shared in the building of the San Diego, Corpus Christi and Rio Grande Railway, a line extending 132 miles from Corpus Christi to Laredo. Begun in 1876 this narrow gauge system was completed in 1880 and then sold to the Mexican National.

The *Santa Gertrudis* continued to grow and with its expansion the herds also increased—until an average of between 75,000 and 80,000 head could be found each year on its ranges . . . but even so, a small empire compared with that the Captain visualized in his dreams.

When a stomach disorder developed and ended the Captain's career at the Menger Hotel at San Antonio in April of 1885, one of his major ambitions remained unfulfilled. He had hoped, some day, to own all the land between Corpus Christi and the Rio Grande.

### Robert Kleberg took up the sceptre left by the captain

When he died he held title to only 500,000 acres!

But his dream would have been a physical as well as a financial impossibility. Mifflin Kenedy and his son, John held a fair-sized chunk of that territory. They had sold the *Laureles* in 1882 to purchase the Kenedy Pasture Company in Cameron county, a domain 30 miles in length and 20 miles in width (with which the son carried on after the elder Kenedy's death in 1895 at Corpus Christi.)

Captain King left all his vast empire to his wife and she asked the family lawyer, Robert J. Kleberg, to help her in the management of the ranch.  Mr. Kleberg already was engaged to a daughter of the Kings, Miss Alice, and after their marriage he assumed active direction of the estate.

The heir took his place among the greater cattle barons of the Southwest.  He took up where the Captain left off. He made still greater improvemnts, both in ranching methods and in stock breeding.  He studied the menace of the cattle tick, which brings on the bovine fevers.  He mixed the first batch of "wash" that ever went on a cow's back, and became the "father" of the modern dipping vat.

He founded the town of Kingsville by donating land; he helped build two railroads through the Nueces country; he helped put through the dredging project which made Corpus Christi a deep water port — and before Mrs. Henrietta King died in 1925 at the palatial *Santa Gertrudis* headquarters her son-in-law had built, she saw Don José de la Garza's original grant expanded into a kingdom of a million acres. And when death removed Mr. Kleberg from the scene in 1932 the land books showed a total of nearly 1,250,000 acres.

ROBERT KLEBERG

Then Bob Kleberg, Jr., a young man in his late thirties, took the saddle as manager of the King, with his mother— the founder's only living daughter—the ruling queen of the *Santa Gertrudis*.  He was to hold the managership until the estate, under the provisions of Mrs. Henrietta King's will, should be divided among the heirs of the old Captain's five children, a group which includes Richard King III, president of the Corpus Christi National Bank, and Richard Mifflin Kleberg.

The new ruler of the kingdom followed in the footsteps of his predecessors—and in some ways went them one or two better. During his regime, for instance, he stretched a thousand miles of new fence, added more acreage, imported and experimented with Afrikander cattle, and busied himself with perfecting the ranch's own breed, the *Santa Gertrudis*—a cross between Shorthorns and Brahmas.

The throne of Bob Kleberg the Younger was at the *Santa Gertrudis*. Down on the. *Norias,* the great division of the south, Caesar Kleberg, a bachelor cousin, was the ruler—living in a ranch house which had a bath tub on the front porch, a house through whose doors no woman ever had passed. Here was the real buffer state between two nations, for the *Norias* had been the scene of many a skirmish with Mexican raiders from over the border; and even today the rifles of the gun rack at the headquarters are kept at the cock.

Captain Richard King . . . Robert Kleberg the Elder . . . Robert Kleberg the Younger . . . each succeeding generation has made a new monarch for the Texas cattle industry; and the royal line might have continued but for the will of the founder's widow.

The ten years of trust before the ranch was to be divided among the heirs expired on March 31, 1935, and on that date the division was announced.

### King Vaqueros grow up with the empire, its law their law

Through purchase of the interests of other heirs, purchases of land in their own name, and by the terms of the will, Mrs. Robert J. Kleberg, Sr., and her children remain at the *Santa Gertrudis* with some 815,325 acres around them. These holdings are owned by the King Ranch Corporation, of which Robert J. Kleberg the Younger is president and general manager, and Congressman Richard Mifflin Kleberg, vice-president. The headquarters and some 30,000 acres had been transferred to Mrs. Kleberg by Mrs. King before her death on account of her action in "having lovingly and faithfully devoted practically her whole life to my care, consolation and aid."

Among other bequests, Richard King, III, received 182,871 acres and the Atwood heirs of Chicago, 112,421 acres.

Few things remain now to recall the days of Captain King. A new breed of cattle has supplanted the longhorns, and nearly 300 windmills dot the landscape on his one-time kingdom. Even the fences are different—the wire running through holes bored in the posts.

But one carryover from the old days still may be found in the country—that in some of the *vaqueros* who work the cattle. Just as the management came down from generation to generation, so it was with some of those who did the work afield. Many grew up with the empire knowing no other law, knowing no other business.

There was, for instance, old Augustine Quintenilla ... so old that none knew his age. In the wisdom of his many years he knew more, or at least as much, about cattle than any man in Texas; and twenty years ago he was made *caporal* of the *Laureles* division. Though he made it a practice to remain in bed during every January to escape the fate of his brother who had died in that month, there was another month. Quintenilla the *Caporal* died in October of 1934, leaving two sons to the empire ... which now, alas, no longer exists in its original form.

And it is just as well, perhaps, that old Augustine Quintenilla never knew ...

BRAND
CAPT. RICHARD KING
RANCH

Photograph by Erwin E. Smith

*Campfire reveries*

# Bos
# Indicus

ABEL BORDEN

BRAHMAS

● How Abel Borden,
Shanghai Pierce's
Nephew, brought
India's S a c r e d
cattle to America

FOUR-HEADED Brah-
ma, Supreme Soul of the Hindus, was a most remarkable and
puzzling deity—both in physical appearance and in his accomplishments.

97

In the beginning he was but an intellect floating in space, and then—desirous of producing different beings from his own self—he created the waters by his own thought, and placed in them seed which developed into a golden egg.

Therein was born Brahma, "Parent of the Worlds," himself. Having dwelt in the egg for a year, that lord by his own thought split the egg in twain, and from the two halves fashioned the heaven and the earth . . . placing in the middle the sky, the points of the compass, and the perpetual place of the waters.

And then, according to legend, the Supreme Soul rolled up his sleeves and went to work on the first creature to be placed upon his new-made earth. The clay took form, developed into a brawny, humpbacked bull—and the great god Brahma, as he surveyed his first day's work, was well pleased.

Hereafter, said he, those who wished to follow his teaching, must regard certain of the Hump-backed Ones as sacred, and damned be he who should kill the holy beast or eat its meat. That is why, even in the India of today, may be found men of certain castes who had rather part with wife than kill or sell his sacred cow or bull.

How, then, did so many of these hump-backs reach the Matagorda country on the Texas Gulf coast? The traveler, knowing the Hindu legend, may well ask himself that question as he wonders at the great beasts grazing on the coastal range.

*Bos Indicus* is vastly different from the common species of *Bos Taurus*. Aside from the hump on the shoulders, the most striking points of distinction between them are found in the large pendulous dewlap, and the loose, pendulous skin in the region of the belly. They are heavy in build, black hoofs prevail, the hide varies in color from cream and chocolate-brown to black, the tail is slender and whiplike—and the bulls do not bellow, but roar, and the cows grunt rather than low.

There are four principal breeding stocks in the species— the Nellore, the Gir, the Guzerat, and the Krishna Valley—and the cross-breeds from these divisions make a pleasing panorama as they roam the plains of the Matagorda. But behind that panorama hides a story unique in the history of the cattle industry—

The first importation of Brahman cattle into the United States appears to have been made in 1849 by Dr. J. B. Davis of South Carolina, who brought over a bull and two cows, but the first alien blood came into Texas through Louisiana—all because an Englishman bought a shipload of sugar cane for milling in Australia.

This Briton voyaged to Louisiana about 1861 to study the cane industry, and when he arrived he put up at the home of a Mr. Barrow, with whom he had contracted for a cargo of cane. He stayed a year, and when his ship at last was ready to weigh anchor for Sydney he offered to pay Mr. Barrow board for that period, which offer was refused.

"Then I'll bring you something when I come back," he said.

And true to his word, the Englishman, when he returned to Louisiana, brought his host a present—three Brahman bulls which in some unexplained manner had found their way to Australia.

Needless to say, Mr. Barrow was surprised, and he appraised the big beasts with quizzical eyes. The Englishman explained:

"When I was here before," he said, "it struck me that your native oxen could do with more strength. I would like you to experiment . . . cross these bulls with Louisiana cows to bring about a hardier, stronger breed."

Within five years the foreign blood began to evince itself slightly in Louisiana coast cattle, and in 1866 Colonel Shannon of Galveston, while visiting the Barrow place, bought a few of the better types at $150 a head. Colonel Shannon, an old Terry Ranger and a former stock buyer for the Confederate army, knew that the cattlemen of Texas would be interested in the possibility of a new beef type. He took a fine black bull to the ranch of J. A. McFaddin near Victoria. The Colonel advised the rancher to introduce the blood into his own herd.

Photograph by Erwin E. Smith

*Steer rider*

"I have found these Brahmans fat when other cattle are poor," he said.

### First Brahma in South Texas was an unpopular beast

At that time probably no more than thirty head with the foreign blood were scattered over Texas. Since livestock men were giving most of their attention to introduction of the Durham strain, Mr. McFaddin was doubtful. So were other ranchers who came to view the strange freak. They served warning.

"Don't let him come around my ranch," most of them said. "Don't let him get out, or he is dead, sure."

This sort of talk had an effect on Mr. McFaddin, and had it not been for his son Al he might have told the Colonel to take his black bull and go. Al wanted the animal and the purchase was made.

From that moment Al M. McFaddin took a devout interest in the India stock. Later, when he drove to market he sometimes would find in the herd two or three steers with Brahma blood, and he noticed that these always topped the market.

After that he began trying to find cattle with the *Bos Indicus* strain. If he saw two or three in a bunch he would buy, but the breed was scarce in those days, and he found no animals which might be called purebreds.

The year 1904 arrived before he was successful in this quest. One day while in St. Louis he attended Hagenbeck's Circus, and in the menagerie tent he was surprised to find a Brahma bull and cow in a cage—being exhibited to the pop-eyed public as outstanding examples of India's sacred bossies.

McFaddin sought out Mr. Hagenbeck and learned that the pair had been imported only the year before "at great cost and with much trouble in breaking down caste prejudice." Before he left the tent McFaddin had title to that bull and cow. He paid $1,000 for each and shipped the beasts to Texas.

On the ranch near Victoria the great experiment started. The cow died before calving, but the bull was used to start the original McFaddin grade herd, the first in the state.

And now other ranchers began to sit up and take notice. They observed that this new type never was bothered by the ticks, that the fatal fever passed them by while taking heavy toll in the native herds. Tom O'Connor, who had pastures on two sides of the McFaddins, took an exceptional interest in the herd and at last tried to buy it. McFaddin refused to sell, but O'Connor finally obtained a few head of "grade" cattle, as did Abel P. Borden, who at that time was executor for the estate of his late uncle, Shanghai Pierce.

Borden was interested, for he had heard the great Shanghai say that these cattle were the only ones he had ever seen which would produce a grade better than the parent animal. He wondered what he could do about building up the Pierce Estate herds.   And then—

"Tama Jim" Wilson came to Texas.

The Hon. James Wilson, secretary of agriculture, was not concerned with cattle when he came to visit A. P. Borden in Texas.   He was more interested in tea.

Photograph by Erwin E. Smith
*Boys receiving the mail*

A year before, Mr. Borden who believed that extensive farming should run hand-in-hand with extensive ranching, had cleared a tract along the Colorado River near the present village of Mackey.   Secretary Wilson had selected this place as an ideal spot to conduct a tea-growing experiment in the South.

He made arrangements with Borden and then sent down J. H. Kinsler, a young scientist, to manage the experiment. Plants were brought in and everything went off nicely for awhile.   Then the plants began to die . . . rot at the roots.

At first Secretary Wilson feared that the young superintendent was at fault, and he ordered Dr. B. T. Galloway, head of the Bureau of Plant Industry, to the scene of action. Galloway had no better luck, and finally "Tama Jim" himself came down from Washington.

Mr. Borden gave the story of that visit to this writer only a few weeks before he died of a heart attack in St. Louis on October 18, 1934.

"Mr. Wilson spent several weeks studying the tea experiment," said the nephew of Shaghai Pierce, "but as he analyzed the problem his attention was attracted to the Brahma cattle, and as time went on he began to show less interest in tea and more in the cattle. Then, one day, he turned to me and said: 'Mr. Borden, if you will go to India and import some of these cattle . . . purebreds . . . I will give you a special commission and place behind you all the agencies of the United States Government.' "

Mr. Borden waved a hand toward a framed document hanging on the wall of the study in his home at Mackey.

"There is the commission," he said. "That piece of paper, dated December 22, 1905, brought the first large purebred herd to Texas."

It wasn't, however, just a simple procedure of going over and bringing back the cattle. Mr. Borden finally brought fifty-one head of the sacred brutes, but he had more trouble with that small bunch than with the collected thousands of long-horns he helped to drive in eight trips over the trail to Kansas in the early days.

Tom O'Connor helped finance the trip, and when Borden sailed for India, Dr. William Thompson of San Antonio went with him.

"A man can buy anything if he has the money," said Mr. Borden, "but we did encounter difficulties in some instances with caste prejudices in India."

He explained that there are various Brahman sects, some of which refrain from killing cattle or using meat for food, others killing and using beef without objection—and some cattle of this type, otherwise called the Zebu, are not regarded as sacred. In a strict sense the term Brahman, derived from the name of the Hindu deity, applies only to certain bulls which have been designated by priests as sacred; and for this reason he could not purchase some of the finer types he wanted to include in the importation herd.

"Once in a pasture near Agra," he recalled, "I came across an excellent specimen, and as soon as I saw it I was determined to buy. In order to find the owner I waited until evening and trailed the animal home . . . only to discover that the animal belonged to a man of the more orthodox caste. The owner said he would as soon sell his wife as the beast, but he would give it to me on one condition . . . if I would agree not to kill the animal or any of its progeny. I could not honestly make such an agreement, and so the importation herd lost a valuable addition."

### The Priesthood was shocked, wouldn't sell animals

Borden tried once to purchase a bull from a priest, but so great was that good man's horror at the suggestion that the Texan thereafter avoided the priesthood as prospects.

After several months, however, he succeeded in assembling a representative herd of 51 head of various breeds and various colors—grays, whites, and blacks and reds. They were loaded at Bombay and started for home—but new difficulties loomed ahead.

The entire consignment was held up in quarantine at New York; and Mr. Borden always suspected that breeders of other types had a hand in the detention. Anyhow, that herd remained in quarantine for nearly six months. The inspectors claimed the animals had Surra disease, and in small lots they were condemned for slaughter.

Borden stood by helplessly and watched the herd diminish. He pleaded with the Treasury Department in Washington and could get no release, and then—after eighteen animals had been killed and the remainder condemned—he went in desperation to President Theodore Roosevelt, always a friend of cattlemen.

T. R. listened sympathetically to the story, and then with little comment, called Lyman Gage, secretary of the Treasury, on the telephone. The cattle were released and Borden went to Texas with 33 head—16 of which went to O'Connor in the division.

Today Brahmas still are bred extensively in the coastal regions. The world-famous J. D. Hudgins herd in Wharton County is one of the leaders in the industry—but Borden, who in 1928 retired as executor of the Pierce Estate and converted his Mackey ranch into a cotton plantation, believed that the day of the Brahma is over in Texas.

He blamed the Fort Worth market, and the rodeo performances at Fort Worth's annual Fat Stock Show, where performers ride the wild "roaring" Brahma steers in the arena.

"The Fort Worth market is to blame for the decline of the type as a meat steer," he told me shortly before his death. "The packers are prejudiced against the South Texas cattle; and the public, seeing the so-called vicious Brahmas in the rodeo arena, gathers the impression that the meat of these battered steers must surely be too tough to eat."

Commission men at the Fort Worth Stockyards will tell you that the market really is prejudiced, but not for this reason. They point out that the Brahmas, when being handled in shipping pens and chutes, are as wild "as a bunch of Bengal tigers," and that in their mad milling and piling up, they sustain bruises . . . and packers do not like bruised meat.

Bengal tigers? Those steers the rodeo-goer sees in the Coliseum are wild and unmanageable because man has made them that way, according to the man who imported the first large herd.

"Like any other animal," Mr. Borden used to say, "the

Brahma is just as mean as man makes it. He is bold, and he is proud ... the only type of steer that can look a man in the eye and not waver. The Hereford will look, then glance away. He remembers something that the two-legged creatures have done to him, and he is ashamed of mankind. But the Brahma has no such scruples; he neither fears nor disrespects the master of the beasts."

Even if the Brahman breed goes tickless and avoids the scourge of fever, the North Texan and the Panhandler can find no place for *Bos Indicus* upon their ranges.

"They can't stand the winters on our plains," they say.

But down in the south the Brahman still is something of a sacred cow. Abel Borden liked them, and so did Tom O'Connor. It was O'Connor who told the boys, when he was dying, to round up a big herd near the house ... so he could hear them "beller" as he left.

BRAND
BORDEN BRAHMAS

BRAND
AL N. McFADDEN

# The
# Jingle-Bob
# King

John Chisum

Boot trouble

● How John Chisum fought
Apaches and Thieves to
found a 200-mile Cattle
Empire

**T**HE Mescalero Apaches
were on the raid.

In the early hours of morning, under the light of a wan-
ing moon, a war party had slipped out of the reservation and
had headed for the flats along the *Rio Feliz.*

107

There was the beef on the *Feliz*, and the Apaches—like their brothers, the gray wolves of the plains—wanted it; and again like their brothers the wolves, preferred to hunt it down and make the kill themselves . . . as in the days before Uncle Sam had seen fit to round up his savage nephews and place them on a reservation under the watchful eyes of blue-coated cavalrymen, whose duties included the unpleasant task of feeding the redskin charges like so many wild animals on a game preserve.

But of late something had gone wrong at the military post. For some reason concerned with graft and greed and politics the officers who played nurse to the Mescaleros had delayed the weekly ration—and the tribesmen, when it came to bread-line etiquette, were not a patient people. Then, too, they disliked being fed from the hand just as much as the cavalrymen disliked to feed them. That's why the war party was heading for the *Feliz*.

It was near noon when the hunters reached the flats and the first herd was sighted. Here was meat—and the young men, riding in advance of their elders, galloped in to cut the herd and pick a dozen beasts for slaughter; but before this purpose could be carried out the older men had arrived to lend their wisdom to the business.

It was then that one of the sub-chiefs, seasoned veteran of many forays, shouted a warning to those who rode among the cattle. He had noticed on the brutes two unusual but familiar markings—a long white streak burned into the hide from shoulder to hip, and an ear slashed through from its tip to head so that it flopped and bobbed in a peculiar fashion while the steer was in flight.

These signs the old man knew, and he held up a restraining hand.

"Jingle-bob!" he said, and: "Captain Chee-sum."

And so the savage raiders rode on—seeking other herds to

harry. Even the younger men, the more reckless and daring warriors, did not wait to argue, for they had heard a name both famed and feared throughout the breadth and length of this wild country—that of Captain Chee-sum, the man of many cattle.

Still fresh in memory was the day when this sanguine person, his patience exhausted by repeated forays on his range, had ridden with a party of armed men into the heart of the reservation itself to shoot down in cold blood the thieves who stole his cattle . . . an act which had brought into deep respect the brand of the long "fence rail" and the cut of the "jingle-bob" ear.

Well, no matter . . . there were other cattle on the *Feliz*. The raiding party rode on.

### A night of storm and stampede, and a herd vanishes

Who was this Captain Chee-sum whose name, mentioned in the waste of the plains, was sufficient to stay the destructive hand of the Apache, fiercest of all the tribesmen in New Mexico? For an introduction, for a proper meeting with the man as he really was, let us shift the scene and change the characters a bit.

The wind had risen in the night, bringing down from the north a swirling, blinding snowstorm which swept the Pecos River country from Fort Sumner to the Texas line. It was one of those sudden, hardstriking northers familiar to that area; and as it howled over the bleak New Mexican plains a few miles east of the river, it found a sorely disgusted Texas cattleman huddled down in an improvised dugout cursing the fate which had brought him from his home range, near Colorado City.

He had been a fool, he told himself, to drive 4,000 head of steers over the trail at this season of the year, and he swore by twice that many horns and hoofs that never again would he heed the lure of fat contracts handed out by the Government at Fort Sumner. So far as he was concerned Apache bellies could go empty in the future; he would drive no more stock over the long trail from Texas. Robert Wiley promised himself that.

Daylight brought a lulling storm and clearing skies, and as Wiley crawled from his dugout to survey the damage wrought in the night he saw before him a farstretching plain blanketed in white—that and nothing more. In all that expanse of snow and mesquite not a hide nor horn was in sight, though Wiley strained his eyes through high-powered field glasses in a vain attempt to trace some remnant of the herd which had bedded down in the dusk. The night, with its driving cold and howling wind, had brought stampede, and the beasts had vanished as though the earth had opened up to swallow them.

Now it is no very pleasant thing to have a fortune on the hoof get up in the darknss and wander away, and Wiley was a picture of despair as he contemplated his predicament. A stranger in the country, he realized the futility of search and so he ordered his trail hands to saddle.

"We'll just git on to th' river and see Old John," he said, "for if any man in this God-forsaken country can help us, he can."

And so the crestfallen outfit jogged west, coming at mid-afternoon to a small store nestling in a clump of cottonwoods on the bank of the Pecos near South Springs. The storekeeper, already having sighted the new arrivals, was at the hitching rail to meet them.

He looked more the vagabond than the merchant. His well-worn overalls, the frayed cuffs of which brushed a pair of heavy brogans, covered a big-boned and lanky frame which suggested the power of a giant. He was tall, slightly stooped in the shoulders, and he wore atop his head an old felt hat, pushed back from the forehead to reveal a few black strings of straying hair.

There was something in the face that marked him apart from the common run of men, though it was difficult to say just what. Perhaps it was in his steely gray eyes; or the firm-set, square jaw; or the thin, straight-lined mouth, which was shadowed by his only mark of elegance—a heavy black mustache which tapered to a needle-point suggestive of the stylish pinch of wax. A case of rugged individualism if there ever was one, this storekeeper on the Pecos.

"Well, Bob," he said, for he had known Wiley in Texas, "light and come in. What brings you down this way?"

"Hard luck, John," replied Wiley, still sitting on his horse. "Mighty hard luck"—and then he proceeded to pour out the whole woeful story.

With a merry twinkle in his eyes the rugged merchant listened attentively to the sorrowful narrative and then, unable to restrain his rising mirth, burst into a guffaw which shook the very rafters of his store. He laughed as a strong man laughs; he even lay down on the ground and rolled. Four thousand steers disappearing in the night! It struck him as amusing, highly amusing—but somehow Wiley failed to see the joke.

"What's so damn funny about that?" demanded the Texan, shifting in his saddle and regarding the old man sourly. "Four thousand head's a right smart bunch of stuff."

"And that's why it's so funny," said the storekeeper. Then recovering his dignity: "What they worth, Bob?"

"Thirty-five thousand, if they're worth a cent," said Wiley sadly, "but that was yesterday."

"Thirty-five thousand, eh?" And without another word the man in overalls turned and went into his store, returning a few minutes later with a roll of currency large enough to choke a longhorn. He held out the money to Wiley.

"Guess I'd better take 'em," he said. "You can get down and make out the paper. The critters probably drifted down and mixed in with the 20,000 I got on the lower range. My boys'll prowl 'em out when I need 'em."

### A Man in rags, but monarch of a 200-mile range

And that's the way John Chisum, the Rail and Jingle-Bob man, did business in the '70's; and that's one reason why he was called the Cattle King of the Pecos—a man in rags, but a monarch whose kingdom extended along 200 miles of river front that stretched from the Hondo to the Texas border.

He ruled with an iron hand, though there was nothing about his rustic makeup to suggest the hard-boiled warrior. He resembled the peace-loving farmer rather than the doughty fighter—and it was difficult to picture him as a man who shot down Apaches on a Government-protected reservation; as a man who some day would look into the muzzle of a Colt revolver and dare Billy the Kid to pull the trigger.

He ruled on nerve, and nerve alone, for unlike most of the contemporaries of that era when the West was in the making, he seldom was seen with the conventional six-shooter dangling from the hip. Peculiar to his type, he lived for many years among some of the worst gunmen who ever graced this continent with their presence, but preferred to go his way unarmed—his faith strong in the unwritten code which protects the defenseless from the pistol of the killer.

It is in such wisdom concerning the balance between life and death that real genius is born, for a man less wise probably never would have lived to boss the greatest range the world has ever known and round out a career which is among the most picturesque in the annals of the West—a cattle career which had its beginning on a comparatively small pasture which extended forty miles south from Denton to cover a part of the site upon which Fort Worth now stands.

John Simpson Chisum was born to the soil. He first saw

the light of day in Madison County, Tennessee, August 15, 1824, the son of a farmer, C. C. Chisum, who moved his family to the north of Texas in 1837. The country, menaced by marauding bands of Indians, was sparsely settled, and old Chisum (whose name originally was Chisholm, it having been changed for pension purposes after an army officer set it down as Chisum after the battle of New Orleans in 1812) settled at Ft. Inglish, now Bonham, later moving to Paris.

Here young John obtained his education, what little the community's frontier school afforded—and here he met the girl whose image he was to carry in his heart as in the years to follow he rode the wild lands of the West . . . an image that instilled in him that one soft touch of romance which was to temper the steel of his soul and leave him, even in his grimmer moments of blood and death, with the simple faith of a child in the greater things of life. She was, in a sense, his destiny—his ever-guiding star.

But something happened—nobody knows just what—and the girl bestowed her hand elsewhere. Disillusioned, young Chisum, at the age of 29, deserted the plow on his father's farm and began to cast about for something more exciting upon which to rest the structure of his career. He chose politics, and after the election of 1853 we find him taking the oath of office as clerk of Lamar County. But he grew restless—because one must suspect the image in the corner of his heart was troubling; and so, after scarcely more than a year, he resigned his place to enter the more appealing business of cattle raising.

The industry by that time, the year 1854, had extended north from the coastal plains, and though the individual herds had not yet become surprisingly large, the settlers throughout the upper portion of the State already were looking upon cattle as the principal means of future livelihood, and the country was filling with stock.

Chisum had little money but found a backer—S. K. Fowler, a New Yorker interested in western speculation. Fowler was willing to put up $6,000 as a starter and, padded with this stake, Chisum set out for Colorado County in the south. There he bought 1,000 head at $6 each . . . the calves thrown in for good measure . . . and he trailed back north to turn loose on the Fort Worth-Denton range, the partners soon adding to the herd 1,000 more animals which they picked up for $2 a head. Then Chisum made a 10-year contract with his financial backer, agreeing to manage on shares.

Photograph by Erwin E. Smith
*Good water*

Such was the beginning of a cattle king—one of the greatest ever to ride the sweeping stretches of the *Llano Estacado*.

It was inevitable, however, that the young stockman soon would be crowded for elbow room—for this range he had chosen was good agricultural land and quite naturally drew to it the ever-advancing tide of homeseekers from the east and south ... and Chisum was a man of vision, possessed of that native instinct which holds itself aloof from the restraints of civilization. So, in 1862, he sought more distant pastures. He found them in West Texas, and with only the Indian and the lobo wolf as neighbors, he settled on the Concho, his ranch the only one for leagues about.

It was a fortunate move. The range along the river was free and open, and the grass was good. Besides, the War between the States was in full swing, and Chisum had scarcely established himself in a prairie dugout before he found himself designated by the Confederacy as government stock raiser, an appointment carrying a contract of $40 a head—an exceptionally good price even if paid in uncertain currency of the Southern states.

Chisum already had become accustomed to long chances but in this instance he took no gamble on Confederate victory and permanent validation of its money. He didn't hoard; rather, when he sold a stock of beeves to the troops the money seemed to burn his fingers until he could get rid of it. He increased his herd, purchasing a dozen longhorns for every one he sold, with the result that his money was on the hoof when at the end of the Civil War the chief value of Southern currency consisted in the area of wall space it would cover.

### Lack of elbow room sent long John westward

Thus Chisum became one of the few cattlemen to profit from the war, but at the same time he disliked dividing those profits with Partner Fowler, and as their contract expired with the closing of the conflict, he was glad to notify Mr. Fowler that all future business would be conducted by Chisum and Company—and, of course, the partner could do nothing else but sell.

Chisum now had the field to himself, and he had little

competition. The few settlers who owned cattle in any large quantities had joined the colors at the pop of the first gun, leaving their herds to shift for themselves. The stock had increased, scattered and as a result the State of Texas, from Matagorda to the Panhandle, was overrun with cattle. The maverick had, in fact, come into its own.

This very situation brought trouble down upon John's head, for as soon as the boys in gray started drifting home again the west of Texas was swept with such an orgy of cow stealing that Chisum soon knew that he must move nearer the setting sun or else continually patrol his ranges with a rifle. Then, too, the elbow space was diminishing. Other cattlemen—like Charles Goodnight, Oliver Loving and the Slaughters of Palo Pinto—already were in business within 100 miles of his pastures. Crowding him out, leaving him scarcely space for proper breathing!

And so he sent his brother, Pittser Chisum, to seek out possible ranch sites in New Mexico. Brother Pittser was absent for a long while, and when at last he returned he brought with him such glowing accounts of the country along the Pecos that John scarcely could credit his ears.

"I'll go and see for myself," he told Pittser, "but I'll take along a small herd to sell to the government agents at Fort Sumner. Might as well make the visit pay."

He traveled over a trail already blazed by Loving and Goodnight—who took a herd to the Fort in '66—and when he arrived in New Mexico he discovered that Pittser had not erred. The range was suitable in every respect and there was a ready market, the government post needing beef for the Indians on the Mescalero Reservation. So Chisum returned to Texas in the early months of 1867 and moved 900 head of steers from the Concho to the Bosque Grande, the first herd to settle permanently in Southeastern New Mexico.

He established a camp, hired hands, secured a fat contract

from the officers at Sumner and then, after leaving Pittser
in charge, returned again to Texas in the spring of '68 to
gather cattle and fill the contract.

With the cow thieves multiplying on the old range the
Texans were only too glad to sell, and soon the dwellers along
the frontier began witnessing a strange, unusual sight . . . for
the herds that John Chisum drove from Texas to New Mexico
carried dozens, even scores, of different brands—an assortment
so varied that people on the westward end of the line were
at loss to understand where John was getting the variety.
No man likes to be called a cow thief, but even so Chisum
kept his counsel—never troubling to deny the charges until
the gossip became so persistent that he had to make some sort
of statement. Then he merely produced a sheaf of papers,
which he carried in a section of old lead pipe.

"Here is my authority," he said, displaying power of attorney for about 200 different marks and brands.

The documents gave the cattleman permission from owners
of the brands specified to drive stock with that particular
marking and to pick up strays found on the range. It was
an unusual arrangement and it called for an enormous amount
of bookkeeping on Chisum's part, but he always made a settlement of some sort with owners, sometimes in cash, sometimes
by note—a practice which in the end was to prove the man's
undoing.

The trail herds often met with trouble; for more than
once the Apaches of the Mescalero Reservation (for whom
the government bought the beef) could see no reason why
they should wait for Uncle Sam's officers to check in the cattle
and pay for them. For instance—

It was John's custom to drive across the west of Texas, hit
the New Mexico line above Horsehead Crossing, and there
deliver his stuff to Brother Pittser and his hands who would

take the beeves in charge and drive them—usually with a troop escort—up the Pecos to the army post.

Early in June of 1869, John arrived at Horsehead with 1,200 head, and Pittser was waiting to carry out his end of the work.  But for some reason Fort Sumner had been unable to furnish an escort and Pittser, with the usual trail hands, started out alone.  He didn't get far.  On Black River a party of Apaches, on "holiday" from the reservation, were waiting. They stampeded the herd on the night of June 12.  Although the Chisum men put up a good fight against long odds and succeeded in killing several of the warriors, the raid, from the Indian viewpoint, was a howling success . . . even if some did die over meat that would have been handed them free within the next few days.

Pittser didn't save a single cow.  The Apaches drove for the Guadalupe.mountains and there they made the kill—1,200 good steers that cost $20 each in Texas.

When John arrived again at Horsehead and heard his brother's story of the donation to Uncle Sam's savage nephews, he merely smiled in his cool, calm manner, pointed to the new herd and remarked:

"Well, here's another bunch;  try 'er again."

The day was not far distant, however, when Chisum's nonchalance in the face of such matters would fall from him.  He had by this time decided that his interests lay in the west. There he had found his market, leaving the northern trails to other stockmen.  Never once did he drive in that direction, although history sometimes has confused his name with that of Jesse Chisholm, the half-breed Indian who opened that avenue of cattle commerce.  The two are said to have been related, but remotely.

### The Jingle-Bob ear crop becomes a famous mark

Thoroughly satisfied with New Mexico, Chisum, in 1870, began a movement to place all his cattle in that territory, but adverse fortune beset him from the very start. On the first Texas round-up the Comanches stampeded his horses by night and the 'punchers had to let the cattle drift until they could go to San Antonio for new mounts.

They tried again in the spring and took the first of the herds through to Bosque Grande; and by the time the removal was complete John had on hand something like 25,000 head. He closed out all his Texas holdings, and in 1872 he was the only ranchman on the Pecos in Southwestern New Mexico, his domain extending for 200 miles along and about the river. He claimed range from Anton Chico on the north

*John Chisum's "Fence rail" brand*

to Seven Rivers on the south, from the White Mountains on the west to Canadian on the east—and no cattleman in the West was more widely known.

And no brand, either, was more widely famed than the long "fence rail"—that streak he burned from shoulder blade to hip that he might confound the thieves who tried so many times to blot his mark. And no other ranchman in the country had an ear-cut like his "jingle-bob", the upward slash that caused the ears of Chisum stock to dangle in fantastic fashion.

John Chisum at this time was approaching the height of his career—approaching, too, the series of reverses, involving war and death and murder, which were to force him from his throne. For he hadn't been long in New Mexico before he was confronted with the same troubles he had experienced in Texas.

First—the Indians. The Comanches and the Apaches began making frequent, and more frequent, forays into his herds. They became so bold, in fact, that on July 19, 1873, they rode up to the store he had established at Bosque Grande headquarters and stampeded the horses from the corral. Chisum and those of his 'punchers who happened to be on hand, entrenched in the store and peppered the raiders with a steady stream of fire, and although they knocked half a dozen redskins from their ponies, Bosque Grande lost 100 horses.

Later in that same month the Apaches charged a round-up party working under Pittser Chisum, broke open the corral, skipped with 40 horses, then turned their attention to another round-up camp working under an employe, one McKittrick. The boys with McKittrick put up a hot fight and lost one man, but as night fell the Indians left with 80 mounts.

Still later in July, at Huggins Arroyo, the savages killed Newt Huggins, a Chisum line-rider; and in the fall they finished off another, Jack Holt, and got away with 60 horses. Then, to add insult to injury, they raided the horse camp at Lloyd's Crossing in the spring of '74 and added 100 more to the tally sheet of losses.

The boss of Bosque Grande, quite naturally, was growing weary—and to make the business worse not only the Indians but the white raiders were cutting in on the herds. The whites became even worse than the reds, for whereas the Apaches usually went for horses, stealing just enough cattle for sport, the whites thought nothing of lifting 1,000 head at a time and vanishing with them into parts unknown. And the range was much too wide to guard.

The King of the Pecos had at this time something like 100,000 head under the "rail" brand, and he realized that if his assets were not to be swept away on the hoof he had better sell—if he could—and get something out of the business before it was too late. True, he was making money from the government contracts—money which he kept in an old safe at his headquarters, his faith in banks never having been very strong—but his profits seemed trifling compared with the losses he was suffering through thievery.

Accordingly, he sought buyers, and early in 1877 made arrangements with the St. Louis commission house of Hunter and Evans for disposal of about 65,000 animals; agreeing, under the contract, to supervise the round-up and make delivery to the purchasing agents.

The story of the deal wasn't long in finding its way to the most remote corners of the frontier, and there started on the plains of New Mexico a robbery festival which made as child's play that which had gone before. The "rustlers," when they heard what was happening, banded together in groups, and as one herd was driven out by the rightful owner another was taken from the range by thieves. Thus started a peculiar sort of race to see who should reap the most profit—the rightful owner or the thief.

Chisum, beset as he was by these difficulties, all but lost his faith in humanity, but not quite. He still carried in his heart that bright and shining image of his youth—a remembrance made even more poignant by the knowledge that the girl had made an unhappy marriage. Men who knew him, and who rode with him, have said that even during this critical stage in his career she was seldom absent from his mind,

and that he spoke of her by many a flickering camp-fire on
the open range.   In all these years he had never married;
he had, in fact, avoided women, preferring to remain faithful
to the image—and without it the thing which was about to
happen, bad as it was, might have been worse.

Emboldened by the success of the white thieves, the Apaches now joined in the wholesale game of robbery . . . not for
the sake of food and gain, but for the thrill of the chase and
the bloody kill.   They would slip by night from the confines
of the Mescalero Reservation, creep silently upon a herd, stampede it, and then drive for the Guadalupes—to kill as they
killed the buffalo in the days before the white man came.
How many animals Chisum furnished for these savage rodeos
he had no way of knowing.   For a long while he was patient—
and then he could stand the strain no longer.

### The Apache Raiders feel the iron hand of Captain Chisum

Hiring 100 men, he armed them to the teeth, mounted
them on good horses, filled his own saddle pack to bulging
with the best and strongest whiskey, then led the company
toward the Mescalero Reservation.   Half a mile from the military post, headquarters for the army officers who conducted
the affairs of the reservation, he reined in and cautioned his
men to silence.

"Wait here 'til I get back," he said, and then grinning like
a school boy bent on mischief the overalled king of the Pecos
rode on to the post.   It was nearly two hours before he returned—to report that the whiskey had served its purpose.

"I had to buy a little, but the whole staff is down and out,"
he said, and then wheeling his horse and kicking in his spurs:
"Come on, boys, let's go!"

Straight into the Mescalero Reservation charged the yelling Chisum "cavalry", pistols popping as the riders galloped
in among the tepees!   The raid was a complete surprise and

many an Apache warrior, his belly filled with jingle-bob beef, died with a pistol ball in his carcass as he emerged from his lodge to see what the shooting was about.

The army officers, dead drunk at the post, heard nothing of the fireworks and they were sadder and wiser men when they awoke to find the corpses of more than 100 Indians strewn about the reservation.

Chisum's "army" already had departed, but the cattle king's vengeance had been complete—so complete that most of the Apache survivors fled panic-stricken from the Government area, to take refuge on Lost River and in the brakes of the Tularosa—but ever thereafter, from Anton Chico to the Seven Rivers, the animals of the long "fence rail" were sacred cows upon the Pecos range.

For instance, after camping one night in the White Mountains preparatory to driving 4,000 head of steers through Indian country, an outfit under Chisum awoke to find Apache raiders in the vicinity. Old John himself started the herd moving, with Frank Baker, Gus Gildea and Bill Henry taking the point. The brutes scarcely were on the way before a party of Mescaleros, well armed and with a chief at the head, rode up and demanded toll for "eating up our grass."

Chisum, his temper somewhat cooled since the reservation massacre, was willing to let the redskins cut out 20 head, but the trail bosses couldn't see it that way. Gildea and Baker argued with the raiders, told them that Captain Chee-sum himself was with the herd, and the chief, receiving this information, wheeled his paint pony and departed with his warriors at his heels.

But even if Indian troubles were over, Old John still had the white thieves on his hands, and he hired detectives to track them down. Not only that, he engaged the services of some of the toughest hombres ever to enter the Territory—"warriors" more familiar with the six-shooter and the Winchester than with the lariat—but Chisum didn't want them to handle cattle.

He hired them for what they were and they did their work well—so well, indeed, that they contributed in part to the situation which brought on the Lincoln County War, that bloody period which banded families and factions together in opposing camps and gave birth to a cattle feud which, after months of murder, cow thievery and general lawlessness, was ended only by interference by United States troops.

Hell broke loose in New Mexico and men like the notorious Billy the Kid helped pile on the coals. At the outset this sallow-faced but sanguine young New Yorker wasn't vastly interested; but before the war was over he had found it ample opportunity to square old accounts and vent his blood-lust with a record of twenty-one killings—one death for every year he lived, until he himself died at the hands of Sheriff Pat Garrett.

Naturally, all this trouble caused delay for Chisum in the work of gathering and delivering his cattle to Hunter and Evans, but when the job was completed in 1880 the count stood at about 55,000 head, with more on the range when the commission firm wanted them. And then the buyers paid off —principally, so it is said, in those same notes which Chisum had given Texas owners in the earlier days, and which Hunter and Evans had collected all over West Texas, taking them up at discount.

It was a hard blow and Chisum was surprised, but he took it standing and without a word of protest . . . just as he did a short time later when his trusted bookkeeper eloped with most of the remaining cash assets.

**A Good trail man and one of the best counters in business**

As they say today, the Cattle King of the Pecos "could take it". More than once he had demonstrated that—as on the day during the Lincoln County War when he had stood in a

Lincoln saloon, one booted foot on the rail, one elbow on the bar, his steel grey eyes gazing straight ahead—into the black muzzle of a .45 calibre Colt revolver.

The business end of this lethal instrument was held in the hand of a frail young man whose ordinarily sallow cheeks were flushed with evidence that the bottle had passed on many rounds, but despite the heavy load of liquor that he carried, the youth pushed the gun slowly toward the other's face.

"You owe me money, John," he said. "Even if you don't admit it, you hired me to help guard your range, and you're going to pay. You're going to pay or . . . "

He pushed the weapon a little closer, until the muzzle was within six inches of the cowman's eyes. But the latter did not move; he did not so much as shift his position at the bar, but the firm, straight line of his mouth became a little firmer. And then he spoke:

"Kid," he said, cooly, "you can't do it. You ain't got the nerve to look me in the eye and pull the trigger."

A sly grin appeared on the face of the sickly-appearing youth. His finger squeezed down on the trigger and the hammer of the double-action Colt started back, slowly and steadily. And then, just before the final click which would blast out John Chisum's life and scatter his brains the length of the mahogany, the rising hammer stopped . . . but it held the attention of every eye in that strangely silent bar-room.

"Well . . . why don't you shoot?" asked Chisum. "I'm waitin'."

The hammer began to fall, slowly and carefully.

"Aw, hell!" exclaimed Billy the Kid. "C'mon, let's have a drink!"

History doesn't say so, but one can well imagine John Chisum adopting that same attitude when he realized at last that his great cattle empire was slipping from his grasp . . . "Aw, hell, c'mon, let's have a drink!"

He retired from the cow business, more or less, after the Hunter-Evans sellout. He never came back. A tumor had developed in his throat and, critically ill, he went to Eureka Springs, Arkansas, in December of 1884. His friends hoped that the change would better his condition but—they carried him back to Texas and buried him in Paris on Christmas Day.

"A good trail man and the best counter I've ever known," Colonel Charles Goodnight used to say. "He was the only man I've ever seen who could count three grades as they went by, and do it accurately . . ."

*John Chisum's grave, Paris, Texas*

# Boss

## of the

## Palo Duro

CHARLES GOODNIGHT

SHOE TROUBLE

● The J A Ranch of today stands as a monument to a man who faced frontier perils

U NDER the light of the stars, which danced like silver lanterns of the gods in the purple velvet of the Texas sky, a man lay asleep on a buffalo robe.

127

Peace held the land enthralled—the silence of the night along the Brazos broken only by the croaking of frogs at the river's edge, and by the restless stirring of the trail herd which had bedded down in the dusk.

But the man on the buffalo robe was restless, too. Once in half wakefulness, he raised himself and listened as a horse nickered in the remuda and a coyote barked in the mesquite. Then, muttering as one who strives to drive away the foggy terrors of a dream, he turned again to sleep.

There was something in the air. His intuition, his long years of experience on the wild frontier told him that, but he was tired—as any man might be after a day's trail through Young county en route to markets in New Mexico.

Peace lay over the land, and then—a pounding of hoofs, a chorus of savage yells, panic among the cattle, and a pistol shot, followed by those swishing whispers in the dark which meant but one thing . . . !

Indian attack!

The big man on the buffalo robe lay very still—for now the moon had risen, and he did not care to silhouette himself against the sky and make a larger target for the deadly dogwood arrows being twanged from the Comanche bows.

One of the feathered shafts, winging through the air like an invisible streak of lightning, struck the edge of the robe, deflected downward, and passed completely under his body. A chance shot, perhaps, but an inch or two higher and the iron spike would have been in the cattleman's stomach.

He was on his feet in a second and running toward the horse remuda, revolver in hand. Everywhere around him was pandemonium. He heard the two night herders plugging out in the dark with their weapons, but he knew what the red devils were after and he hurried on toward the horses. Suddenly a group of moving, mounted figures outlined themselves against the horizon. He raised his revolver and fired . . . once, twice, three times . . . and the shadows melted into the night.

On the right and left other revolvers spurted flame as the trail hands joined in the melee, and at intervals the long crack of a rifle split the early morning.

And then—a pounding of hoofs again, a tattoo on the prairie that grew fainter in the distance. The Comanche raiders had been put to flight. They had skittered away into the west with the night's prize—one mule from the remuda and a few steers from the edge of the herd.

The man of the buffalo robe . . . his name was Charlie Goodnight . . . made a rapid survey of the situation. He made sure that the night riders had the longhorns well in hand, and then indulged in a sigh of relief. This was not the first time that he and Oliver Loving, a neighboring ranchman, had taken cattle over the trail to New Mexico, and there always had been trouble of some sort, always certain narrow corners—but what could one expect on the Texas plains in '67? Thankful for the turn of fate which had prevented grim disaster, he made his way to camp.

The fire of the night before was but a glowing mass of embers, but as Goodnight approached the spot the first faint flush of dawn revealed a little knot of men working over a figure stretched prone upon the ground.

"What is it, boys?" he called.

"It's Long Joe," said Oliver Loving. "He's got an arrow spike behind the ear."

Goodnight leaned over the injured cowboy and with his fingers probed the wound, a deep cut that had missed a vital spot by a hair's breadth.

"Not bad, but the spike's still in," he said, by way of diagnosis.

"Then yank it out," said the cowboy, "an' get 'er over with."

*Veteran hands on the J A ranch*

Goodnight reached into a pocket, took out a heavy pair of harness pliers, and with these crude forceps extracted the pointed piece of metal. Rough surgery, but these men were rough men—and Long Joe was back in the saddle when the herd pointed west again that morning.

It was all in the day's work, this sort of thing—just a prelude to such hardships as those to be found in the ninety-six miles of waterless country that waited ahead—but Charles Goodnight never was one to let trouble stay him from his purpose. Otherwise he might not have won his place on the roster of the Texas cattle kings. For him, as well as for Long Joe and Oliver Loving, the Indian raid on the Brazos was just another incident. He had known hardship and danger all his life.

Even in that early day Charles Goodnight had seen a great deal of West Texas.

### Two young men find Texas a good sized place

Born in Macoupin county, Illinois, in March of 1836, his father died when the son was five; and then, after the remarriage of his mother in 1846, the family had moved to Texas to settle on a farm in Milam county. As a result young Charles had spent the greater part of his boyhood behind the handles of a plow, a rifle strapped across the implement just in case the Indians interfered with his agricultural pursuits.

He knew little of school, but at the age of nineteen he broke away from farming to learn a more lasting lesson in geography than can be found in any book. Goodnight and J. W. Sheek, a young man of similar age, had heard alluring tales of gold in California, and the more they heard the brighter grew the rainbow pointing to the pot of treasure at its end. They invested their savings in a heavy wagon and bull team and set out for the Golden West to make their fortunes.

They reached the banks of the San Saba after many weary

weeks of travel, and there for the first time they began to realize the vastness of the country.

"Texas," observed Goodnight thoughtfully, "seems to be some-sized place. Sure thought we'd be in California afore this."

And Sheek was thinking about the same thing.

"Maybe we could do better in Texas, after all," he suggested. "Maybe all that gold's been taken, anyways."

*Roundup—Calf caught by the heel*

And so, after a night camp on the San Saba, the tongue of the bull wagon was pointed east again—over one of the few back-trails Charles Goodnight ever was to take. Even so, they didn't back-track all the way to Milam county—for on the Brazos they met a Johnson county cattleman, spent the night with him, and received an offer to handle cattle on shares.

The range was free, the cowman said, and they could pick what part of it they would, and then at the end of the year claim as their own one-fourth the increase in a herd of 400.

It seemed a good bargain; so good, indeed, that Goodnight

and Sheek insisted on a nine-year contract, which they received—and then they gathered the cattle and moved them to the Keechi Valley in Palo Pinto county. Thus the beginning of 1857 saw a new cattle king in the making.

Before the dawn of another year, however, it became plainly apparent that some change must be wrought if the two young men were to prosper in the business, for when the count of newly-branded calves was made the score was only 32, or a joint profit of about $95 for the year's labor. But a contract is a contract, and they held on.

Meanwhile, Goodnight found time to fulfill his civic duties. The "Kiwanis" and "Rotary" clubs of those days met in the field, and not at the banquet board. It was the hey-dey of Comanche raiding through the north of Texas and many times after the fierce tribesmen had swept through the settlements on lightning sorties, the young cattleman threw in with the Minute Men companies of Captains John Baylor and Jack Cureton to take the trail and teach a lesson to the culprits.

Suffering one atrocity after another, it was a time of sore trial for the isolated settlers. There were many who became, in self-defense, almost as savage as the Comanche himself in the business of lifting hair from the human head; but despite the scalping horrors he witnessed on many campaigns with Baylor and Cureton, Goodnight never became particularly embittered against the First American.

Under the circumstances, of course, he became an expert in the shoot-and-run game with the redskin ... became, in fact, one of the best scouts in all the northwest country. He could give and take as conditions demanded, and even in this affair of life and death the Indians came to respect him for his fairness—a thing which would stand him in good stead during the years to come.

Meanwhile, the share herd on the Brazos increased steadily, and when the time came for settlement of contract Goodnight and Sheek found themselves not only with 4,000 head of their own, but enough money to buy out the share of the original owner.

Into the midst of this good fortune, however, crept calamity. The Civil War had been in progress, and Goodnight—because of his experience—had been called upon to act as

Photograph by Erwin E. Smith
*Day herder J A*

scout for Cureton's Texas Rangers, assigned to protect from Indian raiders the family and property of northwest Texans who had gone to fight under the Stars and Bars.

The Cureton company made a good job of it, but in saving lives and homes they couldn't possibly watch that portion of the country's assets which moved on the hoof. Therefore, when Goodnight returned home again he found most of his cattle on the lost, strayed or stolen list. Just as in the south, and in other sections of the State, the thieves had been busy and the herds had been pretty well combed.

Disgusted, Goodnight thought of seeking other pastures, and he did make one trip to the Rio Grande in search of a new location; but the party returned short of its destination when one member, C. C. Slaughter, was wounded by an accidental shot.

Back in Palo Pinto county the thieving had grown worse, and Goodnight thought of New Mexico. He conferred with Oliver Loving, the Jack county rancher and trailmaker who already had driven two herds out of the State, one to Illinois in 1858 and one to Colorado in 1859. The two got together. In 1866, after mustering eighteen men and a herd of 2,000, they started for Fort Sumner—opening that cattle route which has gone down in history as the Goodnight-Loving Trail. It led from Palo Pinto county to the Concho, westward to Horsehead Crossing on the Pecos, and thence up the Pecos to Fort Sumner, New Mexico, and later was extended to Pueblo and Denver.

And laying a new trail in those days, across a trackless plain infested with Indians, wasn't altogether child's play. To lay the course they studied maps and drew on Goodnight's exper-

Photograph by Erwin E. Smith
*Water hole*

iences on the frontier; and then with two men as pointers to lead the stock, started the drive.

**Across a 96-mile desert on the way to market**

Mounted on a good horse, either Goodnight or Loving would ride twenty miles ahead in quest of water holes, and then, when one was found, return to the herd, inform the drivers, change to a fresh horse, and begin a new search—keeping up the system until the destination was reached.

And the desert country—that was the worst of all.

"On my first drive across the ninety-six mile desert that lies between the Pecos and the Concho rivers, I lost 300 head of cattle," said Goodnight in a description he once wrote of the 600-mile drive. "We were three days and nights crossing this desert and during this time we had no sleep or rest, as we had to keep the cattle moving all the time in order to get them to the river before they died of thirst."

"I rode the same horse for three days and nights, and what sleep I got was on his back. As the cattle got closer to the water they had no sense at all and we had to hold them back as well as we could. When they reached the stream (the Pecos) they swam right across and then doubled back before they stopped to drink . . . but after this trip across the desert we made it systematically and there was no more loss.

"We would leave the Concho at noon and drive that afternoon and all night, the next day and the next night. About 10 o'clock in the morning we would reach the Pecos. The mess wagon was always sent on ahead in making these drives and the men would eat and drink as they passed it with the suffering cattle."

And so a new trail was blazed to Fort Sumner, the government post where supplies were bought by Uncle Sam for his Indian wards on the reservations—the same trail which Chisum, the Jingle-Bob King, would take the following year when he moved his first 900 head from the Concho to Bosque Grande to settle the first permanent herd in New Mexico.

Colonel Goodnight and Oliver Loving sold their stock at a good price, eight cents a pound, and when they were paid off, they received about $10,000—in gold and silver coin.

Now that's a lot of loose and heavy change to carry about in one's pockets, and the two partners sat down to figure out some method of taking their fortune back to Texas. No other course suggesting itself, they finally loaded it on pack mules and started on the back trail. They were, of course, enthusiastic over the success of the venture and they made all possible haste, planning as they went the collection of another herd for a repetition of the drive.

But mules always have been uncertain creatures, and in a night camp on the trans-Pecos plains one of the animals, frightened perhaps by the solo of a loafer wolf, broke his mooring and galloped for the great open spaces. That the mule should be carrying $6,000 in coin was bad enough, but the calamity was made worse by the fact that he had upon his back all the provisions for the eighteen men in the party.

The money was saved when Goodnight caught the beast—but never did cash seem to have a smaller value. The outfit couldn't eat it, and they couldn't use it to replenish the stock of provisions—now scattered for miles about the countryside.

The men pushed on and, needless to say, they were a hungry lot when they reached the Pecos and encountered the wagon train of one Honey Johnson, Indian trader. Honey furnished food and . . . of all things . . . watermelons!

Arriving home at last, Goodnight and Loving gathered a new herd within a few weeks and took the trail again. On the homeward journey this time they used a wagon instead of a mule and the silver came back safely. The Fort Sumner market by this time was taking on the aspects of a bonanza, but good luck always doesn't last and the next trail was to prove the reverse of the so-called third time charm.

It was on this drive that the Indian attack in Young county occurred . . . the fight in which an arrow was driven under Goodnight's buffalo robe, and in which Long Joe received an arrow wound behind one ear; but that wasn't the worst of the trip by any means. Beside that trail waited tragedy . . .

After the Young county raid Goodnight and Loving decided that travel by night would be safest. As the drive proceeded past Phantom Hill and across the Concho country, the herd was settled during the day and put on the move every evening just as dusk was deepening.

Photograph by Erwin E. Smith
*J A Chuckwagon*

Naturally, this slowed progress and when the outfit reached the Pecos a week later Loving was fearful, since other herds were beginning to trail to New Mexico, that some rival stockman might push ahead and snare the Indian feeding contract at Sumner . . . and so he made a proposal to his partner.

"I'll take One-Armed Bill with me," he said, "ride on to the Fort and close a deal, then join the herd as you bring it up the Pecos."

"Too dangerous," protested Goodnight. "The country's full of Comanches and Apaches, and two men wouldn't have a chance."

But Loving was obstinate.  He argued, said there was danger of others grabbing the contract, and at last Goodnight consented to the plan on one condition—that Loving and Bill Wilson ride only by night to avoid war parties that might be abroad.  The two promised, and after leave taking, rode away toward the West.

Charles Goodnight never would ride with his partner again, for the prophecy made on the banks of the Pecos was to hold true.  The country was filled with roving Indians, and within a few weeks Goodnight was to get the details.  Loving did meet Indians—but the account of what occurred on the banks of the winding river belongs only to the tragic story of Oliver Loving himself.

With the death of Loving, and with Indian raiders cutting the profits from trail herds, Goodnight felt the first symptoms of discouragement; but for three years he continued the drives to the New Mexico and Colorado markets.

The last year on the trail, 1871, he was associated with John Chisum, and his profit for the year was $17,000.  It was then that he ventured into matrimony—taking as his bride Miss Mary Ann Dyer, the daughter of a Fort Worth attorney, Joel Henry Dyer.  Now his days of trailing were over, or at least Goodnight thought they were, and he decided to become a farmer.

The couple moved to Colorado and settled on a tract of land near Pueblo, but Mr. Goodnight soon branched out in the banking business—just in time for the panic of 1873 to swallow his entire fortune, with the exception of about 2,000 head of cattle.  He lost all that he had made with Loving, all he had made with Chisum.

**Into a new, wild country to found the great JA**

Faced with the task of recouping,  his thoughts naturally turned first to cattle, and he remembered that during his service as an Indian scout with the Rangers he had seen a large canyon in the plains of the Texas Panhandle which, though somewhat isolated from the world, would make an ideal ranch site. It was a country inhabited only by the buffalo, the Indian, the wolves, and the winds...

Accordingly, he and his wife and a few teamsters took the trail in 1876 for the *Palo Duro* country. It was a long, hard journey. Upon arrival they found the terrain too rough to

*When Mrs. C. Adair, one of the owners of the J A, came from England during her last years for a visit at the ranch, the boys, some of them wearing ties for the first time in years, dress up for the occasion.*

follow the cattle through the entrance to the canyon. Goodnight took the wagons to the rim, and with ropes let the wagon parts and supplies down into the great cut.

Here, 200 miles from the nearest outpost, and with the herd of 2,000 salvaged from the panic, was the birthplace for one of the greatest ranches in all the broad sweep of the Panhandle, a venture which still stands among the larger empires—the JA.

The ranch itself took its name, and ample backing, the following year when Goodnight, revisiting Pueblo, formed a partnership with John Adair of Wrathdair, Ireland, one of the many British investors lured to the West by the romance of cattle and the promise the industry held for rich reward.

Adair was willing to invest nearly half a million, and with this stake Goodnight bought the *Palo Duro* canyon and surrounding territory section by section until the JA became one of the greatest kingdoms of the West—a 600,000 acre pasture grazing 60,000 head of cattle.

In fact, the JA boasted 63,000 head in 1888 when Adair and Goodnight dissolved partnership, the latter taking over a division known as the *Quitaque*—a mere "milking lot" of 40,000 acres compared with the domain of the parent ranch, which today still is managed for the Adair estate.

In the earlier days it had been the custom of the Boss of the *Palo Duro*, when he found a buffalo calf on one of the ranges, to drive the "dogie" home and care for it in a pen especially constructed for the purpose; and so when he took over the *Quitaque* he owned one of the largest herds of "humpbacks" in all the world.

On the *Quitaque* he built a sturdy eight-foot fence to hold the aggregation and began experimenting with the "cattalo," a cross breed between the domestic cattle and the giant rovers of the plains, but results never were highly practical.

"Light, come in and rest your saddle"—those always were the unwritten words woven into the doormat at the JA and the *Quitaque*, and among the visitors came the enemies of old . . . the Indians of the past, warriors with whom Goodnight himself had traded lead in many a fight across the prairies. But now they came in peace because they wanted to visit with the "*Bueno Noche*," as the Apaches used to call him. Sometimes, too, they begged him for a buffalo—that they might run it down and make the kill, and relive for one rare moment the happiness of wilder, braver days.

One old employe tells how a band of Comanches camped for two weeks near the ranch house and made almost daily petitions to the Big Boss for a bull from among the shaggy monarchs. Goodnight, preferring not to set a precedent, held out for a long while but finally told Charlie Beverly, a wagon boss, to cut out one of the brutes.

"And I'll never forget that day," says the old employe. "When Charlie cut out the bull the Comanches started for 'im; you'd thought the earth was cavin' in. That buffalo didn't stop for nothin' and I guess, all told, he musta knocked down half a mile o' fence before the Indians got 'im. They rode 'im down and made the kill with arrers and then . . . well, they just let him lay and went ridin' out acrost the prairie, sorta sad-like. Guess they knew they'd never hunt again, 'least not that way."

### Goodnight respected his men and they respected him

Though milder-mannered and kindlier than many another among the Texas cattle kings, the Boss of the *Palo Duro* permitted no rough stuff, say the men who one time rode his ranges. He had a particular set of rules for his cowboys. If they fought, they soon were seeking work elsewhere. If two men met in some far corner of the range and stopped for a session of talk it was the unwritten law that they should dismount and ease the saddle girth. If a puncher was caught raking a horse with spurs, he was fired on the spot. He even made the boys wash up saddle blankets once a week. But even with this set of steadfast rules the men respected him— and he respected them.

"The cowboy of the old days was the most misunderstood man on earth," he used to say. "Few young people today realize that the western men—the cowboys—were as brave and chivalrous as it is possible to be. Many of the greatest

and richest men of present-day Texas were cowboys, and of
the hands I employed there are now at least three million-
aires.  Fewer cowboys," he would add, "have been tried for
crime than any other class I can name."

He would champion the cause of the cowboy anywhere, and
with all the zeal and enthusiasm he displayed as a leader among
ranchmen in numerous fights on cattle convention floors.  He
was a born fighter, and the training he received when he rode
with Cureton's Rangers against the tribesmen came to the sur-

Photograph by Erwin E. Smith
*Three Circle Boys working the breaks*

face more than once—as in the trail days when he stood as
a northern barrier against the herds which trekked up from
the south to spread the Texas fever;  as in the days when he
played a leading role in the famous Grass Lease fight—the
three-cornered Panhandle war between cowmen and "nesters"
and the cowmen and the state government.

He lost some of his grip as he grew older, but never the fight in his system. At the age of ninety he was left alone when death took his wife. After that he broke rapidly. A short time before his own death in the late '20's he married twenty-year-old Corrine Goodnight, who had been corresponding with him because their names were the same, and who had stopped at the ranch to see him while on a trip through the country.

The cattle kingdom that he left may not have been as great as it once was, but the name "Goodnight", which is attached now to one of the towns in the area, remains among the greatest on the Plains. "The Boss of the Palo Duro" is buried there.

BRAND
CHAS. GOODNIGHT

# The Odyssey of Oliver Loving

OLIVER LOVING

DAY HERDERS PLAYING CARDS

● The Saga of the man who blazed the trail to outside markets in the 'Fifties.

**O**LIVER LOVING knew his business well—better perhaps than any other man in all the western cattle country—but just the same Colonel Charles Goodnight, his partner, was uneasy.

*Out where the West "is"—white faces moving to new pasture*

Photograph by W. D. Smithers

The Colonel made no secret of that as he watched the sandy-haired *Palo Pinto* ranchman and one of the trail hands, One-Armed Bill Wilson, ride off up the Pecos toward Fort Sumner. Goodnight, all through that Spring day in 1867, had argued against the journey.

"Better lose the contract, or even a few more steers, than get a skinful of arrows," he had told Loving, "but if you're bound to go ride at night. With the country full of Comanches and Apaches as fleas on a hound's back, two men have no business out alone. Bad enough with eighteen."

It had been pretty bad. The outfit had lost more than 200 steers since it had started with 2,500 head from the home range in Jack and Palo Pinto counties. Indians, in swift night raids, had accounted for some; others had been left on the ninety-six miles of waterless alkali desert between the Concho and the Pecos; and the remainder had gone in the mad stampede of thirsty brutes at the latter river. There the hands had earned the two days of rest they took before continuing up the Pecos toward Horsehead Crossing.

There Loving had made his proposal to push on with Wilson. He knew that other drivers were on the trail, and that the herd which first reached the Fort probably would make up the next beef ration Uncle Sam dispensed to his Indians. He wanted the Government contract which was waiting at Sumner . . .

Had his partner been any other man, Goodnight might have put up a more vigorous protest, but Oliver Loving had been first on the trails. He knew his business.

A native of Hopkins county, Kentucky, he was at this time about fifty-four years of age. Behind him was a life of experience that qualified him well for the journey he was undertaking. Loving had brought his wife and five children from Kentucky in 1845 to settle in what was now Lamar county. The following year the family had moved to Collin county, where Loving farmed, dealt in livestock, and freighted by ox wagon for merchants and army posts between Houston and Shreveport. But in 1855 he began to feel that the area was becoming too populated for proper elbow exercise, and so he sold his 640-acre farm and established his family in the north-

Photograph by Erwin E. Smith
*Chuck-wagon and cook*

eastern part of Jack county, in a place called Loving's Valley.

There he turned all his energy to stock raising, and by 1858 his herd had increased to such proportions that he felt forced to find a market. Accordingly, he went in with a neighbor, John Durkee, collected a herd, and headed for Chicago—on the first northward drive ever made from Texas. They went through . . . and the steak of OL steers found its way onto the platters of the north . . .

Encouraged by the profits from this venture, Loving returned home to plan another. The spring of 1859 found him on the trail again—but this time to Colorado. With three companions, Sylvester Reed, John B. Dawson and J. W. Curtis, Loving left Palo Pinto on May 15, striking northwest to the Arkansas River, following it to Pueblo, and then hitting for Denver, where they peddled out the few hundred head in the drive.

Nearly a year passed before Loving came home again—to find that the Indian raids had become so numerous on the frontier that his family had sought safety in the more civilized precincts of Weatherford. He remained with the family awhile and then went away to secure a beef contract with the Confederate troops operating on the Mississippi. With the close of the Civil War he returned home, where soon he formed the trail driving partnership with Colonel Goodnight, then of Palo Pinto.

They had made several trips previous to the incident on the Pecos and Goodnight felt that Loving, with his experience and background could ride the 250 miles to Fort Sumner if anybody could ... if only he would remember his promise to ride by night.

Loving really had intended to keep that promise, but after two days, during which not an Indian was sighted, he told One-Armed Bill that the country appeared safe enough to traverse in day-light hours.

"We'll do it," he said. "We can make better time ... and we've got to hurry if we want that contract."

And with those words he sealed his fate ... uttered, so to speak, his own death warrant.

### A race against Death and a fight on the Pecos

The two riders, at the time, were below the present site of Carlsbad, and as they took the trail on the third day the countryside, as Loving had pointed out, seemed peaceful enough. They rode throughout the morning, crossing the Blue River shortly after noon and then, about five miles beyond the crossing, Wilson reined in. He had caught a glimpse of something out across the mesquite-sprinkled mesa.

"Indians!" he said. "an' as near as I c'n tell, Comanches ... about eighty or ninety of 'em!"

"And they've seen us," replied Loving, who was sizing up the landscape from under the shade of a hand. "Ride for the river," he ordered. "Come on, let's go!"

He flicked his bridle rein and wheeled his horse.

A short distance to the left lay the Pecos, where the mesa broke off abruptly into the water. Once there, they might find some degree of safety, certainly more than afforded by the open plain. They spurred their mounts into a run; the Indians, on their fleet ponies, whooping along behind.

Even the horses seemed to sense the terror of the moment, and they fairly flew across the ground. Sometimes during the race which followed, Wilson and Loving, glancing back through the cloud of alkali dust kicked up by flying hoofs, glimpsed the brown of a naked body as the distance between pursued and pursuers closed. And then, at last, the river.

At that point the Pecos takes a curve and near the bank at that time a sand dune extended out into the river. A patch of cane grew near the water's edge and on the bank behind was a small clump of mesquite which obstructed the view from the plains. Had Wilson and Loving searched for miles along the stream they could not have found a spot more favorable to the emergency. It was as though a blind fate had led them in their flight, and after swinging from their saddles and tying the horses to the mesquite, they cut for the river along the dune.

There ... again quite by accident ... they stumbled onto a cave-like hole which an *arroyo* had cut into the bank on the south side of the curve. It wasn't very commodious, especially for two men needing elbow room to handle rifles, but the cattlemen weren't very particular at that moment. They tumbled in, thankful that the hole was so situated in the jutting dune that it was protected on three sides by the river. Hence

the savages could come at them only from across the river
or over the dune . . . which, of course, could be raked by rifle
fire from the hole.

The two men were scarcely settled in the cramped quarters
before the entertainment started. The first of the Indians arrived to find Loving set and waiting. He edged his rifle
across the lip of the hole, drew a bead, and squeezed the trigger . . . and out on the dune a man went down, with a sort of
gurgle that told a story all its own.

The Comanches, expecting easy prey, had come upon a
wasp's nest, and after the initial sortie there were few in all
that howling horde of painted warriors who were courageous
enough to expose themselves to the deadly fire from the dune.

Wilson's rifle was older and less serviceable than that of
his boss, but he had a cap-and-ball revolver which could do
noble work upon occasion, and everytime the one-armed puncher sighted the glint of a naked body he let go a slug of hot
lead which warned the ambitious redskins that death, swift
and sudden, lay behind that strip of sand. The Indians, growing more cautious, decided to play a waiting game . . .

Slowly the sun drooped down toward the rim of the West,
throwing long shadows from the clump of cane on the water's
edge. Soon night would be closing in, and the two men in
the hole realized that then their position would become even
more perilous . . . so Wilson attempted a parley. He called
to the Comanches in Spanish, saying that he and Loving desired only peace, that they wanted only to continue their way
unmolested.

"Then put down your guns," came the reply, in the same
language, "and you can come out unharmed."

Wilson, however, wasn't so easily taken in. He had heard
savage promises before . . . made in one moment and broken in
the next.

"Keep an eye on the cane," he whispered to Loving. "Pick 'em off if they try to slip in there."

But the words were scarcely uttered before a burst of rifle fire came from that quarter. A bullet kicked into the sand on the edge of the hole, and Loving cried out in pain. The slug, a hand-hammered affair, passed through Loving's left wrist, and penetrated his left side.

Wilson popped a few shots into the cane and then turned to the relief of his wounded companion.

"They've got me," said Loving. "You'd better get out . . . if you can . . . and save yourself. Find Goodnight and tell him what has happened. . . "

Wilson refused to budge. He could see that Loving was fast losing blood, and knew that something had to be done at once. Working as rapidly as his one arm and the cramped quarters would permit, the cowboy tried to pad the wound with clothing, and partially succeeded. He made Loving as comfortable as possible and then—lying on his armless side, his six-shooter in his one hand—he awaited the next move.

A tense period of silence, broken only by the slurping of the river, followed . . . then a rustle, ever so slight, from the cane. Wilson thumbed back the hammer of his revolver, but this time it wasn't Indians . . . for as the rustle ceased there came to the man's keen ears a familiar and oft-heard sound, the ominous rattle of a snake. Then, in the already failing light, Wilson saw it—a large, mottled-backed fellow which slithered out of the cane and glided directly toward the hole!

Fascinated, the two men watched as the rattler twisted across the strip of land toward them, and they shuddered a little as they realized that the reptile apparently was bent upon sharing their place of refuge. And that is exactly what the snake intended to do . . . and did. It came to the lip of the hole, hesitated a moment, and then plopped in . . . to coil its fat body and sway its horrible head within a few inches of Wilson's knees.

### A desperate situation—one foe within, one outside

There they lay—two men and a yard and a half of grisly death. Satan himself could not have devised a more diabolical situation, for now Loving and Wilson had an enemy within and one without.

If they moved, if they so much as shifted position in that cramped hole, the swaying, cold-eyed head with its long white fangs, might strike. If they evacuated the hole, as they were sore tempted to do, almost certain death waited on the dune. The whisper of arrows as they sank into the sand near the hole was proof enough of that. It was merely a question of choice between two evils—the stab of fang or arrow spike.

Loving almost forgot his wounds in the trying half hour which followed, and cold perspiration stood out in little beads on Wilson's brow. Their muscles cramped almost unbearably, and they became obsessed with an almost uncontrollable desire to shift position, but they dared not.

And then, as night spread her blanket over the land, the rattler slowly uncoiled, slipped its scaly body across one of Wilson's boots and, like a twisting line of shadow, left the hole and disappeared into the cane.

Death had gone its way, but not from Oliver Loving's mind. He felt certain that he had reached the end. He still was losing blood from the wound in his side, and the pain in his wrist was causing nausea; he was growing weaker.

"There isn't a chance for me to get out," he told Wilson, "but maybe you can make it. I want you to take my rifle . . . it's the best of the two . . . get out and try to find Goodnight. Bring him back, and if I'm still here . . . all right. But if I'm not . . . well, just tell the folks about it . . . "

The one-armed puncher again protested.

"You know I can't leave you here," he said. "What if the devils take you?"

"But they won't," promised Loving. "I'll shoot myself first. But you've got to do it, Bill, it's the only chance."

Oliver Loving knew something of Indian tortures, and he really had no thought of allowing himself to be captured alive; and he argued that two men need not die when one already was almost certain of death.

Finally Wilson agreed. He helped Loving load every chamber of his cap-and-ball revolver and charge the rifle which was to be left behind; and then, after slipping off his boots and pants, he took Loving's rifle and started crawling over the dune toward the river.

He negotiated the strip of land in safety and with a slight splash slipped into the water, but he had no sooner done so than he realized that he, a one-armed man, could not expect to swim far with a rifle. Accordingly, he hid the weapon under the bank, then silently started paddling downstream, unarmed . . .

Loving, lying in the hole, strained his ears to catch some sound from his departing friend, but he heard nothing . . . nothing except the incessant croaking of frogs and the far-away howl of a prowling loafer.

The night wind rose. It whispered through the cane at the river's edge and stirred the mesquite on the flat above the bank . . . while Loving, his finger on the trigger of his cocked rifle, listened and waited.

Sometimes he thought he sensed a shadowy movement on the dune and his heart pounded a bit faster, but always the shadows dissolved and he saw nothing before him but the blackness of the night. Had Wilson escaped? He wondered.

A new strength was coming over him. The wound in his side was ebbing but little now, but the shattered wrist still throbbed. Through the long hours it ached and burned, then mercifully grew numb as the first streaks of dawn began to appear in the eastern sky.

Daylight came on rapidly, like the sudden lifting of a curtain, and it revealed to the wounded cattleman the reason for those noises he had heard on the dune during the night. The Comanches had been busy digging a tunnel through the sand toward his place of concealment, and not twenty feet away he could see, even now, the scalplock of a brave. Loving raised the rifle with his good hand, rested the barrel on the edge of the hole and fired. The Indian coughed and fell, face forward.

More than once through the following morning the Indians tried to reach him by way of the trench, but by the time the cattleman had put bullets into a couple more warriors the enemy abandoned this method of attack. Instead, they retreated to the high ground behind the hole, gathered up boulders and began throwing them over in the hope that one would find the unseen target.

Luck was with Oliver Loving that day. Some of the stones came uncomfortably close ... close enough to hurl sand into his face ... but none found the mark.

By mid-afternoon he was growing weaker again, more from lack of water and food than from the pain of his wounds. A few feet away the swollen Pecos swept by, and every ripple served to increase his thirst, but Loving dared not venture out. The sky, however, was becoming overcast. There was hope in that.

Night brought the rain—in torrents—but if it soaked Loving to the skin and banished his thirst temporarily it also increased the dangers of his predicament. The downpour soaked his powder, even rendering useless the charges in his revolver and rifle. Now he gave himself but a few hours at the most— unless, by some chance, Wilson had reached the herd and Goodnight was leading a party to his rescue. Again he wondered if Wilson had managed to slip through. He still was wondering when day dawned . . . bleak, cold and gray.

Loving felt certain that the Comanches would attack at daylight but after an hour had passed, then two, there came neither sound nor sign of the enemy. He waited still another hour before daring to hope that the storm had driven away the savages; and then, warily and painfully, he crawled from the hole and staggered to his feet.

The wound in his side was less painful now, but the injured wrist seemed to be growing steadily worse. He felt that he might get along somehow if he could find a few mouthfuls of food to give him strength.

Unsteadily, he started up the river toward a spot where he knew the trail herd would seek a crossing. That, he reasoned, would be his best course. Several times, as he went along, he raised his rifle to fire at some small birds he saw, but his water-soaked powder failed to respond to the spark. Discouraged, he staggered on, coming at last to a clump of mesquite and china trees on the bank above the Pecos.

### How Bill Wilson wandered—in his under-clothes

Here, with his powder and caps, he attempted to make a fire that he might parch and eat his Mexican gloves, but he was unsuccessful. He was becoming weaker with each passing moment, and he was thirsty again. He put a piece of his shirt on the end of a stick, dipped it into the river, pulled it back, and sucked eagerly at the cloth . . . then lost consciousness.

And now let us return to Bill Wilson. What had become of him? After swimming down the river, under water part of the way, he had come clear of the enemy and had crawled from the stream to go in search of Goodnight. But as ill-fortune would have it, he had become lost on the mesa and had wandered about for three days in his 'long-handled' underwear. Like Loving, he too had been unable to find food on the barren plain; and when, toward the end of the fourth

day, he contacted the herd quite by accident, Colonel Goodnight had some difficulty in recognizing the man as an employe who had left him only a week before.

Goodnight lost no time. After listening to Bill Wilson's
halting story and obtaining a description of the spot where the
fight had occurred, he took six men and rode at once to Loving's relief.

The party found the hole in the sand, all right. It was
easily identified, surrounded as it was with arrow shafts and
stones; and they found Wilson's clothes and the rifle he had
hidden under the bank... but the group found no trace of
Oliver Loving.

Photograph by Erwin E. Smith
*Map in the sand*

The men searched the countryside for miles around and
then, despairing, Goodnight and his six rejoined the herd and
continued the trail to Fort Sumner. But they rode in silence,
for Oliver Loving was greatly respected by all who knew him.

Seventy-five miles from the Fort they met a man... Burleson by name... who had a strange story to tell. Oliver
Loving wasn't dead at all. He had been found on the bank
of the Pecos by three Mexicans and an American boy who were
on their way from Mexico to the Fort, and Loving had given

them $250 to carry him to Sumner in an ox drawn wagon.

Burleson said that he, himself, enroute home to Texas, had met the wagon on the way and had ridden back to the Fort for a carriage ambulance ... with the result that even now Loving was at the Government post recovering from his wounds.

Goodnight, of course, could scarcely credit his ears. He immediately saddled a fresh horse and started ... and he rode that seventy-five miles in eighteen hours.

As Burleson had said, the Colonel found Loving doing well. The wound in his side was fast healing but the doctors still were having difficulty with the wrist. It was, needless to say, a happy reunion, and after resting a few days Goodnight started for the mountains between Las Vegas and San Jose to recover some stock stolen the previous year.

He found the stock and was returning to the Fort ... was, in fact, only thirty miles from the post ... when he was met by a courier. Gangrene had set in on Loving's arm, said the messenger, and the doctors would be forced to amputate. Loving wanted Goodnight present.

Next morning the operation was performed, to be followed ten hours later by another. Loving began to weaken, and as the days passed with his strength failing, he realized that he was nearing the end and called Goodnight to his bedside.

"I have a request," he said. "Don't leave me in this ... foreign soil. Take me back to Texas."

**They were the trail blazers for the Texas industry**

And Goodnight did as he was requested to do. When Oliver Loving died, three weeks after the operation, there was some difficulty at first in obtaining a suitable casket and it was found necessary to inter the cattleman, temporarily in the "foreign soil" of New Mexico. After a few weeks Goodnight freighted in a metallic coffin, removed the body from the grave, placed it on a wagon, and with an honor guard of six men, began

one of the strangest funeral marches in early Texas history—
a slow, sad trek through the mountains and across those same
plains over which Oliver Loving had driven one of the first
herds ever to take the trail from Texas.  Among the riders
who accompanied the wagon was the late W. D. Reynolds
of Fort Worth.

After many weary weeks the body was delivered to the Jack
County rancher's family, which included James C. Loving, a
son who later helped organize the Texas and Southwestern
Cattle Raisers Association, of which a great grandson of Oliver,
the late E. B. Spiller, was secretary for many years.

The Lovings are still in the cattle business in Jack County.
One grandson of the pioneer, another Oliver, became a banker
at Jermyn;  and two others resided in Fort Worth—the late
Horace Wilson, a livestock commission man, and James C.
Wilson, judge of the United States Court.

It was with the latter, that Colonel Goodnight, a few years
before his own death, left a token of his affection for his former
trail partner.   It is a picture of Goodnight and Oliver Loving,
framed with saddle leather and carrying commemoration plates
in silver.  It hangs today in Judge Wilson's Fort Worth home,
and the plate under the photograph of Goodnight carries this
inscription, written by the Boss of the *Palo Duro* himself:

### Loving and Goodnight

*Started from Young County June 6, 1866, thence south-*
*west to the Pecos River, following said river to Fort*
*Sumner, New Mexico, thence northwest, crossing the Ar-*
*kansas River below Pueblo, crossing the Divide seventy-*
*five miles east of Denver, delivering at the Mouth of*
*Crow Creek on the South Platte, Colo., seventy-five*
*miles north of Denver.*

And under the picture of Loving  the brief story of the
first established trail from Texas to the West:

## OLIVER LOVING

*The first to seek an outlet for Texas cattle. Leaving Palo
Pinto County May 15, 1859, north to the Arkansas
River, thence following the river to Pueblo, thence to
Denver.*

BRAND
OLIVER LOVING

# A Cattleman
# in the Pulpit

REV. GEORGE WEBB SLAUGHTER

COL. C. C. SLAUGHTER

● Parson Slaughter
fought Indians,
branded calves, and
preached with a
pistol in his belt

O N AN AUTUMN Sunday in the year 1860 the good people of the village of Palo Pinto fidgeted nervously on the hard benches of the Baptist Church as they listened to the Word interpreted through the mouth of a tall and bearded man who appeared not at all to heed the visible signs of distraction in his flock.

The Reverend George Webb Slaughter had a message to deliver, and, God willing, he intended to deliver it—even if he had to use the brace of pistols which hung from his broad belt; even if he had to resort to the long-barreled rifle which leaned against the pulpit, within easy reach of the hand which was raised at intervals to call the congregation to prayer.

The Reverend George Slaughter was a devout young man, and he had no intention of allowing a few pesky Indians, such as those who loitered even then about the settlement, to delay the work of the Lord.

The brethren of the faith, as I have pointed out, were a bit nervous. They cast uneasy glances toward the door, shifted handholds on their own rifles, and at times pricked up their ears to listen—but even in the face of threatening danger they heard every deep-spoken word uttered by the pastor . . . for the Reverend Slaughter was a man of parts. His was a voice crying in the wilderness, and here in this wild land on the border of a new frontier was a people eager to hear.

For the gentleman in the pulpit was not only a minister— he was doctor, neighbor and friend, but as a preacher his sermons sprang from the fount of inspiration. He had little time to prepare his dissertations as pastors do today; he was much too busy on week days with the lariat and branding iron— too busy laying the foundations of a ranch kingdom which one day would be among the greatest in all the State of Texas.

The parson had, even then, about 1,500 head of longhorns and a few horses—his remuda having been cut by an Indian raid—but with all the care required by the livestock he still found opportunity to carry the gospel into the settlements. He was, after a fashion, circuit rider for the frontier, filling appointments all over the countryside—traveling by horseback; the Bible, a few psalm books and provisions in his saddlebags;

a couple of pistols at his waist and a rifle in the saddle scabbard under one knee.

Sometimes these journeys took him fifty miles across the wilderness, and often he camped alone on the trail at night, but everywhere he went the frontiersmen were ready and willing to listen to his talk . . . for the personal history of the man was closely allied with that of the new State.

George Slaughter was born in Lawrence county, Mississippi, The family moved to Louisiana in 1825, and it was then that young George received his first and only elementary schooling—a period of educational instruction which lasted only three weeks.

In that day and time there were more important phases of education than the traditional "three R's," the pistol and the rifle being more widely used than the pen and parchment; and George was to find this knowledge an advantage when in 1830 the family crossed the Sabine and settled at Nacogdoches, then an important city in the Mexican state of Texas-Coahuila.

For it so happened that the *alcade* of the municipality, one Colonel Piedras, was a despotic type of major-domo whose one great ambition in life was making as much misery as possible for the American settlers of the place. Continually he took unto himself wider powers until in the spring of 1832 he felt himself safe in taking one of the boldest steps of all. A devout Catholic himself, he caused the arrest of every Protestant minister in Nacogdoches; and, of course, the members of the American colony boiled.

Who, they asked, was Piedras, to dictate to them the methods of their own worship? They met, selected a delegation to wait upon the Mexican and plead for tolerance, but the ensuing conference came to naught. Piedras turned a deaf ear and the colonists, despairing of results through diplomatic efforts, held a mass meeting in San Augustine and decided to force the argument in good old frontier fashion.

It was an exciting June day, and twenty-year-old George enjoyed it all. He was, in fact, one of the first to strap on weapons when the Americans, about 400 strong, began mustering for a march on Nacogdoches. The party started and then at the outskirts of that town halted to send forth another delegation, in the hope that the matter might be settled amicably and the ministers released without bloodshed. But the Colonel was a hard man—he met the flag of truce with a cavalry charge.

That day, however, the Texans were not running. They pulled down with long rifles and in the first volley emptied a few saddles among the onrushing dragoons. The charge wavered, halted, and then turned into a mad retreat, the Texans following close behind.

Young Slaughter, marching in the van, saw an uncle, G. P. Smith, fall with a rifle ball through the breast, and he pushed on, determined to help make the rout a complete success. The Mexicans fell back toward the Angelina River but swollen as it was by recent rains, there was but one point for crossing, and that point eighteen miles away.

### The Parson counted Houston among his early friends

Realizing this several of the mounted Americans made an encircling move and reached this position in advance of the enemy, and the Mexicans arrived to find a trap. Caught between two fires, the cavalrymen surrendered after a brief renewal of the skirmish, and Colonel Piedras received his orders—to depart from Texas and return no more, a pledge he failed to keep. The Protestant ministers of Nacogdoches were, of course, released.

This incident is related merely because of its bearing upon the future course of Slaughter's career, for it is highly probable that a remembrance of Colonel Piedras influenced him to a great extent in the days before he was ordained to take the pulpit.

After the fight on the Angelina our subject took a freighting job between Texas and Louisiana. While on one of his
trips to the Louisiana town of Natchitoches he met a man who
caught his romantic fancy . . . a strange and unusual character
who soon was to lead him into one of his greatest adventures.

This gentleman was picturesque, even for the frontier. He
wore buckskin clothes, a scalplock and the accompanying feathers, together with various ornaments common to life among the
Indians, but with all his wild appearance he claimed to be a
lawyer—proving it by engaging young Slaughter to haul his
law books into Nacogdoches.

Their paths did not cross again until two years later, outside San Antonio. The gentleman in buckskin then was in
command of the Texas Army and, with scalplock and feathers
gone, the young freighter had difficulty in recognizing General Sam Houston, his former lawyer friend.

Slaughter was in a company which reported directly to the
General for duty. He served in the "grass fight"; he was
in the ranks as the woefully small army awaited the advanc-
ing hordes of Santa Anna; and it was he whom General
Houston sent as courier to the Alamo, asking Colonel Travis
to evacuate and take his garrison to open country. Had Travis heeded the message carried by Slaughter one of the greatest tragedies in Texas history would have been averted, but
Travis didn't. Instead, he drew his sword, scratched a line
upon the ground, and asked all loyal followers to cross. All
crossed, Slaughter rode back to General Houston—and the
Alamo became bloody history.

As Houston's courier Slaughter also carried similar messages to Colonel J. W. Fannin, entrenched at Goliad and refusing to move, but Fannin had ideas of his own on the conduct of warfare, and the Mexican butchers likewise got his
little party. All that is history, and for that reason there need
be no explanation here of the events which followed—the

"strategic retreat" of Houston which led Santa Anna into the trap at San Jacinto, and the ending of the war for freedom. Slaughter participated throughout the campaign, and then returned to Nacogdoches to marry Miss Sarah Mason. The newly-weds moved to Sabine County, where Slaughter re-entered the freighting business.

But a soldier must return to the wars, and in 1839 we find Captain Slaughter leading a company of militia against the Cherokees on the Neches River in the first of the campaigns made by General Rusk to exclude the Indians from the Republic. He was in the fight which ended the career of Chief Bowles, and he helped chase the fast retreating enemy all the way to the Bois d'Arc fork of the Trinity. Then he returned home, disbanded his company and again resumed his freighting business.

It was at this time that he began to interest himself in those two great professions—medicine and the ministry. He studied the former until he had qualified as a practicing physician and then, in 1844, two years after deserting Methodism to embrace the Baptist faith, he was ordained to preach.

Like most frontier people, the dwellers in the Sabine country were not heavily burdened with worldly goods, and although the freighter cracked his whip behind a team on week days and occupied the pulpit on Sundays, he soon discovered that even the combined jobs did not hold a future rosy enough to provide for his growing family.

The livestock industry, though still something of a gamble, was just coming into its own, and cattle caught the preacher's fancy—and so, in the early part of 1852, he packed his family and personal belongings into wagons, gathered up the 100 head of cattle he had acquired, and set out for Freestone County to establish a ranch near the town of Butler.

The stock increased and five years later, with a herd that now tallied 500, Parson Slaughter drove to Palo Pinto County and set up on 2,000 acres he had purchased near Golconda, a few miles north of the present county seat.

It was here we find him as this story opens—branding calves on week days; preaching the Word on Sundays, a rifle barrel within his reach. And that weapon wasn't a mere gesture— the parson really used it when necessity made the call. Fortunately this never occurred within the precincts of his church but there were times when the good man did not allow the Commandment in *Exodus* to rest too heavily upon his conscience.

In 1861 he fought a singlehanded skirmish with half a dozen Indians on Cedar Creek and succeeded in putting them to flight; and in '64 when the Comanches lifted all his horses during a raid on the ranch, seriously wounding his son John, the preacher again squinted down the sights and popped away at the redskins during the better part of a morning, but in vain; the enemy got away.

He had better luck a short time later while driving a small bunch of cattle on Dry Creek near Graham. Attacked suddenly by thirteen warriors, the Rev. Mr. Slaughter dismounted, took careful aim with his rifle, and let go into the thick of the raiders.

With a yell of pain one brave went down, while his companions scattered like a covey of quail, reforming to hold a council of war, and then coming back to take the parson's scalp. The Rev. Slaughter was ready and waiting. Stretching himself on the ground, he opened fire with first one pistol and then the other. He drove off the savage charge, saved not only his scalp but all of his cattle.

#### The Comanches make a raid and are taught a trick

While all this riotous business was occurring, the herd on the range had increased until the owner was able to count, in 1867, about 12,000 head, pastured both in Palo Pinto and Young counties. Most of these he sold to a neighbor ranch

family, the Lovings of Jack county.  Then he formed a partnership with his oldest son, C. C. Slaughter, to make the trail
drives into Kansas—a partnership almost dissolved by tragedy
in its early stages.

The very next year while driving a trail herd through
Young County in the vicinity of Flat Top Mountain  the
Slaughters, with fourteen men, camped at night within a few
miles of the spot where hostile Indians were massacreing thirteen drivers of a government wagon train.  This gruesome
work at an end the Comanches turned their attention to the
cattlemen, hoping to stampede and kill the 500 steers that
made up the drive.

"But they won't get 'em!" exclaimed the parson as the first
signs of attack became evident.  He tolled off six men.  "You
take the stock," he ordered, "and get 'em on the move.  The
rest will stay and put up a fight.  Get going!"

The herd had scarcely started before the Comanches closed
in for the raid, which might have been successful but for the
cunning of the preacher.  Remembering his military days he
devised a trick which was carried out in this wise:  While two
trail hands helped the Slaughters pour on a steady fire from
behind the shelter of their horses, the other members of the
party slipped away unobserved by the enemy, passed down a
ravine, and attacked from a different angle.  The Indians
naturally suspected that reinforcements had arrived and they
fled . . . without a single steer.

Through the first half of the '70's Slaughter and Son made
the Kansas drives, shipping from cowtowns there to St. Louis
and Chicago markets—laying the financial background for the
great cattle empire which would become the Lazy S—and then
ill health forced the pastor to retire from business.  He sold
out, returned to his Palo Pinto place, and except in a minor
way, dealt no more in livestock before his death in March of

Old-time chuck wagon on the Plains. Before the days of "flys" the old-time cowboy depended on the "black spot" beneath the wagon and his hat to provide shade and shelter.

1895. His son, destined to become even a greater cattle king, carried on.

C. C. Slaughter had been born to the business. As a lad he had helped 'tend his father's original hundred head down in the Sabine country; he had driven one of the wagons when the family migrated to Freestone County in 1852; and he had helped the parson start the ranch in Palo Pinto. Thus his early environment left him in no doubt as to the career he should follow.

Even as a youth he had made his entry into the cattle business by hauling a load of lumber to Dallas County, where he sold it, bought wheat with the proceeds, and then returned home with the flour to sell at a profit of more than $500. With this money he bought a small interest that an uncle held in his father's herd.

But under the stress of the times in that wild and rugged land young Slaughter could not devote all his days to cattle— for in 1860, about the time his father was holding forth in the Palo Pinto pulpit, the son, as a member of Captain Jack Cureton's Ranger company, was out a great deal on Indian scouts, a duty which included participation in the Sul Ross campaign against Nocona's Comanches—the expedition which rescued the white Cynthia Ann Parker from her Indian captors. And then, when Governor Sam Houston ordered organization of Minute Men companies to act as guards for the frontier, C. C. Slaughter was elected captain of one unit.

After the Civil War, Slaughter, with several other cattlemen of the area—Charles Goodnight, Kit Carter, George Lemley and Dick Jowell—discussed the possibilities of large scale ranching in Old Mexico, and with this in mind they started by pack mule for the border on a tour of investigation. But they got no farther than the Devil's River country, where an accidental discharge from Lemley's rifle sent a ball through Slaughter's right shoulder.

One of the earliest livestock shows in New Mexico, at Roswell in 1907 . . . The central figure in the picture is Colonel C. C. Slaughter of Texas Lazy S fame. It was he, who about the turn of the century, startled the range world by bidding in Sir Bredwell at $5,000. In this photo he is at left center holding the halter of the big bull.

It was a serious wound and for weeks he was without expert treatment.

His companions feared the worst, but he pulled through and was carried to the settlements on a litter suspended between two pack mules. Safely home again he spent 1867 convalescing. In the following year he went up the Chisholm Trail for the first time as prelude to the many drives he was to make with his father and younger brother.

Then, after dissolving partnership at his father's retirement, C. C. Slaughter began buying land and importing from Kentucky some of the Shorthorn cattle which in time were to eliminate from the picture such rangy "moss horn" types as those which the parson drove to Abilene and Dodge. He became at that time one of the greater factors in the Texas cattle industry, and with J. C. Loving, Burk Burnett, Kit Carter and others he helped organize, in the shade of a tree at Graham, the organization now known as the Texas and Southwestern Cattle Raisers Association.

His herds increased; and his land holdings, located principally west of the Colorado River, grew into a kingdom fifty miles wide and eighty miles long—a great cattle empire which took as its coat-of-arms the far-famed Lazy S.

C. C. Slaughter later became a Dallas banker, but his interest centered always on the range; and until his death, no cowman in the State was better known—for few men in all the West ever put more beefsteak on the platters of the world.

The great cattle kingdom no longer exists in its entirety, having been divided among his heirs, but even today in the pens at Fort Worth stockyards may be found steers that carry the brand of the Lazy S . . . for C. C. Slaughter, Jr., who lives in Dallas, has kept his father's iron.

BRAND
C.C.SLAUGHTER
RANCH

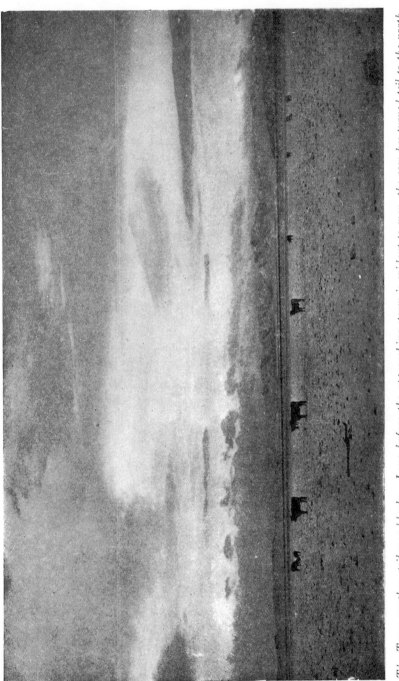

*The Texas norther strikes suddenly. Long before the approaching storm is evident to man, the cow has turned tail to the north and is trekking for the "breaks."*

# Reynolds
## of the
## Long X

George T. Reynolds

W. D. Reynolds

● Carved out an Empire in
the Trans-Pecos in midst
of gun smoke and Indian
raids

T HE WIND sang in the
mesquite, and low on the horizon a fast-growing mist foretold
the approach of a blue norther—but no thought for the weather was in the minds of the seven saddle-weary riders who

dropped their reins at McCamus Ranch near the junction of the Concho and Colorado Rivers.

On that cold January day in 1864 these men had ridden many long miles and their chief concern at the moment was in the promise the ranch held for "civilized" grub like boiled potatoes, bread, or a pot of beans. Venison and buffalo meat grow tiresome after three or four days of nothing else.

The travelers were not disappointed. Good, civilized food was to be had at the McCamus, and when they returned to the trail in the morning they felt that life again was worth the living.

The seven, led by young George T. Reynolds and his brother-in-law, Sam Newcomb, were out prospecting—seeking a ranch site which might be comparatively free from the dangers of Indian raids, if such a thing were possible. Back home, on the Clear Fork of the Brazos in Stephens county, the settlers were experienceing troubled times.

George's father, B. W. Reynolds, who had come into the country from Georgia by way of Alabama and the two Texas counties of Shelby and Palo Pinto, was having increased difficulty in keeping together his small herd—which he had purchased three years before from J. R. Baylor, giving as part payment a negro slave girl valued at $1,000.

During the War between the States the Indians had grown bolder in their raids across the unprotected frontier; and the end of the civil conflict had saddled upon the country a horde of discharged soldiers who seemed to prefer cattle thievery to the usual pursuits of honest men. Between the two evils no man's herd could remain his own unless he kept almost constant vigil. That's why the elder son was looking about for new pastures —preferably a more westerly place which would be guiltless of human presence.

George Reynolds, born in Alabama, had been in Texas since the age of three. He was at that time about twenty—blond, blue-eyed and slender—but despite his youth he already had put behind him several episodes or real adventure.

Only the year before he had ridden with Colonel Nat Buff-ord's 19th Texas Cavalry on raids through Arkansas and Miss-ouri, and near the close of the war he had come home with a wound, a horse, a saddle, and a pocketful of practically use-less Confederate money.

These were about his only assets as he rode with Newcomb and the others up the Concho. They were headed for the springs on Kickapoo Creek, where they hoped to find the de-sirable ranch site, but the party failed to reach that destina-tion . . . fate having arranged an interlude along the way.

### An Indian Party is routed and a grim trophy seized

One day's ride from the springs the seven came suddenly upon a small band of Comanches who were driving a herd of horses, and since the Indians showed undue haste in seeking the horizon the whites grew suspicious.

"Stolen stock!" ventured young Reynolds. "And I think we'd better go after them."

The other Texans needed no urging. They unslung their rifles, kicked in with their spurs, and gave chase. The Indians, however, had a good start, and by laying on the rawhide lashes they gained enough time and distance to desert jaded mounts and swing onto fresh ones. Thus they saved their own skins, but lost the horses—one of which was carrying, as tragic proof of some unrecorded skirmish, a blood-stained Texas saddle.

This fact alone eliminated all doubt as to the character of the horses and after rounding up the frightened herd the white men conferred on the proper course to pursue. They decided, finally, to dive for Fort Mason and attempt to find a clue to the owners, but unfortunately, they ran into unexpected diffi-culties along the way.

A company of Texas Rangers was encamped at San Saba

and, true to the traditions of the old Frontier Batallion, these men were an inquisitive-minded lot. They wanted to know the history of those horses ... and much of their questioning centered, naturally, on that bloddy saddle.

Reynolds attempted to make explanations but the Ranger captain thought the business looked queer, and said so.

"I reckon," he said, when the inquisition was over, "that we'll have to be holding you boys 'til we know more about the stock."

Mr. Reynolds protested. This, he said, was mighty sorry treatment for men who were trying to right a wrong and return stolen property to rightful owners, but the Ranger captain was not to be moved.

"Lock 'em up, boys," he ordered, "and corral the horses."

The jail at San Saba in those days wasn't much to boast about. It was a one-room affair, and that eight feet by ten. It was poorly lighted and poorly ventilated, but that wasn't by any means the worst of it ... as the seven young men from the Brazos soon discovered.

The place was fairly alive with vermin, a fact which became evident a few minutes after the lock had been snapped on the door. Reynolds and his companions tried to make the best of a bad situation but they failed to get much sleep during the three succeeding nights. The Rangers seemed to make little progress on their investigation, but on the fourth day one member of the company, who had been absent from camp at the time of the arrest, came to the jail to view the captives. He recognized George Reynolds.

"Why, I know this man," he said. "I used to work for his father in Palo Pinto county. He wouldn't steal a horse from any man, an' he wouldn't travel in company with men who would. You got the wrong boys, Cap'n."

And the Captain lost no time in emptying the guard house and offering his apologies. Disgusted for the time with exploration, Reynolds and his companions saddled and rode for home. The ranch on Kickapoo Creek could wait awhile ... how long they had no way of knowing.

### Satanta, wolf of the north, goes on the warpath

The party arrived home to find the settlements menaced by Indians as never before. Satanta, notorious war chief of Kiowas, was abroad in the north of Texas with 500 warriors at his back ... sacking homes, killing occupants, and running away cattle.

The old wolf of the north had just visited the scattered settlements along Elm Creek in Young county, where his painted followers had killed nineteen whites and kidnapped several children. Simultaneously one group of warriors, eighteen in all, had struck at Fort Bragg. They had burned all the buildings and then had scampered back to join the main party ... unaware that half a dozen settlers had received news of the affair and had cut in on their trail.

George Reynolds was in the group, which came upon the savages suddenly in a place where they were planning to camp for the night. The whites charged at once, and in the first rush Reynold's horse which had been ridden for several hours, dropped from sheer exhaustion. But he soon had a new one, an Indian pony whose rider he killed with a well-aimed rifle ball.

During the next twenty minutes a hot fight raged through the mesquite, and before the enemy decided on flight Reynolds heard the whistle of several arrows about his head ... but he came out unscathed, except for a missing pants leg which had been ripped away in the wild chase through the brush. Besides the victim of Mr. Reynold's rifle, the Indians left three others for the waiting wolves.

After the bloody raids in '64, which served to teach Satanta he was not dealing with timid men, the settlers enjoyed a

brief period of peace, and it was during this lull that young
Reynolds made his first venture into the cattle business.

He purchased 100 head of steers, and in 1866 moved to
Throckmorton county and leased the old Stone Ranch, to which
he moved his father and family.  But even here the Reynolds
brothers—George, William and Ben—could not shake off the
Indians.  In June of that year, during the absence of the father
and sons, the Comanches swooped down on the ranch and
chased away the entire herd of cattle, which by that time had
increased to about 500 head.

The raiders also took every loose saddle horse on the place,
but the loss, disastrous as it was, failed to discourage the Reynolds.  The brothers took up hunting in an effort to recoup
the family finances and in less than a year took the hides from
nearly a thousand buffaloes.  It was during this time that
George and Ben killed the only albino buffalo ever seen on
the plains, a great shaggy white beast that stood out in the
herd like a snowball in a coal heap.

But during this period of hunting the brothers never found
an Indian trail but they followed, hoping to even the count
somewhat for the stock stolen the year before, and one of these
adventurous expeditions brought disaster.

On April 3, 1867, George and William, with eight others,
started on a trail which led to the mouth of the Double Mountain Fork in what is now Haskell county.  There they found
their Indians—but a great many more than they expected.

The Comanches, a hunting party of thirty or more, were
busy skinning a buffalo when the Texans rode up, and they
showed fight immediately.  One of the braves, a sub-chief
who could speak a little English, dropped his skinning knife
and advanced on foot . . . a revolver in either hand, a volley
of oaths punctuating his yells.

He opened fire at long range, first with one revolver and
then the other, but George Reynolds noticed that the guns

were held in such position that the lead was being thrown much too high to find a mark.

"Hold up, boys," he said, as some of the men prepared for action. "Let him come closer. I'll take him . . ."

There was no denying that the Indian was more courageous than cautious. He kept coming and firing until both revolvers were empty. Then he unslung his bow and strung an arrow, but before he could draw back the buckskin George leveled his heavy navy revolver, took careful aim, and fired.

"Got him!" shouted Si Huff, who rode beside Reynolds. "I heard it hit."

Even so, the Indian kept his feet. Though shot through the body, he turned to run, but at this moment Reynolds fired again. The Comanche swayed and fell . . . his neck broken by the second bullet.

Then, with a yell, the Texans charged, firing both right and left as the Indians deserted the kill and took to their ponies. They scattered like scared quail, and as the party of whites split to begin pursuit Reynolds and Huff found themselves riding together.

Before them in the mesquite the hoofs of half a dozen hard-pushed mustangs kicked up the dust as their riders tried to urge them out of range . . . but Reynolds and Huff gained with every stride their horses took.

It was then that one of the hard-pressed Indians slowed his mount and strung an arrow. He half turned, twanged back the string, and let go . . . just as George Reynolds was jerking back the hammer of his revolver. He never pulled the trigger, for in the next second he felt a sharp pain in the abdomen as the iron head of the arrow struck just above the belt. Reynolds dropped his weapon and toppled toward the ground..

Reynolds sensed, before he hit the earth, that he was done for; but to his own amazement he did not lose consciousness

—though the experience might have finished off another man at once.

Protruding from his stomach—sunk almost to the feathers on the dogwood shaft—was a Comanche arrow! He tugged at the wood, and it came out . . . but not the iron spike. That terrible piece of metal, after penetrating his abdomen, had lodged in the muscles of his back and had pulled loose as the shaft came clear.

Si Huff, after seeing George Reynolds fall with an arrow in his stomach, rode back to investigate.

"No use, Si," said Reynolds. "They've got me. You'd better go on and help the boys, I'm shot clean through."

Huff took in the situation at a glance and he evidently formed the same opinion on the efficiency of the arrow, but he wasn't willing to let matters stand as they were.

"Do you know which Indian did it?" he asked. "Tell me . . . quick!"

"Yes . . . the one with the red shirt."

"Then I'll have the - - - - 's scalp!" exclaimed Si, wheeling his horse. The animal jumped at the touch of the rider's heels, and Huff was gone.

### Indian with red shirt twangs his last 'Arrer'

Reynolds, half dazed by pain, waited for what seemed hours, but it was really little more than fifteen minutes before his friend came riding back . . . carrying in one hand a tuft of matted hair.

"Here," said Huff, displaying the bleeding scalp. "Here's your man with the red shirt! He's shot his last arrer."

A few minutes later William Reynolds and the other five arrived on the scene. They brought with them, as grim souvenirs of the chase, four additional scalps, but these trophies were all but forgotten in the alarm over George's condition.

William examined the wound and the shaft which his brother had removed with his own hands, but could think of no way to get at the arrow head.  He guessed, and correctly so, that it was a case calling for expert surgery, but he held no hope that his brother would live to reach a doctor . . . not with home sixty miles away, and the nearest medical aid an additional hundred miles to the east.

In desperation, he did the only thing left to do—lifted George on a pack horse and started for the Stone Ranch.  How the sorely wounded man survived the ordeal of that jolting ride of sixty miles across the mesquite flats remains to this day one of the mysteries in the annals of the West, but George Reynold's physical strength was as great as his courage—and twenty-four hours later he was in his own bed.

Even then no hope was held for his recovery and a rider was dispatched at once to bring a doctor from Weatherford, more than a hundred miles.  Five days passed before the messenger returned with the man of medicine, and by that time the wounded man was out of danger.  The physician said, however, that he could not remove the arrow head, which remained securely lodged in the muscles of the back.  The spike stayed in—for fifteen years—being removed, finally, by surgeons in Kansas City in July of 1882.

Mr. Reynolds was soon up and about, and when he was again able to sit on a horse he visited the scene of the fight. The five Indians scalped by the whites remained where they had fallen . . . except that wolves had passed that way.  A sixth, who had been fatally wounded after his horse had been shot from under him, was found under a pile of rocks.  Since this warrior had saved his hair by crawling into the brush to die, the Indians had given him burial in accordance with the tribal custom of paying funeral honors only to unscalped braves. But they had scalped the horse—for failing its rider in a time of need.

Before the fight at Double Mountain George Reynolds had been a frequent visitor at the Shackleford county ranch of a neighbor, J. B. Matthews, and with his recovery he and one of the neighbor's daughters, Miss L. E. Matthews, began to think of a wedding date.   Miss Matthews was fifteen.

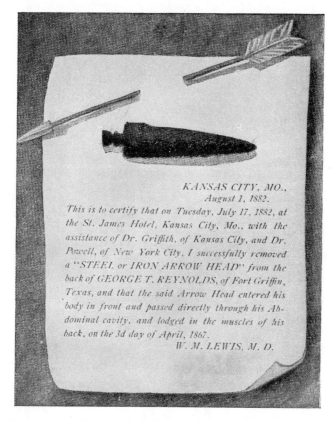

*Here is the arrow-head taken from the back of George T. Reynolds, and the certificate of the doctor who removed it fifteen years after the cattleman was shot by an Indian.*

But first Mr. Reynolds must needs travel to the village of Palo Pinto to take out a license ... and for many months Mr. Reynolds had stayed clear of that little town in the cedar-studded hills.   There was good reason why this should be ... for the sheriff was just awaiting an opportunity to place him under arrest.

All the trouble had come about because of Jacko, a lad who had accompanied George and his future father-in-law on a cattle hunting trip. This Jacko, having been left one day in charge of camp, had so far succumbed to temptation as to take the best horse in the outfit, load it with all the blankets at hand, and depart for places unknown.

But he hadn't quite succeeded in escape. George, together with Si Huff and Tom Crammer, took up the trail and caught Jacko in Parker county. They were returning, intending to lodge the boy in the Palo Pinto jail, when they were met by one J. C. Darnell, who expressed surprise that they should waste valuable time on such a prisoner.

"Why not hang him now?" suggested Mr. Darnell, "and have done with it?"

Whereupon the unfortunate Jacko was led beneath a post-oak where a rawhide rope—incidentally, one of the stolen items—was placed about his neck. The thief asked for, and was granted, time to pray, and he ended his supplication with such a piteous petition for mercy that the cattlemen decided on a flogging rather than a hanging.

George Reynolds himself applied the lashes, a penitentiary offense in those days, and though a hanging might have gone unnoticed, the Palo Pinto county sheriff felt bound to interest himself in the case. The good officer had been looking for Reynolds ever since . . . and now Reynolds had to visit Palo Pinto to obtain his marriage license.

**Mrs. Reynolds rode the trails when they were wild**

Unhesitatingly he went to get it, and two friends rode with him, and they met not the slightest opposition from the sheriff—perhaps for the reason that each of the three carried, in addition to a double-barrel shotgun, four revolvers at the belt.

The couple married—and Mr. Reynolds, needing money to buy additional cattle, found a job hauling from Leon County the timbers used in building stockades at Fort Griffin, the army

Photograph by W. D. Smithers

*Holding a herd in a Big Bend shelter*

post being erected about fourteen miles from the old Stone Ranch.

In the spring of that year he pooled his resources with his brother William, who, having been on the last trail made by Charles Goodnight and Oliver Loving, had just returned to Texas with the body of Loving, dead as a result of the fight with Indians on the Pecos. The brothers made purchases and then decided to try their luck farther west.

And so, in the summer of 1868, George hit the trail for Colorado with a herd of a thousand longhorn steers. With him, in addition to about a dozen hands, went his brother Ben, and his wife.

It was a hazardous trip, but to her last days Mrs. Reynolds looked back upon it as the most thrilling journey in her eventful life—for more than once, when the Indians swooped down to harry the herd and stampede the horses she found herself in that narrow corner which holds the uncertainties of fate.

She rode in a hack and she once sat in it at Horsehead Crossing on the Pecos while her husband, sitting beside her with a rifle on his knees, watched through a spy-glass the movements of a band of Indians who were attempting to encircle the herd.

Only the night before the savages had stampeded the horses, taking six of the best mounts; and in the dawn they had followed the herd to the Pecos in the hope of making a successful attack before the hands could get the longhorns across that swollen stream.

The outfit was caught between the Comanches and the rolling river—a plainsman's equivalent for being caught between the devil and the deep blue sea—and for two tense hours the situation appeared none too bright. At the first hint of attack, which seemed almost inevitable, the Reynolds brothers posted their men in strategic positions around the cattle. Then George climbed onto the hack with his wife. There, in case worst came to worst, would be the last stand.

"If it does come to that," Mrs. Reynolds told her husband, "promise me that you'll save one bullet . . . for me."

But Mr. Reynolds pretended not to hear; he was too busy with his telescope, watching the indecisive movements of the enemy.

Sometimes he felt certain that a charge was forming, but the Indians hesitated a bit too long. They had the odds in numbers, but the better armament of the white men made up the difference; and besides, the cattlemen could draw small but effective reinforcements from the riders with another herd which had crossed the Pecos the night before, and which even then was waiting on the opposite bank. Finally, the Reynolds decided to risk a crossing, and the outfit went over. The Indians lost their prey.

The herd wintered near Raton Pass. In the following spring it was trailed on to Colorado to be turned loose near La Junta. There the family established headquarters on the open range—the beginning of the cattle empire which later was to be known through every country which grazed a steer as the Long X.

William Reynolds brought out more Texas cattle in 1870, and from that day until this the Reynolds Cattle Company has been a major factor in the livestock industry of the West.

More trails followed—to Salt Lake City and to Cheyenne —and on some of these Mrs. Reynolds went along in the hack, sleeping at night beside lonely campfires while the wolves howled to the moon and the mocking birds sang to the stars. Amanda Burks, famed "cattle queen of Cotulla", went up the Chisholm Trail to Kansas but her journeys from the south of Texas could not compare with the trails followed by Mrs. George Reynolds over the Indian-infested mesas of the West...

There were times when she never saw another woman for months, once for so long a time as four months, but even so she would not have traded those days for any since.

The Reynolds remained in Colorado four years and then returned to the old home in Texas, where George Reynolds had another narrow escape from an Indian arrow.   Immediately after the return he went to Weatherford where he purchased a herd of cattle from Charlie Rivers, son-in-law of the first Oliver Loving.

The transaction was closed and the steers were to be rounded up next day for a drive to Utah, but during the night, while Reynolds lay sleeping with Rivers, the camp was attacked by Indians.   An arrow whispered through the blackness, skimmed over Reynolds, and found a mark in his companion.

### The Long X still goes onto Texas steer hides

Rivers lived but a short while, but before death overtook him, sent for his brother-in-law,   J. C. Loving, who was camped nearby.   He told Mr. Loving of the deal made the previous day and requested that the cattle be delivered according to contract . . . and then he died.   The herd was driven through to Utah by William and George Reynolds, who added to the profits of the venture by delivering a herd of horses in Colorado on the return journey.

Back in Texas once more, and this time to stay, William married Miss Susie Matthews, a sister of his brother's wife.

The brothers bought land in Shackleford, Throckmorton and Haskell counties and before many years they had under control more than 100,000 acres, across which grazed 20,000 head of cattle.   They began specializing in Herefords, and then they branched out into other lines of business as well.

They both moved to Albany, where they became principals in the organization of the First National Bank;  and during the famous "Run of 1889" which opened Oklahoma Territory to settlement, George went to Oklahoma City, set up two barrels in the street of the mushroom town, laid planks across them, and stepped into the role of paying and receiving

*Out in the Big Bend the herd moves across the flat to a corral or loading pen*

teller.    Thus the First National Bank of that city was organized.

Later the families moved to Fort Worth, but the brothers
retained until they died extensive ranch holdings.    The five
sons of William Reynolds manage the livestock enterprises of
the Reynolds Cattle Company and the separate holdings and
the separate brands of the W. D. Reynolds Trust—and though
the longhorns which the brothers once drove to New Mexico
and Colorado are gone, and the blooded Herefords have come
to take their place beneath the sun, down in Culberson and
Jeff Davis counties in the Trans-Pecos country, in the western Panhandle, as well as back east, an old familiar brand
still finds its way into the fire . . .

And Texas steers still wear the Long X on their hides.

BRAND

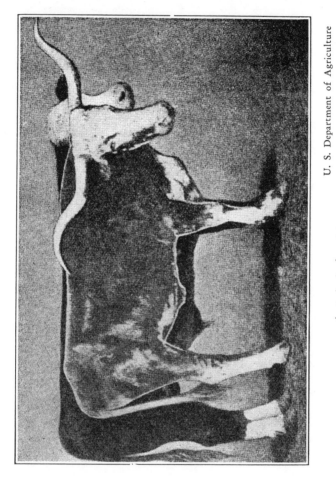

*A study in breed improvement*

U. S. Department of Agriculture

# Androcles
# of the
# Plains

SATANTA

RANGE DUEL

● How the gift of a gun to an Indian saved the life of a Cattleman from the fate of a white prisoner

**Y**OU have heard the story of Androcles and the lion—how the escaped slave of Rome removed a thorn from the paw of a beast in the wilderness; how the slave was captured and condemned to die in the arena

193

of the Coliseum; and how his life was spared when the lion selected to devour him turned out to be his old friend of the wilderness, recently snared by the huntsmen. You have heard that story, but listen—

Evander Light had taken a bride in Denver and the young couple, ignoring the fact that all western country was an untracked and dangerous land in those days... the year 1863 ... had packed their belongings and started east for Kansas.

It was common knowledge in every outpost that this was a perilous season to be abroad—that some of the tribes were in conflict and that travelers might expect to meet with trouble —but Evander Light, a New Yorker by birth but a westerner by preference, was not one to allow wars and rumors of wars to keep him from his chosen honeymoon. There was some satisfaction, however, in being able to travel with a military train... just in case of difficulties.

And there was ample opportunity for mishap. Between Denver and their destination, Fort Leavenworth, their route led directly through the "happy hunting grounds" of the Pawnees, the Kiowas and the Comanches... happy because the tribesmen were lifting far more scalplocks than buffalo robes.

The ox teams struggled on, straining hard at the creaking wagons; and then, at a point near the Arkansas River, came the first alarm. At first it sounded as the distant echo of brief, stacatto claps of thunder, a sound half smothered behind the rolling hills ahead, but the members of the troop escort and the veteran plainsmen of the train listened with growing uneasiness. Even the horses pricked up their ears for they, like some of their masters, knew gunfire when they heard it.

Somewhere back of the hills a battle was in progress but the leaders of the caravan lacked the inclination to investigate. Instead, they urged the oxen forward, and yokes groaned under the strain as the long bullwhips cracked and popped. The

Arkansas, a liquid snake meandering through the lowlands, lay just ahead ...

And then out from the hills galloped a lone rider. He seemed, at first, little more than a cloud of dust on the horizon ... like one of the devil-dusters which swirl across the prairies in time of drouth ... but as the cloud drew close enough to be identified as horse and man, the bullwhackers recognized the rider as an Indian.

A short distance from the caravan, which had come to a halt, the stranger stopped and held out a hand in sign of friendship, but even this gesture hardly was enough to convince the whites that they were dealing with a man of peace.

The warrior, half-naked from the waist up, sat bare-back on a paint pony, his buck-skin covered legs dangling lower than the animal's belly ... but an eye less practiced than that of a physician could readily see that the man was wounded in several places. The more experienced among the travelers appraised him carefully and then knew him for what he was —a Kiowa, and to all appearances, a head-man of the tribe.

"Tough lookin' hombre, ain't he?" observed a grizzled sergeant of the troop, and then cocking an eye toward the distant hills: "But that ain't ary picnic out yonder."

There was silence for a moment and then the Indian fixed his gaze on Evander Light, whom he evidently believed to be the leader of the train, and explained himself.

"Peace, friend," he said, in his halting, short-clipped English. "We are Kiowa ... on warpath. We fight Pawnee. But my gun ... I have lost him."

He went on to say that he had dropped his weapon somewhere in the midst of the melee, and would the white captain be good enough to supply him with a gun, just as a loan. The battle was close in honors, and even now he feared that the Pawnees might be taking the chance of victory.

Evander Light did not hesitate. Moved by the gallantry

of the savage, he took from one of his holsters a cap and ball revolver and passed it butt first to the wounded man. The latter glanced once at the gun, gazed steadily for a moment at his benefactor, and without a word kicked his pony in the ribs and dashed back toward the hills ... again like a devil-duster swirling out across the prairie.

The wagon train pushed on to the Arkansas, and on to Fort Leavenworth.

Let us now pass briefly over the record of two years—a period which brought the rails of the Union Pacfic pushing across the great expanse of the West in the trail of stations established by that pioneering business enterprise, the Wells Fargo Express Company. The West was sitting at the back door of civilization, with only the hostile Indian jealous of the encroachment.

### Civil War's end brought many new faces to Texas

Soon the longhorns would be following the weary trail from Texas to board the railway cars for eastern markets; soon new towns would boom along the line, Dodge, Abilene, Wichita. The Civil War was at an end and discharged soldiers of both armies were pouring into the new country, bringing the vice and dissension and crime which tags the advance of civilization. It was an era which brought gun fighters, bandits and honest men ... adventurers, too.

In this latter group came John W. Light, younger brother of Evander. Lately discharged from the Sixth New York Heavy Artillary, and still troubled by wounds received in the Wilderness, young Mr. Light arrived in Fort Leavenworth primed and cocked for whatever adventure the plains might have to offer.

He found it almost immediately, Brother Evander arranging that he go as driver with a wagon train just leaving for Santa Fe, New Mexico. The trip out was lacking in unusual incidents, but on the return he lost his oxen in a Western

Kansas snow storm, and he was compelled to leave the wagons and push on to Leavenworth afoot. In the spring the Light brothers made an unsuccessful hunt for the property, and returning by way of Fort Larned fell in with Buffalo Bill Madison, who at that time was engaged in trading with the wily savages of Western Kansas and the Indian Territory to the south.

Madison, like all good traders, also was an excellent story teller and he regaled the brothers Light with such entertaining tales of adventure in the field that they decided to link their fortunes with Madison and another trader, Fred Jones, and help carry the message of calico and beads to the red brethren of the Kiowa, Comanche and Cheyenne divisions.

Photograph by Erwin E. Smith
*The wagon*

With four trinket-loaded wagons they headed south—little suspecting that Act One of a drama in which they were to participate even then was being staged in Fort Leavenworth.

Colonel Leavenworth, then in charge of the Kansas Indian agencies, had a problem on his hands. Some of the bad boys among his wards had slipped down into Texas to drive away several thousand head of cattle. This crime might have been overlooked by the authorities—for steers were cheap just then —but the Indians had carried matters a bit too far by also bringing back a white woman and child they had captured on the raid.

The Colonel, meeting with a committee of sub-chiefs, did not mince words. He demanded unconditional release of the prisoners, but the Indians had chosen to plead ignorance of the crime—a denial which angered the knowing officer to the very depths of his soul. The chiefs could get out, said he, and they need not trouble to show their faces around the agency until they felt disposed to bring in the woman and her child.

Now it was the turn of the Indians to display anger. Sullen, ill-tempered, and crying injustice they rode away to the south—to overtake, as chance would have it, the trading wagons driven by Madison, Jones and the Light brothers.

The Cheyennes and the Kiowas, for the party was made up from both tribes, were in the mood for any sort of mischief and they took immediate charge of the rolling stock. Pleased with the whatnots in the wagons, they appropriated everything in sight, made the traders prisoners, and continued the trek southward.

On the second day they came to a Kiowa village and then the fun started. The bucks came out with their bows and arrows and pistols to amuse themselves by shooting at the feet of the white men and demanding that they dance; and then, tiring of this and similar other diversions, they placed their prisoners in a tepee until such time when the chiefs should decide upon a course of action.

John wanted to know what fate he might expect.

"No use to worry about that," counseled Evander. "We'll just have to wait and see, but whatever it is it'll be plenty."

John was of the opinion that nothing could be much worse than the food—which consisted principally of dried buffalo meat and raw tallow—but Evander, wiser in the ways of the red brother, advised him to gulp down the mess and like it.

"There's a sight o' things worse'n dried meat an' tallow," said he. "We've still got our scalps an' that's somethin'."

Six long weeks they took that bill of fare, and then arrived the fateful day when they were led before Satanta, principal war chief of the Kiowas, and known among his people as "the orator of the plains".

He soon was to win the right to yet another name, this chief who later was to kill himself at the Texas Penitentiary

*Texas prison system calf with Lone Star brand*

after being sent there to serve a life sentence for his part in the murder of wagon teamsters during a raid into Jack county.

### A Savage remembers, and shows his appreciation

Satanta raised his eyes to look at the prisoners as they were led into his presence, and his attention seemed to be centered on the face of Evander; and while Light wondered where he had seen the Kiowa before the chief arose from his place, rushed to his captive and threw both arms about him in fond embrace.

He murmured but one word: "Arkansas!"

Then Evander Light knew—knew that the battle of two years ago had been won and that the lion had come safely from the hills; realized, too, his own role in the drama—that of an Androcles of the frontier.

Thus John and Evander escaped they knew not what fate. Satanta told them to take their wagons and go in peace—all because a revolver had been placed in his hands at a time when sorely needed.

Of course the incident had little to do with it, but it served as a prelude to John Light's advent into the cattle business. His experience with the savages of the Territory taught him that the trader's life was hardly one to recommend.

The following year found him supplying the district commissary and the Kansas military posts with beef, which he purchased on the hoof and sold on the block for ten cents a pound. He made money, sometimes thousands a month . . . but good fortune seldom abides forever with a man. He made some bad deals and by 1874 had lost all he had taken in as profit. In the markets, however, he had made friends with numerous Texans, and he decided to go south in an attempt to recoup his fortunes.

When John left Kansas that year he had eight dollars in his pocket, but upon his arrival in Mason County he found employment on the farm of Ben Gooch, who was willing to pay him as much as $40 a month.

A year later Light found backing, bought Gooch's farm and his 2,500 head of cattle on a three-year credit, and with the financial aid of Seth Mabry of Austin built the herd to 5,000 by the spring of 1876. Then he drove to Ogallala, Nebraska, and came home with a profit. Through similar enterprises he paid off his debt and began buying more land and cattle. Before the turn of the century he sold and went to Chickasha in the Indian Territory to spend the remaining days of his life.

He was a lesser and a minor king, as cow royalty went on the *Llano Estacado* in those days, but at the same time an example of how more than one man made his start in the business. . . .

With an initial capital of $8, sometimes slightly more, sometimes slightly less. . . .

BRAND
G. E. LIGHT
RANCH

*The horses ....*

# Bugbee
## of the
## Quarter Circle T

THOMAS BUGBEE

MANHANDLED

● He scooped a dugout in plains and from it built a 450,000 acre cattle kingdom

A TRAIN of wagons crawled across the sand-scourged desert toward the saw-toothed mountain range which bit into the crystal sky.

Shimmering wraiths of heat floated through the dust raised by the creaking wheels; and far in the distance a lake, green and blue and dancing, caught briefly the reflection of the towering peaks, and then was gone. . . another mirage swallowed in the grim but gorgeous pageantry of sand and sun.

In the deep silence of late afternoon all the western land seemed weighted with the majesty and mystery of death; but there was, too, a certain beauty—the pendulous white bells of the *yucca* swaying gently under the hot breath of devastating winds; the weird, pencilled shadows which crept from the *saguaro* and the *cholla* as the rays from the sloping sun attacked that giant cacti of the wasteland.

Sand and sun, mirage and shadow, a land of nothingness from which came no sound—other than that stirred by the forty-five wagons of the freighters, pushing across the desert for the Great Salt Lakes of Utah.

The far peaks already were outlined in crimson as the lead wagon came to a halt and the driver scrambled down from the spring seat. He had seen something out beyond a dune and as he went to investigate other drivers reined in, to peer out from under canvass-covered bows and inquire of one another the reason for delay. Then, one by one, they ambled up the line of wagons to see for themselves.

The lead driver had found something in the sand. He stood silently atop the dune, looking down on the charred fragments of half a dozen wagons . . . but there was something else. At his feet lay a human skull, bleached white as the sand which half covered its skeleton, and grinning with sightless eyes into the sky.

A little way apart was still another . . . perhaps that of a woman, for beside it lay the skeleton of a child . . . together with a dozen others who had found under that dune the end of a westward trail.

Who were these wanderers, and what fate had overtaken them? The mystery was easy of solution—a few iron-tipped arrows, broken in the dust, was quite enough to tell the story.

It was near sunset when the last spade of desert was turned
and the last word had been uttered in the prayer for the burial of the dead, but the freighting train pushed on a few more
miles before making camp for the night.  Even then the men
of the wagons talked but little of the incident—perhaps because they themselves rode so close to death in those dangerous days of 1866—but as the fires were lighted within the
circle of wagons there was one among the teamsters who wondered.

"So this," mused Thomas Bugbee, "is adventure . . . adventure at thirty-five dollars a month?"

Thomas Sherman Bugbee was twenty-three, and was getting
his first taste of western travel.  Lately arrived from New
England, he had joined the Salt Lake-bound supply train at
St. Joseph, Missouri.  Even though he had come from far
north in Yankee-land, he had seen enough danger to know his
way about.

At the age of fourteen, in his native Maine, he had left
home to take up employment on a farm.  Then in 1860,
having chosen agriculture for a career, he had homesteaded on
eighty acres in the western part of that state.  He was just
beginning to make progress at the opening of the War between the States, and then quite suddenly had found himself
in the 10th Maine Infantry, on his way to Baltimore to guard
trains.

He saw action, too.  Wounded at Cedar Mountain, he took
part in Antietam, Fredericksburg, the second Bull Run, Lookout Mountain and Gettysburg; and when he was mustered
out in 1864 he went to Washington seeking work.  He took
a job as conductor aboard one of the horse-drawn street cars
on the Washington to Georgetown run, but tiring after a few
weeks, turned in his cap and started for Maine.

He had trouble en route, for about the time of his departure from the capital Abraham Lincoln was assassinated in

Ford's Theatre and the police of the country were on the lookout for the slayer. Imagine, then, young Mr. Bugbee's discomfiture when, upon arrival in Boston, he found himself in the clutches of the law ... suspected of being John Wilkes Booth! After several hours, however, he succeeded in proving his identity and was allowed to continue northward.

### A Risky trail—across the desert to Salt Lake

Finding post-war Maine suffering an economic depression, Bugbee decided to cast his lot in the West—where at least adventure, if not a fortune, waited. At St. Joseph, where he arrived in due time, he found the supply train ready to roll for Utah. Here was a chance for travel, and he signed on as a teamster—at $35 a month.

Then the desert and, at last, Salt Lake.

Thomas Bugbee learned a great deal on the journey, and when he arrived at the capital of Brigham Young he immediately went into business for himself ... as a freighter. Beginnings, of course, were small, but after awhile he was branching out into Idaho, with the result that the fall months of 1868 found him with a surplus of $35,000 needing investment.

"Cattle are cheap in Texas an' meat's high out here," suggested an Idaho neighbor. "A man could make a poke-ful of money if he could drive out a herd, but ... "

"A good idea," said Bugbee, "and worth looking into."

"But as I was saying," went on the neighbor, "the risk would be too great ... with the desert and the danged Injuns. A man would be liable to get his hide shot full o' arrers."

Maybe ... but Thomas Bugbee believed the chance worth taking, and so did two of his friends, M. M. Shea and George Miller, who also had a little money waiting investment. The three rigged out a wagon and started ... on one of the most roundabout journeys ever made into Texas from the West. They drove first to Green River City, where they boarded the Union Pacific to ride into Omaha. A few weeks later they were in Vicksburg and on their way by water to Shreveport, from which city they traveled by hack to Marshall in East Texas.

There, they bought saddle horses and equipment, then set out for Collin county in the north to visit a cattleman acquaintance of Mr. Miller. This gentleman, John A. Knight, was glad to see them.

"Sure," he said, when the venture was explained, "I can furnish as many cattle as you want. There are plenty on the ranges to the south . . . down around Fort Worth."

Miller 'allowed' that 1,200 head would be quite enough for a small outfit to handle, and the four rode down to Fort Worth, where the three partners saw such sights as the small city afforded while Knight made purchases throughout the vicinity.

When the steers were delivered, at $11 a head, Shea, Miller and Bugbee hired five hands, and headed north. They drove to Sherman, crossed the Red River, trekked through the Indian Territory, crossed the Arkansas—where they fought off a small band of Indian raiders—and came at last to the Snake River country of Idaho. There they took the profits, selling the $11 steers at $45.

The following year Bugbee and Shea returned to Texas, bought on the Brazos and drove 1,500 head to Colorado. The venture being highly successful, Bugbee withdrew from the partnership to go on his own. He back-tracked to Texas, bought in Burleson county, and hit the trail for Kansas with 750 head; but he arrived during the "great rush" of 1871 which glutted the Kansas rail terminals with trail herds from all over the south of Texas.

The Lone Star cattlemen had "discovered" the railroad, which meant a market outlet, and since 1866—the first year of the drives—more and more steers were going up to Abilene and Wichita. The total reached 350,000 in 1870, but 1871,

*Holding herd....*

Photograph by Erwin E. Smith

the year Bugbee went up, was destined to see 600,000 animals at the terminals.

The market already was glutted when Bugbee arrived with his 750, and since $2 a hundred was the best price offered, he decided to winter in Rice county, west of Abilene, and hope for improved prices in the spring.

The winter was wet, and driving northers swept down across the plains, with the result that the spring roundup revealed the absence of all but 315 steers. He sold these at a sacrifice, bought 225 head of two year-olds, and held them on the open range near Sterling.

Summer brought new hope . . . and romance. Bugbee had been calling at the home of Thomas Dunn in Sterling and on August thirteenth of that year, he married Mr. Dunn's daughter, Mary. The couple loaded their belongings into a wagon, and after Mr. Bugbee had hired several hands to drive and handle the cattle, they started for Western Kansas on a honeymoon—and to search for a ranch location.

Although the Bugbees were constantly on the alert against Indians, the journey into Western Kansas was made without unusual incident, except for two semi-humorous episodes. The weather was warm and the couple slept under the wagon, and one night the grease in their supply of bacon melted, dripped down through the cracks of the wagon bed and onto the head of the bride. She gave herself a shampoo in the waters of the Arkansas, but the very next night, while sleeping under the opposite end of the wagon, a keg of sorghum molasses sprung a leak with similar results.

The couple followed the river through a country abounding with buffalo until at last they came to a spot suitable for ranching. There, near the spot where the town of Lakin later would stand, Mr. Bugbee scooped a dugout from the soil near the river bank and turned loose the herd.

In this lonely outpost beyond civilization the cattleman's

bride counted it a rare occasion when she saw another woman, but she managed to avoid loneliness by taking a keen interest in the cattle, keeping an eye open for Indians, and by shooting buffalo.

In fact, this latter business proved the salvation of the ranch during the first two years, the Bugbees deriving enough income from buffalo hides to pay the salaries of the five men employed to help with the cattle. At the end of that time Bugbee began buying young animals, shaping them and driving them to nearby rail markets.

#### They lived in a dugout with buffalo hide curtains

The couple remained in the dugout on the Arkansas for nearly four years. One day in early October, 1876, after Indians had made several attempts to raid the herd, Bugbee consulted with his wife as to the wisdom of seeking a change of climate.

"The Indians are getting worse every day," he said, "and I think we'd better get out of Kansas while we have some stock to move. We've had luck so far but we don't know when it'll change."

They considered a new range, and finally decided on the south. They loaded the wagon, gathered up the herd, and started for No Man's Land—that narrow strip of the Indian Territory which, jutting westward from the Territory proper, touched the borderline of Colorado to form a county-wide dividing line between the states of Texas and Kansas.

Below the strip lay their goal—the Texas Panhandle, at that time a "terra incognito" practically devoid of inhabitants except for Colonel and Mrs. Charles Goodnight and the hands they had brought with them to the founding of their ranch in *Palo Duro* Canyon earlier in the year.

The Bugbee outfit, with 1,800 head, started its trek south at the beginning of a misty, fog-laden day; and the cattle, wild after long months on the open range, were hard to hold.

Many small groups detached themselves from the main herd and scattered, making it necessary for the outfit, after crossing the Cimarron and arriving at Beaver Creek in the Strip to camp a few days while the cowboys back-trailed to collect strays.

Then, with the herd in hand once more, Bugbee pushed on into Texas and turned loose on the banks of the Canadian River . . . to become one of the first two resident ranchers on the high Panhandle.

The ranch house wasn't at all pretentious at first—just another dugout, but it did have certain improvements, notably buffalo hide curtains for the windows, and a meat supply service right at the front door.

The buffalo were even more numerous here than on the Kansas plains. Unmolested for centuries except by the Indian bowmen, they ranged in unbelievably large herds along the banks of the Canadian; and since they had not learned to fear the roar of a gun it was possible for Mrs. Bugbee, when she wanted to stock the larder with fresh steaks, to do so by simply stepping to the door of the dugout and downing a cow or young bull with a rifle.

No exaggeration, that—but if the hump-backed animals furnished meat in over-abundance they also created a problem as they cropped passively at the green grass along the river. That was just it—grass. The buffalo left little feed for the cattle, and Bugbee realized that something had to be done about it.

Consequently, he did what Goodnight had been doing on the JA to the south, and what newly arriving ranchmen soon were doing—he hired men for the sole purpose of keeping the humpbacks off a certain area of range.

That such a thing should be necessary seems almost like pure fiction in this day when the last traces of once great herds may be seen only in parks and private herds, but in those days before the great slaughter—when men worked buffalo as well as cattle, but for different purposes—strange and sometimes humorous, incidents occurred.

There was the case of a neighbor, Leigh Dyer—the Dyer later to be identified with the T-Anchor brand west of the JA's. Dyer, while riding the Goodnight range with a companion, decided to rope a buffalo cow. He galloped up to the herd and then . . . but let his companion of that day tell it.

"He threw his rope onto a buffalo cow and shot her twice. The cow then commenced comin' for him; and his horse, getting scared, let in to buckin' an' spilt Leigh on a rock. He got bad shaken, and for two or three hours could not move at all, and I had to move him when he had to change positions. The first thing he said was, and is, I believe what everybody has in their minds when they get bad hurt, 'I tell you, Hugh,' he said, 'this kind of life is a mighty uncertain kinder business.' "

But already the buffalo was joining the Indian on the way to oblivion. Bugbee, with the help of his hired riders, kept his 1,800 cattle on the grass, and more and more animals began wearing the mark of the Quarter Circle T, the brand he had adopted.

The dugout was abandoned and the Bugbees built a small ranchhouse, which became famed throughout all the north country for its hospitality—which, according to old-timers, included the best glass of buttermilk to be found between the Cimarron and the Rio Grande. Never a traveler passed that way but he was invited to "light, come in and eat," or, if the pause had to be brief, to have at least a glass of buttermilk.

### Bugbee established famed brand called Shoe-Bar

And so there were many who regretted the transaction through which Bugbee, in 1882, disposed of the Quarter Circle T. He had at that time 12,500 head of cattle. He sold to the Hansford Land and Cattle Company for $350,000.

He invested part of this amount in Kansas City real estate, but the following year marked his return to the cattle business.

With O. H. Nelson as partner, Bugbee bought 8,000 young cattle from the JA and 7,000 from other ranches. The herd was put on Red River in Hall county. Then Mr. Bugbee formed another partnership, this time with C. W. Word of Wichita Falls. They bought 26,000 head and put them on 225,000 acres they had leased in the Cheyenne country of the Indian Territory, at two cents an acre.

Word and Bugbee put in 65 miles of fence at a cost of about $200 a mile, but this project was no sooner completed than the Government issued orders instructing whites to leave the Indian country, and leave immediately.

Part of the big herd was moved to Hall county, but 6,000 were lost through scattering. The remainder were sold and the company closed out at a loss, Bugbee returning to Hall

Photograph by Erwin E. Smith
*The Shoe Bar trail herd files down to water*

to buy out Nelson. Here would be the scene of his greatest operation—on a pasture of 450,000 acres, a tract 132 miles around. Soon he was running 20,000 head under a brand which was to become famous in the Panhandle—the Shoe Bar. Later, on still another but smaller ranch in Knox county, he was to have yet another brand—the 6 9.

The great ranch remained intact until the country began filling with settlers in the late '90's.  Then Bugbee began selling off small tracts until, at last, the ranch consisted of a mere 60,000 acres in Donley, Hall and Armstrong counties.

Thomas Bugbee went to Kansas City, managing his ranch affairs from there, but the lure of Texas proved too strong. He wanted to see how his son, John, who still resides in the Panhandle, was making out.  Thereafter, until his death on October 18, 1925, Thomas Bugbee remained near his ranges. When death overtook him he was in Clarendon—a town not many miles from that spot on the banks of the Canadian where so many years before he had scooped his dugout to become one of the first two cowmen on the broad sweep of the high Panhandle Plains.

There is some question which was first, Bugbee or Colonel Goodnight, and the issue--important or not--still furnishes excuse for much conversation in the high country, but whatever the case the dates of their arrivals are so close together that solution of the controversy couldn't mean much, one way or the other.

BRAND
THOS. BUGBEE

# A
# Calf Starts
# a
# Kingdom

LASSOED BY THE HEEL

● Henry C a m p b e l l, founder of the great Matador, left a lasting mark on Llano Estacado

HARRY CAMPBELL

$S$OME BOYS like dogs, others ponies, but young Henry Campbell wanted more than anything else he had seen in his fourteen years of life—just a calf.

His father had promised him the next one that should be left in the barnyard of the Campbell's Waller county farm, but even so, Henry could scarce credit his good fortune when he learned that a faithful cow had been obliging enough to fill the order.

Fourteen-year-old Henry had become, overnight, a Texas cowboy and cattleman; and as he carefully appraised his wobbley-legged "one-head herd" for the first time he felt a strange and almost overwhelming satisfaction. If the boys back in North Carolina, from whence the family had just come, could see him now!

Every day the lad watched the progress of the gangling, moon-faced suckling. He helped wean it from its mother's side and then, as it began taking its first experimental nips from the green floor of the earth, young Henry made it his daily task to lead the calf to spots where the grass grew thickest.

But as time went on he realized that something was lacking. At first he didn't know just what it was, then, quite suddenly, he saw it...he was afoot! How could he ever expect to be a real cowboy without learning to ride, and how could he learn to ride without a pony? If a man is to succeed in any business, he told himself, a man must first familiarize himself with the details of his chosen business. He pondered awhile and then decided upon the next best thing—he would break the calf.

The little critter had grown, and as Henry looked him over he was assailed by doubt—for this would not be his first experience at "bronc busting".

In the days before the calf there had been a goat on the Campbell farm, and when Henry had crawled upon this animal's middle to give him a ride, the Billy had piled Henry so quickly that the boy had lost some of his ambition to fork high-rollers. Of course, he knew enough about livestock to realize that goats didn't count among cattlemen, but just the same the incident stood out like a warning in his memory as he prepared a rope surcingle and proceeded with the business in hand.

He led the motley-faced critter to a convenient flat, knotted the rope about its middle, and swung aboard. The surprised calf, feeling a strange weight upon his back, quivered. Then he ducked his head, let out a bawl of protest, and humped. The front feet hit the ground with a thud and the hind legs came up with a jerky little kick, but Henry kept his seat.

He did slip a little sideways, but he managed to straighten out before the calf started a series of long running bucks, into which he put every instinctive trick he knew in an effort to shake loose the weight on his back. But the boy stayed up, and finally the calf quit his bawling and began running in circles. Then he stopped altogether, and the weight removed itself.

Henry Campbell had "busted" his first mount . . . and it is hardly necessary to add that he was proud of the accomplishment. From that day thenceforward he was a cowboy and a cattleman.

"This particular calf," he often said in later years, "became the object of my constant care and solicitude. It was a companion. I studied its wants and habits, and became intimate with its every instinct as it grew into mature oxhood. From this time on my life was constantly associated with cattle . . . in driving, tending herds, and handling oxen. Whatever measure of success I have enjoyed must to a great extent be attributed to my intimate knowledge of cattle, acquired by careful observation and study in early life."

Thus a single calf became the moving power behind an inspiration which some day would bring about one of the larger ranches of the Texas Panhandle, the great Matador. But between a barnyard calf and the Matador lay many years and many events . . .

When the family of F. Campbell moved to Texas in 1854

from North Carolina, where Henry had been born fourteen
years before, the frontier boasted few schools.  That caused
Henry little worry.  He attended classes for a few weeks
after the family migrated to Grimes county in 1856 but he
soon put aside his books to drive an ox team for his father.
He hauled cotton to market for the neighboring farmers, and
when the Campbells moved on to Ellis county in '59 he took
an ox team to East Texas and brought back the pine lumber
which was used in construction of a new home.

### He bought a saddle on monthly payment plan

By this time, of course, the calf had long since gone to cow
heaven, but Henry sometimes thought of the critter . . . and
day-dreamed of the time when he could follow his natural
bent by entering the cattle business.

He might have realized his ambition sooner but for the War
between the States.  Henry was twenty-one, and with three
of his brothers he enlisted in the 20th Texas Regiment for
service in Missouri, Kansas, Arkansas and the Indian Territory.

After participating in numerous skirmishes his active cam-
paigning came to an end when he was carried off the field at
Honey Springs, Arkansas, suffering from two wounds.  By
the close of the war he had completely recovered.

With a discharge in his pocket he rode back to Ellis county
on a horse he had captured after his own had been shot from
under him in one of the minor engagements. And he straddled
a saddle which he had bought from a friend for $27—the
money to be paid in twelve monthly installments.

Just as in the days when he owned a calf and no pony, he
now owned a horse but no cattle, and he set out to remedy
the situation.  He finally contracted management of a small
herd on a one-fourth share basis but, as previous chapters have
disclosed, those were difficult days in the livestock industry.

Campbell failed to make substantial profits on his initial

post-bellum ventures, but he persisted—until the year 1869 found him on the trail to California, driving a herd of 1,200 for Charles Foster, Ben Lacy and Clabe Allen, who had agreed to pay him $75 a month.

This herd trekked over the route later taken by the Texas and Pacific Railway, but the cattle failed to reach the West Coast. The plan had been to hold and shape up near Phoenix, Arizona, until the following year and then push on to market with fattened stock, but the driver was caught by a severe drouth, which seared the grass and dried the water holes. So, instead of California, Campbell chose Nevada, where he sold for $25 a head.

He was lucky to get even that far, because more than once the beeves were saved from hungry Indians only for the reason that the trail outfit was made up of a dozen well-armed men. Even so there were times when the braver among the Indians would "sashay" up within hailing distance, try a few experimental whoops just to test the effect, then turn tail and run as a lanky puncher would shoulder up and let go with a heavy-bore buffalo gun.

All in all, it had been a trying trip, trying on frayed nerves, and by the time the Nevada market was reached the trail hands were bickering among themselves. One by one the cowboys began to desert, until at last Campbell found himself alone. Nothing daunted him, however. He stowed the proceeds of the sale in his money belt and made preparations for the long trail home. On the day of departure he was approached by a negro, one Henry Bledsoe, who was homesick for his native Texas.

"Marse Henry, take me wid you" pleaded the dark-hued cowboy. "I was brung up in Texas an' I pines to get back."

Campbell couldn't find it in his heart to refuse ... and besides, he was glad for company. It was a tough and irksome ride, that journey. The Apaches of Arizona and New Mexico were on the jump, roaming the mesas like empty-bellied wolves, and many a day the white man and the negro holed up in a canyon, or took shelter in a clump of trees, not daring to venture abroad until night had cast a black blanket of safety over the landscape.

It was on this homeward ride, which gave ample time for meditation, that Campbell first conceived the idea which was to develop into one of the major cattle kingdoms of Texas.

He believed there was money . . . and big money . . . to be made in the beef business if only a man could take it up systematically on an extensive scale. Therefore, after delivering the Nevada profits to Messrs. Foster, Lacy and Allen, he approached several prospective backers on what he had in mind—a really big Plains outfit like that of Shanghai Pierce in the Matagorda, or like that of King and Kenedy in the Brasada.

The financial support was not forthcoming, and for the time he let the matter drop and began collecting cattle for drives to New Orleans. He paid no cash; he merely contracted with each owner for a certain number of head, jotted down the total and the agreed price in a small pocket ledger, and drove for the Louisiana port.

The drives continued several years and he returned home each time with a neat profit, part of which he used in '78 to shape up a herd for Chicago. He bought in Texas for $9 a head and sold in Chicago for $23, but the financial success of the venture was quite overshadowed by something else. He found the backing he wanted.

On that October day in 1878 when Col. A. M. Britton accepted an invitation to a luncheon which several fellow bankers of Chicago had arranged for a prominent Texas cattleman and trail driver, the Colonel was more interested in food than anything else.

But during the meal the conversation turned, naturally

enough, to cattle; and before dessert Colonel Britton was busy
with pencil and paper—jotting down and analyzing raw figures of the livestock industry as they came from the lips of
Henry Campbell.

**At this dinner the far-flung Matador was born**

Colonel Stickney of the Stock Yards National Bank, had
been asking questions. He wanted information on Texas cattle, how they were handled, how they were driven to market,
and what profit the cattleman might reasonably expect to make.

Britton's attention had been caught by the last set of figures.
The profit... that was the thing; and Campbell was using
his current experience as an illustration.

"Those cattle I sold here today," he said. "You know
what I got for 'em...twenty-three a head. And they're the
same steers I bought in Texas for nine...a profit of $14 a
head. Figure it up for yourself on a thousand or two."

Colonel Britton did, and when the luncheon was over he
sought out the Texan and gave him a straight-from-the-shoul-
der proposition.

"Campbell," he said, "you know the business and I have
the money. Let's go into this thing on an extensive scale.
Let's buy land and stock it; let's build one of the biggest
ranches in Texas."

Henry Campbell rode south—to the realization of a dream.

He had in his pocket a large wad of the Colonel's money,
to be used in the founding of a cattle enterprise in which
Campbell himself was to have a fifth share. He carried, too,
an oral power of attorney which left to his own discretion
such matters as location and manner of organization.

Campbell, in his enthusiasm, wasted no time. He chose a
spot at the edge of the Caprock in what is now Motley county.
It was southeast of the JA headquarters and south of the Prairie Dog Fork of the Red River. Here he scooped out a dugout to be used until he could throw a ranch house together,

*Henry Campbell—Founder of the Matador*

Photograph by Erwin E. Smith

and after hiring a few hands, began purchasing cattle on the *Llano Estacado*—one lot being 8,000 Chisum "jingle-bobs" which Tom Coggins and Bob Wiley had taken from old John on a mortgage.

Thus, the Matador, one of the greatest of them all, was born.

The cattleman's wife, who had been Miss Lizzie Bundy of Navarro county before her marriage to Campbell in 1871, found the Panhandle a rather lonely place at first. Other than the wives of a few widely-scattered settlers, she had but one woman neighbor, Mrs. Charles Goodnight of the JA, 70 miles away.

Up near Adobe Walls on the north bank of the Canadian was the Quarter Circle T, home of Mrs. Thomas Bugbee, but that was rather far away for casual visits. Dwellers on the Plains, however, visited little in the '70's.

There were other distant neighbors. The LX's were on Pitcher Creek north of the present site of Amarillo; George Littlefield's LIT was just west of the LX; the Bar-CC and the Turkey Track outfits were up near the Territory line; and over near the tail of the *Palo Duro* Canyon Leigh Dyer was starting the future T-Anchor. There were others, but when Mrs. Campbell came to the ranch in 1879 nobody was crowded for room—yet.

The ranch house was a two-room structure constructed of lumber which Campbell hauled from Fort Griffin, but in this land of dugout dwellers the modest home was indeed a palace . . . the social center for that section of the *Llano Estacado.*

The Panhandle social "whirl" really started in 1882 when the gracious queen of the Matadors gave a Christmas ball at headquarters, a three-day festival in which not only Campbell's cowboys, but the riders from the other ranches participated. The JA's came, and likewise the Spurs, whose ranges lay to

*The calves are worked over—Branded, Castrated, and Vaccinated.*

Photograph by W. D. Smithers

the south . . . some fifty or more men who were more at home in the saddle than tripping to a fiddle.

Mrs. Campbell, in addition to providing wild turkey, hog meat, jellies and all the trimmings, also arranged for the presence of five more women; and as Ben Brock, the cook of the Matadors, scraped his fiddle, they tripped the light fantastic for long and weary hours.

Thereafter the Christmas ball became a regular event at the Matador, being held in the mess hall built for the men the summer of '83. And the cowboys on far distant ranges looked forward throughout the year for those days of revelry.

In the first few years of the Matador one of the several men interested in the project with Campbell and Colonel Britton was S. W. Lomax, and Mrs. Campbell sometimes visited with Mrs. Lomax, who preferred to live in Fort Worth rather than on the open spaces. Lomax had cut loose from the Matador company in the early '80's to take managership of the more southerly Spurs, but it had been he who gave the Matador its name . . . the result of his interest in Spanish literature. He also named the Espuela Cattle Company, which controlled the Spur.

### The British and Scotch begin showing interest in ranching

It was about this time that British and Scotch capital became intensely interested in western ranching, and at the end of the third year Colonel Britton, Campbell and associates sold out to a Scottish syndicate. They received a million and a quarter, and since the ranch had not yet suffered the withering experience of a major drouth, the Caldonians felt they had a bargain.

Campbell had been a good manager. He had continually increased his herds, bought new land, and leased new pastures . . . and the Matador was moving up near the million mark in acreage when the transfer was made.

At the request of the Scots, Campbell stayed on, and the

property did not stunt itself. It continued to grow until the day arrived when it was not at all unusual for 10,000 calves to be branded in a season, and for a working outfit of 100 men to be following the wagons on roundup. Between fifty and seventy-five thousand head were being run on the ranges when friction developed between Campbell and the home office in 1890, at which time Campbell resigned and was supplanted by Murdo Mackenzie, a Scot.

The following year Motley County was organized and Campbell was elected county judge. He was re-elected for another term, but somehow he couldn't get away from the lowing of the herds. Perhaps he thought of the calf his father had given him ... anyhow he bought a small ranch on the Pease River where he made headquarters until his death.

As long as the Panhandle remains a cattle country—which probably will mean just as long as humanity eats its beef-steak—Henry H. Campbell will be remembered as one of its greatest and most respected pioneers, holding as he does a place in the annals of the cow camps with Colonel Goodnight and other of like calibre who called him friend.

The Scots still boss the Matador, which today is running about 50,000 Herefords on 1,000,000 acres in Motley, Old-ham and Hartley counties and on ranges in other states. If you should have business with the company you would go to the Motley County town which bears the company name—or to the United States National Bank Building in Denver, where Murdo Mackenzie's son John directs not only the Texas hold-ings but pasturage in Kansas and Montana.

But if your business is such that it requires the attention of the powers behind the throne you would catch a boat for Scot-land ... for the big "ranch house" is in Dundee.

And, as an old employe on the Texas division once told me:

"Great cattle people, the Scotch. We never buy a hobble rope on the Matador but that they know about it in Dundee.

And they're great on accuracy. I remember once when Scottish headquarters wrote to ask how many calves we would brand in a certain year. A guess was made and Scotland told 'about ten thousand,' It was a pretty good guess, too, for when the actual count was made we were only twenty-seven under that number."

And was Dundee pleased with this close figuring?

The Old-Timer grinned.

"Well," he said, "we got a letter from 'em after the report went in . . . they wanted to know what happened to the other twenty-seven!"

Photograph by Erwin E. Smith

A rare picture of the Matador Outfit made fifty years ago showing at the extreme right H. H. Campbell who established the ranch and Murdo Mackenzie, with black hat and beard, at the time he took over the management of the ranch

# Mackenzie

# of the

# Matador

MURDO MACKENZIE

HEREFORD

● A cowman from Scotland assumes management of Matador from Campbell, organizes 10,000,000 acre Brazilian cattle kingdom, but returns to his old love the Matador

IN A SMALL parish school in the North Country of Scotland a twelve-year-old boy labored over his numbers.

The master had been watching with concealed interest the progress of this particular pupil, for he seemed to sense that

229

this lad—son of a farmer on the nearby Estate of Balnagown —was somehow different from the others.

Young Murdo Mackenzie had a natural talent for arithmetic which kept him so thoroughly occupied that the teacher seldom found it necessary to raise against him the rod he carried both as a symbol of discipline and as a reminder that each child, as he came to school in the morning, was supposed to bring with him a block of peat to help heat the room.

And the master's interest in the ability of the twelve-year-old was justified. Before the end of that school year—it was in 1862—Murdo was able to present the result of his num-

Photograph by Erwin E. Smith

*Matador bunk house and mess hall*

erical research, a new plan of accounting for use in his father's flock of sheep.

A great many years have passed since that time, a great many sheep have been shorn and countless cattle have gone to market, but—strange as it may seem—that same plan of accounting forms the basis for the herd record used today by the Matador Land and Cattle Company.

There is good reason; for until the spring of 1937, as manager of that vast enterprise, the schoolboy of Balnagown sat behind a desk at the company's general headquarters in Denver . . . but at the age of eighty-six instead of twelve.

It is a far distance from the bleak moors and highlands of Scotland to the plains of Texas and the highlands of Colorado, but the story of how Murdo Mackenzie came that distance in the process of carving out his unusual career holds several elements slightly stranger than fiction.

He admits that the gypsies had something to do with it—those wandering Romany tribesmen who oft-times, when Murdo was yet a lad, pitched their tents near the Estate of Balnagown; for in that period, the period when he was still working with his accounting plan, the boy found in the gorigo camps his only contact with the outside world. Evening after evening he sat beside the fires of the gypsies, helping them to make horn spoons, listening to their thrilling . . . and, to him, colorful tales of travel and adventure in far places.

### Even the Gypsies couldn't have guessed his future

He was at an impressionable age and this contact, naturally, carried an influence; but even the Romanies, with all their imagination and worldly wisdom and reputed ability to peer into the future, could scarcely have visualized for their young visitor a future which would make him some day the ruling monarch of an empire which would stretch out over nearly ten million acres of land—a domain almost as large as his native Scotland!

The *Pampas* of South America would see him, and the *Llano Estacado* of the Texas Panhandle—until there would arrive a time, as it has today, when many in the livestock industry and not a few historians of the West would come to regard him as the greatest of living cattlemen. This, the story of his career, is explanatory of that attitude; but let us go back to Balnagown.

At the age of fourteen Murdo Mackenzie, done with the elementary school, entered the Academy of Tain, and upon completion of his course four years later entered a law office as an apprentice.

At the end of eighteen months, however, it became apparent that the legal profession was not the field for his talents, and he decided to accept a position in a bank at Rio de Janeiro, Brazil. But just at that time a vacancy occurred in the bank at Tain and he was given that post, the terms of his employment being that in payment for his services he would be permitted to learn thoroughly the work in each department. Here he remained for three years, learning the business and making acquaintances among the clientele, and when he resigned he was presented with a ten-pound note, which represented the only cash transaction between the bank and himself.

It was one of the bank's clients who gave Mr. Mackenzie his opportunity for advancement. The Factor of the Balnagown Estate asked him to become his assistant, and it was then that Mackenzie returned to live upon the land where he was born.

The estate comprised about half a million acres and included a sheep farm carrying a flock of twelve thousand head, farms for two hundred tenants, and a deer forest of nine thousand acres, thus making the young banker's duties innumerable and diversified. The life proved interesting, but after ten years . . . when he was thirty-five years of age and his salary was $1,200 a year . . . Mr. Mckenzie began to feel that he was fitted for promotion and change.

Opportunity offered itself almost immediately; for that year, 1885, a visitor to the estate asked the assistant factor if he would consider a job in the United States.

The gypsies, in stimulating the mind of a farm lad, had done their work well, but still Mr. Mackenzie, with the canniness characteristic of the Scot, was hesitant.

"It depends," he replied, "upon the work and the nature of the contract."

And then the visitor told him what he had in mind—the job of assistant in the management of the newly-formed Prairie Cattle Company. It was the beginning of that era when many Scots and Britons were catching the ranching fever and preparing to invest millions of pounds and shillings in Texas land and cattle, but the Prairie was to be the first company of Scottish origin.

Photograph by Erwin E. Smith
*Telling off the riders*

The idea appealed to Mr. Mackenzie and within a few days he was on his way to Edinburgh to accept the position and sail from Clydeside for the beginning of a new life overseas.

During those early years in the United States Mr. Mackenzie learned his lessons well. He gained first-hand and invaluable knowledge of running cattle on the open range and the problems that daily confront the cattleman. More important, he learned the customs and the trend of thought of the inhabitants, as well as the code of honor that prevailed on the frontier. And so he was well equipped when, in 1891, he was asked to take over management of the Matador to succeed Henry Campbell.

The history of the Matador and the problems it encountered are little different than those of other cattle companies operating in the early days, but when a delegation from the board of directors came over from Scotland at the end of Mr. Mackenzie's first year as manager he recommended three changes in policy:

1. That the number of cattle in the herd be reduced to 70,000 head.

2. That the two-year-old steers be sent for maturing to Montana and Dakota pastures and from there shipped to market at the age of four years.

3. That the range herd be improved in quality by the use of purebred Hereford bulls. It is by strict adherence to this practice of infusing purebred blood that the Matador herd has reached its present high standard.

The Matador Company is the only one of the large cattle outfits of Scottish origin, organized in the '80's, that is in existence today, and Mr. Mackenzie attributed its survival to the fact that the board of directors in Scotland cooperated with the management. Mr. Alexander MacKay, the present chairman of the board, was its secretary when Mr. Mackenzie took over in 1891, and during fifty-two years the company has been operating in Texas Mr. MacKay only twice has missed making an annual visit to the ranches. To quote Mr. Mackenzie: "Mr. MacKay's sound judgment and keen wisdom are invaluable, and he has never uttered a word of discouragement."

And there was plenty to discourage foreign capital on the Texas plains in the earlier days—drouth, the dreaded Texas

fever, not to mention cow thievery and the more minor ills
that assail the industry.

But there is something about the cow business which always
has attracted the Scot and the Briton and in 1911, after most
of the Scotch and British syndicates had been forced to close
books and sell off herds,   an enterprising group in London

Photograph by Erwin E. Smith
*Claud Jeffers, old-time Matador bronc-buster*

conceived the greatest outfit of them all, and in it the principal role was destined to be thrust upon Murdo Mackenzie.

In the summer of that year the manager of the Matadors
was asked to come to Denver to meet Mr. Percival Farquhar,
the international financier—but let Mr. Mackenzie tell the
story in his own words:

"Mr. Farquhar stated that he was interested in the formation of a cattle company in Brazil and wished me to go with
him to visit one of the large western cattle ranches.  We decided upon the King Ranch as being the one that would give

him the information he particularly desired, and it was while enroute to that ranch that I became acquainted with this amazing man with whom I was to be associated for the following few years.

"He was not only a seer, but a human dynamo, and his mental capacity was a revelation to me. I believe that every bit of information given him was registered in his mind and never forgotten, and I have since regarded my association with Mr. Farquhar as one of the most interesting and gratifying events of my life."

### Mackenzie catches a vision and set himself to work

Together the Londoner and Mr. Mackenzie traveled down into the Nueces country of Texas to inspect every division of the King, that 1,250,000-acre cattle kingdom which has stood for so long as a "buffer state" between the Republic of Mexico and the United States—the only great ranch in the State where conditions are similar to those which might be encountered in South America. And then the two turned north again.

"While enroute to Chicago from the King Ranch," resumed Mr. Mackenzie, "Mr. Farquhar told me that he had arranged for the formation of a land, cattle and packing company in Brazil that would be operated under one management. He asked me to accept the position as manager.

"I quickly declined the offer, since I was then sixty-one years of age and had the feeling that my pioneering days were over. However, as he enthusiastically unfolded his plan in detail my imagination began to work, and I caught a glimpse of his vision—the establishment of a giant cattle kingdom in the heart of Brazil.

"Mr. Farquhar's researches had disclosed that a new source must be found for supplying European countries with beef, and the favored spot, as he saw it, was the interior of Brazil. Land was cheap, was covered with an abundance of grass, was well watered, and the cattle were of a type that would respond to the infusion of pure blood.

"A nucleus of land had been purchased in the State of Matto Grosso, and he wished to start immediately to block up this tract with other lands adjoining, as well as to purchase large areas in other localities."

The magnitude of the project, as Mr. Farquhar continued to unfold his dream, was quite enough to stagger even the imagination of the man who managed the great Matador.

Percival Farquhar was no piker; he intended doing things on an enormous scale. He wanted to start, without delay, the purchasing of a herd of half a million head of cattle!

"He told me," recalled Mr. Mackenzie, "that a credit of $25,000,000 would be placed at my disposal for the purpose of organizing the company, purchasing land and sub-dividing it into pastures and enclosing same, erecting headquarters, buildings and camps, planting pastures of fattening grass, and erecting a packing plant near the city of Sao Paulo where the cattle could be processed for export. I was to realize later Mr. Farquhar's wisdom in uging that no time be lost in getting his buying campaign started and continued with as much haste as was consistent with good business."

As Mr. Mackenzie said—he had caught the vision; he began to forget his sixty-one years, and his belief that his pioneering days were over.

"By the time we reached Chicago," he related, "I did not feel as old as I did when the position of manager was offered me, and a few weeks later I signed a contract for a term of five years and agreed to start for Brazil as soon as the Matador Company could release me."

Mr. Mackenzie began at once to make plans. In the fall of 1911 he sent his son, John, and James R. Burr, both former Matador employes, down to Brazil for the purpose of locating and inspecting suitable lands, and they were followed shortly by two other Texans, John Molesworth and Richard Walsh.

It was early in March of 1912 when Murdo Mackenzie himself reached Sao Paulo.   Land purchases were going forward and by the end of that year 1,000,000 acres had been blocked into one ranch.

The details of the purchases were not simple matters, since often the properties were owned by several different people, and since many of the estates had not been settled legally, titles to the land had to be cleared.   But the buyers went ahead—taking one tract here, another there—until ultimately the aggregate company holdings were near 10,000,000 acres! A great cow kingdom—a ranch which in size has never had, and probably never will have,  an equal  on the face of the earth.

Meanwhile, cattle were being purchased . . . by the tens of thousands.   And before general offices in Paris, France, sent orders to cease buying, because of financial difficulties arising out of the beginning of the World War, Mackenzie and his associates already had bought 250,000 head.

Headquarters were established on five different divisions in the interior of Brazil—three in the state of Matto Grosso, one in Minas Geraes, and one in the state of Parana—and Mr. Mackenzie had engaged trusted and experienced cattlemen from the United States, principally from Texas, to superintend the ranches.

Dave Somerville was his chief ranch supervisor, assisted by E. L. Roberds, Homer Vivian, James R. Burr and J. G. Ramsey.   T. G. Chittenden was office manager and John Mackenzie assisted both in the office and on the ranches.   Dr. J. H. McNeil, now chief of the New Jersey Bureau of Animal Industry, had full charge of the imported cattle, the first of which arrived from the United States in 1915.

**One division of great ranch covered 4,500,000 acres**

Brazilian stockmen had been skeptical about the plan to in-fuse purebred stock with the native breeds. They said it just couldn't work; that the North American cattle could not adapt themselves to the climate and conditions of the South. They were openly pessimistic, freely forecasting that most of the importations would die on the way down—and Mr. Mackenzie admits that the Brazilians had him worried before the first boat load docked.

"But contrary to predictions," said Mr. Mackenzie, "the cattle reached Sao Paulo in first class condition, only five out of a shipment of 945 head being lost. A number of Brazilian cattlemen came to the port to learn first hand the fate of the shipment and they were astounded at the result. And so the next shipment brought down contained a number of animals for the Brazilians."

The type of the offspring of native cows sired by Hereford bulls was a revelation to all livestock men. A native cow with her half bred calf was exhibited at the Livestock Exposition held later at Rio de Janeiro, and they attracted much attention, the calf appearing to be a pure Hereford.

The management of an outfit the proportions of the Brazil Land, Cattle and Packing Company—especially in a land where graft is usually the rule rather than the exception— required an almost superhuman amount of work and energy; but Mr. Mackenzie, in systematizing his organization, gave his personal attention to all financial transactions. Those who were associated with him in those days say that he was not diplomatic, as the term is generally accepted, but succeeded, through honest dealings, in winning early, the respect of those with whom he came in contact. Like a true Scot, he refused to pay one *milreis* of graft but demanded, rather, that his negotiations proceed with reasonable promptness—and they did.

In recalling some of the difficulties, Mr. Mackenzie said:

"Perhaps the most difficult ranch to operate was the *Des-*

*calvados* property located on the Bolivian border. This ranch comprised 4,500,000 acres and carried a herd of 140,000 wild cattle, which virtually had to be captured at roundups.

"But even after a herd had been collected it was often stolen by outlaws, the border country being infested with thieves and renegades of almost every nationality. They had things pretty much their own way until John G. Ramsey, better known as Jack in his home town of Miami, Texas, took over management of the division.

"He organized a police force of picked men as fearless as himself, and in the course of a few years was operating the ranch without difficulty—the outlaws finding the neighborhood an unhealthy place in which to live. Mr. Ramsey remained on the ranch until his death in 1933, and no man in Brazil was more highly respected."

The first major blow to the great enterprise came when the Paris office cabled Brazil to cancel all contracts for the purchase of land and cattle and to cut operating expenses to the bone. Europe was at war and financial support must be withdrawn, at least for a time.

This announcement was little short of calamitous, because herds had been contracted for and were then on the trail to the ranches.

Mr. Mackenzie took quick action. He notified the owners to sell their trail herds to other buyers, and promised that his company would pay off any losses sustained by reason of contract violation. The outlook was discouraging, but Mackenzie was determined to surmount the difficulty and keep the company in operation.

It so happened that a representative of the National City Bank of New York was visiting in Brazil at the time, and Mackenzie went to him. He invited the banker to visit the ranches and together they made a careful inspection and then, upon return to Sao Paulo, the Scot asked for a credit of

$500,000 with which to buy cattle for fattening, the company property to secure the loan.

Next day he was informed that the credit had been established, but that the loan had been made to him personally, because the bank had faith in his ability to carry out the agreement.

With money drawn on this credit cattle were purchased, fattened and sold, and when accounts were settled and the

Photograph by Erwin E. Smith
*Some old hands—Matador Outfit*

borrowed money repaid, the company had a profit of $200,000 —and had been saved from oblivion.

The Brazil Land, Cattle and Packing Company still is operating at a profit, still owns its vast acreage and its giant herds

—largest cattle empire in the world.  It is now being managed by J. D. Fleming, one of Mr. Mackenzie's associates in the days of organization.

Mr. Mackenzie returned to the United States in 1919 to become associated with Thomas E. Wilson in an advisory capacity for the purpose of better understanding between producer and packer—but in 1922, when John MacBain died, Mackenzie returned to his old post, manager of the Matador. He resigned in the spring of 1937 and his son John took his place.

He died on May 30, 1939, at the age of 88, but as long as cattle roam the range the names of Murdo Mackenzie and the Matador will be synonymous.  In fact, the Matador might well be called the Mackenzie—and any old-time cowhand would know exactly what it meant.

BRAND
THE MATADOR

# Ike Pryor
## of the
## 77

IKE PRYOR

BURRO "SHERIFF"
YOKED TO "OUTLAW"
STEER

● From plowhand to cowhand, an orphan boy becomes one of the major kings and ace trail drivers of the Nueces

**W**E were sitting in the San Antonio skyscraper office which, in all reality, serves as general headquarters for the "77", that famous ranch which stretches across one hundred thousand acres of the Texas cattle country that the Mexicans of the Border call the *Brasada*.

A kindly-faced gentleman of many, many years drummed with his fingers on the surface of a flat-top desk.

243

*Ready for the roundup . . . this photo shows a "77" wagon and part of the outfit near Colonel Ike T. Pryor's headquarters on the Nueces.*

With a black skull cap on his head, and with just the suggestion of a twinkle in his eyes, which did not see as well as
in days gone by, he resembled more the retired tradesman
than one of the last among the truly great cattle kings of
Texas—a man who was one of the greatest among all the
trail drivers who ever headed their herds up the dusty overland route to the Kansas markets.

But at the moment Colonel Ike T. Pryor, in the wisdom
of his eighty-four years, wasn't speaking of the "77" and his
herds on the banks of the Nueces.

"Phrenology, that's the thing . . . one of the greatest sciences
in life," he said. "If you want to know what a man's best
fitted to do . . . what he's cut out for . . . have a phrenologist
feel the bumps on his head. Those bumps tell you what is
in that head."

He stopped to answer the telephone, then continued:

"I've been trying to preach that to Dean Kyle down at
A. & M. College," he went on. "I've been trying to tell the
dean that before he gives those boys diplomas at graduation
he should have their heads felt of . . . then put it down on
the diploma what every boy is best fitted for in life. Why,
that's what put me in the cattle business . . . phrenology."

But before going into this matter of bumps on the cranium,
let us look back more than three-quarters of a century for an
insight into the romantic start of Colonel Pryor's career—a
career which finds few parallels in the history of the cattle
industry or in the chronicles of any other business.

Strange as it may sound, since he became one of the great
cattle kings of the world, Ike Pryor never saw a herd of cows
until his eighteenth birthday.

The third of three boys, the future boss of the "77" was
born in Tampa, Florida, on June 22, 1852, and at the age of
five, after the death of both his parents, was put in custody
of an uncle in Alabama. This uncle, a doctor, was rather a

strict man and young Ike did not get along well with him, with the result that he was passed along to another sister of his mother within six months.

"She was a widow with six children and she had married a widower with a similar sized flock," he said, "and naturally I was picked on by the other children. But there was one that I loved—Cousin Sally Lightfoot, my aunt's oldest daughter. She was eighteen, and if ever there was an angel it was Cousin Sally."

A strong attachment grew between the two and both were heartbroken when it was decided that Iky had best go to live with Orville McKissack, another uncle who lived at Spring Hill, Tennessee.

### Little Iky runs away, and is caught in a battle

Iky, the orphan, was six at the time and he didn't want to go, but there was little he could do about it, and he went. He remembers the following three years as one of heartache ... pining for Cousin Sally, his foster mother, and wondering if he would ever see her again.

And then one day, shortly after he was nine, he heard that his idol was married and had gone to Nashville to live. That decided little Iky. Surely Cousin Sally would take him into her home if he could but find her, but he dared not mention the matter to his uncle. So there was but one thing to do— run away, and do his best to find her. The Civil War was raging in the country about his home but that, in his childish mind, was a matter of little importance compared to a reunion with his cousin.

So it was that he struck out from his uncle's house in the night—to meet one of the strangest adventures ever to befall the lot of any small boy.

Without knowing why—and he can't explain it yet—he loaded a sack with scaly-bark nuts before he left his uncle's house, and with this bag thrown over one shoulder he took the road to Nashville.

"Funny thing about those nuts," he said, with a smile. "As soon as I took the road I started throwing them away, first to one side and then the other; and I've since heard that for quite a piece along that highway out of Spring Hill there's some of the prettiest hickory trees you ever saw."

Young Ike made nine miles before the night was far gone, and came at last to the home of an old lady, who gave him supper and a bed and tried to persuade him against continuing toward Nashville.

"Don't you know about the war?" she asked. "And don't you know the soldiers are fighting along the Nashville road?"

But a little thing like war wasn't going to stop Iky. When he set out in the morning he walked right into it!

He had gone only a few miles when he heard rifles popping . . . saw men running and others chasing them. That was near Franklin, where the Federals had made a suprise attack on the Confederates and put them to rout.

But the troopers, having troubles of their own, were far too busy to take note of a small boy who had hidden himself in the brush and was watching the conflict in wild-eyed amazement.

Finally the chase passed, the battle rolling south, and Ike, now within the Federal lines, crawled out of his place of concealment and hurried on toward Nashville, which was now in the hands of Union troops.

That battle changed, perhaps, the course of his entire career —because his uncle, after missing him from home, had sent several men in pursuit, but they had turned back when they ran into the fight.

Then Nashville—cavalrymen, guns, infantrymen, men and horses on the move everywhere. Nine-year-old Iky felt his heart sink within him as he entered the town. He had never visited a big city before and he didn't know just where to turn, but at last he reasoned that he had best ask someone where to find Cousin Sally. He approached a soldier with the question.

"Cousin Sally who?" asked the trooper.

And then little Iky realized that he had forgotten, before leaving home, to find out Cousin Sally's name now that she was married.

That was the start of one of the most heart-breaking searches a small boy ever made. From house to house, from door to door went the orphan lad, always putting his question:

"Does Cousin Sally live here?"

Sometimes, in some of the houses, he found a Sally, but never the right one. Two days passed ... three ... and then a week, with little Ike living as best he could, taking food from soldiers and kindly householders, sleeping under any shelter he could find.

"I suppose I went to hundreds of houses," recalled the Colonel, "until finally I gave up the hunt as hopeless. Then I attached myself to the camp of the Third Ohio Cavalry."

### The boy saw action with the regiment

It so happened that the proprietor of the regimental canteen had a portable printing press and this gentleman conceived the idea of putting out a newspaper, at such intervals as were convenient, and using Iky as a newsboy.

Thus the orphan became the regimental mascot of the Third Ohio. He slept with first one soldier and then another, and when his clothes wore out they gave him old uniforms, which he could manage to wear by cutting off the trouser legs and tying up the seat until he could make them fit at the waist.

For two years he remained with the Third Ohio Cavalry. He was with them at Lookout Mountain and at Missionary Ridge. He acquired a stray horse and it was shot from under him at Murfreesboro.

The waif was eleven now and, being popular with the troops, he had made money with his paper selling. Before Chickamauga was over he had saved one hundred dollars, which he kept in a purse he had fashioned from the skin of a mole he had killed. But in the beginning of his third year with the army he lost his purse and all it contained, becoming penniless again.

It was about this time that the regimental surgeon, a Dr. Wirth, began to take an interest in the boy, and one day the doctor told him that he was leaving the army—that he had arranged for a furloughed soldier to escort Ike to the doctor's own home in Ohio.

"But that only made matters worse," said the Colonel. "Away from the excitement of the battlefields I began, once more, to pine for Cousin Sally. And after several months of brooding I decided to run away again, and might have done so but for news from the front."

The Third Ohio was before Vicksburg and, having run out of forage, a captain was sent to Nashville with an order on General Rosencrans for supplies. At that point Fate took a hand.

The captain, seizing supplies in Nashville wherever he could find them, entered one day into a house and took certain property, telling the housewife the Government would pay for the articles taken. While he was writing out a list of things taken the woman told him she had a question she asked every Federal soldier she saw—if he had ever heard of a small boy who joined the Union forces in Nashville three years before.

"Is your name Sally?" asked the captain.

And when she said it was, the officer told her the story of Iky and where he could be found. Cousin Sally immediately wrote to the Wirth home in Ohio and to Army headquarters in Washington, and before many weeks the orphan lad found

himself on his way to General Rosencrans headquarters for a
meeting with his cousin—and a happy reunion it was.

For three years he remained at the home of his foster-
mother, and then they moved back to Alabama.  It was here,
in 1870, when Ike was eighteen years old, that he again met
one of his older brothers, who had been roaming around in
Texas.

And that was about all that his brother could talk about—
Texas, and what a future it might hold for a man willing to
work.  It all sounded mighty good to the younger brother.
Soon he was on his way down the Mississippi River, to catch
a New Orleans boat out bound for Galveston.  He landed
there with few more than the clothes he wore on his back, a
small amount of money furnished by Cousin Sally, and a
Bible.

With all these worldly goods he made his way to Austin
where he wasn't long in finding employment—as a plowhand
with a farmer named Neil Cain.  Here, on the farm ten miles
east of the capitol, he worked from dawn to dusk for the sum
of $15 a month, but his plowshare alone didn't raise all the
dust over that field.

Beside it ran the great cattle trail from the south of Texas
to the Kansas rail terminals, and ofttimes the eighteen-year-
old boy reined in his mules and stopped between the plow-
handles to watch a passing herd of longhorns.  Sometimes, he
would shout a greeting to the cowboys and ask them where
they were going.

The answer might be Abilene or the Territory.  Again, it
might be Nebraska or Montana.  The adventure of the business took hold on the mind of the plowboy and he often
dreamed and hoped that someday he would be driving on that
trail.

He might have continued farming, however, had it not been
for a man named Fowler who was attracting quite a bit of

attention in Austin, and at this point we return to the subject
of phrenology.

Phrenologist Fowler had been laying hands on some of the
best heads in the capital city. So young Mr. Pryor decided
one day to ride over to town and get an analysis concerning
the contents of his own head.

"I left the farm about daylight," recounted Mr. Pryor,
"and when I arrived at Fowler's office I found a number of
people waiting to have their heads felt of. Finally my turn
came and I went in. Mr. Fowler felt all the bumps on my
head and after a time wrote something on a piece of paper,
and said that would be $10. I paid over the money, three-
quarters of a month's salary, and read the paper. It said:
'All your life you will be under the influence of some woman'."

"Then I took the road home, thinking as I went, and before
I reached the farm I had decided what I would do."

Perhaps Farmer Cain was surprised because, as Mr. Pryor
told it himself, he walked in to his employer, waved the paper
and said:

"Mr. Cain, all I know in the world is written on this piece
of paper. You can take your plow and go to hell."

Ike T. Pryor was about to enter the cattle business.

**He pointed the tongue of wagon toward North Star**

Almost immediately he got a job as a cowboy—with Bill
Arnold of Llano, and within a few weeks he was making his
first trip up the trail with 2,500 head bound for Coffeyville,
Kansas.

Up the trail to Kansas! Ike Pryor wondered why he had
ever plowed. He took to the new life like a steer to corn,
and he was well initiated on the journey, which took six weeks.

"I remember how we used to point the tongue of the wagon
in the direction of the North Star every night so we'd be sure
of the direction in the morning," he said. "And we had one
stampede."

The following year he was trail boss, and in the second year he went to work on a ranch for Charlie Lehmberg, to become manager of the ranch before another twelve months.

After driving a small herd to the Government Reservation at Fort Sill, Indian Territory, he returned home to find that his employer was thinking of quitting the cattle business, Lehmberg offering to sell his twenty-thousand acres and 1,500 head of cattle on any terms that Pryor cared to make. The Colonel, now twenty-four, found backing and became a ranch owner.

The following year he assembled a herd of 1,500 head (250 his own) for a drive to Nebraska. So well did he profit that the next year found him going up with 3,000 head all his own.

Pryor doubled his trail total the following year and then, after taking 12,000 to market in 1880, he was able to double the size of his ranch near Mason.

In that year he went into partnership with a brother. For four years they prospered so remarkably that in 1884, Pryor Brothers put over the trail a record-breaking number of long-horns, fifteen herds of 3,000 each—45,000 head in a single year!

The profits were good and they put them into more cattle, to drive to acreage they had acquired in Southern Colorado; and then, with all the world looking right and with about 20,000 head on the range, the big blow came.

In that year a group of Cleveland, Ohio, men had bought large tracts near the Pryor Colorado holdings and they made a bid to buy the Pryor interests. Colonel Ike, sensing a good deal, went to Cleveland and after several days of negotiations sold out, receiving $100,000 cash as an advance on about $500,000 or $600,000, the full amount depending on the count in the spring.

Elated, Colonel Pryor started for Texas. He had reached

Chicago when he was notified that a blizzard, the worst in years, was sweeping the Colorado ranges, that the snow was eighteen inches deep, and that cattle were freezing by hundreds.

And they did die—not only by hundreds, but by thousands—for when spring came and the roundup was made, only about $65,000 worth of beefsteak under the Pryor brand could be found.

That left the Pryor Brothers $35,000 in debt. They paid off with one hundred saddle horses at $50 each and 3,000 acres of land, at the same time dissolving their partnership.

At the same time the Colonel owed $30,000 to a St. Louis commission house and the house was wanting security. He went to St. Louis and returned with an extension on the debt and with an additional $70,000 to his credit. He went back into business with this capital and by the time the notes became due he could pay.

He made what is commonly called "a cleaning" as a result of the Spanish-American War. While hostilities were under way he sent a Spanish speaking agent to Cuba to watch the situation. This agent notified Pryor as soon as the war was over and it was safe to ship cattle, and within two weeks after the close of the conflict the Colonel had eleven shiploads of steers in Havana—steers which he bought for $15 a head in Texas and sold for $85 in Cuba; and on seven or eight thousand head that runs into money.

Those profits helped him acquire the now famous "77" down in Zavala county on the Nueces.

Just after the turn of the century he bought that 100,000-acre tract for $1.40 an acre, and the Colonel liked to tell how valuable that land has been, not only from the standpoint of cattle raising.

"In 1902 some folks got stuck on the ranch and offered me $400,000 for it," he related. "I sold, receiving $30,000 as an option. They never paid the rest. And then again, in 1906, I sold for $600,000, the down payment $40,000. The notes were not met and I kept the 77."

The Colonel smiled.

"And that's not all." he said. "Somebody got stuck on that little piece of property again in 1910. I got $200,000 and eight notes to meet the remainder at a price of $10 an acre. The notes brought it back to me again."

*Frank McGill of Alice (left) and Joe Sneed of Amarillo looking over some white faces. Mr. Sneed is now (1939) president of the Texas and Southwestern Cattle Raisers Association. He succeeded Mr. McGill.*

The Colonel was long identified with the Texas and Southwestern Cattle Raisers Association. He was first vice-president in 1902, and was elevated to the presidency in 1906, to be re-elected in 1907. He also served as head of the National Livestock Shippers' Protective League; and in 1917, at Cheyenne, Wyoming, he was elected to the presidency of the American National Livestock Association, succeeding himself the following year.

**He saw one of the last of the thundering herds**

He liked nothing better than to talk of those old days on

the trails, and there's one—it was in '75—that particularly
stuck in his memory, when he and his hands were on the way
to Colorado with 3,000 head.

The usual route was to cross the Red River out of Texas,
drive to Dodge City, then head west to Colorado, but on this
trip the Colonel wanted to save time and decided to head west
immediately after making the Red River crossing. The outfit
was warned by buffalo hunters not to risk that route, but the
outfit paid no heed. A couple of days on the trail—and one
afternoon the Colonel saw a cloud of dust on the horizon, a
cloud soon recognized as the dust being raised by an approaching herd of buffalo.

The cattle were hurriedly bedded down and left under the
care of five men while seven rode out to meet the buffalo at
a distance of a quarter of a mile. When the lead buffaloes
were in range the men started shooting into the thick of them,
but instead of turning the herd aside the shots merely split it,
sending one section around one side of the herd, with the other
section going around the other flank. And there they were—
cattle and men—completely surrounded by passing buffalo for
most of the night.

"I'll tell you," he said, "during that year's drive when
we sent 45,000 head up the trail, we lost about 1,500 head,
all wearing the letter P ... our road brand ... on the loin.
They would stray away or get mixed in with other herds
headed, maybe, for Montana or Nebraska. Well sir, for five
years afterward, at cattlemen's conventions all over the country, Wyoming, Fort Worth and elsewhere, I'd have men walk
up to me and ask: 'Colonel, what was your road brand in
'84' And when I'd tell 'em they'd sometimes take out their
check books and say: 'Here, I owe you for three steers that
got in among mine.'

"And now," added the Colonel, with some emphasis, "can

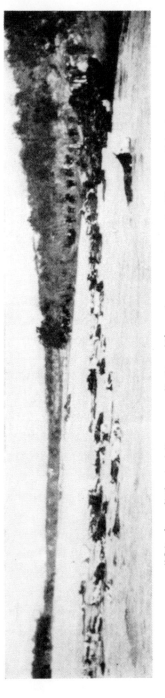

"Git along little dogie" . . . a small thing like a river never stopped a Texas trail herd. This photo shows the cattle fording a Texas stream.

you show me any other class of people on earth who would do that?"

One other thing he liked to talk about in the days before his death in September of 1937—and that was Cousin Sally Lightfoot Ewing. She died in Paris, Texas, at the age of 95.

Dwight Chapin, an old-school cowman who has trailed herds both in South Texas and in Brazil, manages the 77 empire from the rambling old ranch house on the banks of the Nueces, and his favorite story about Ike Pryor is one that the Colonel seldom told.

It appears that the Colonel, in trailing one herd up to Kansas, was met in the Indian Territory by a particularly persistent Osage chief who demanded three steers for beef. Pryor dodged the situation very neatly with a compromise— agreeing to give the trail-side racketeer one beef and an order on the following trail boss for two more. He cut out a sorry old critter and wrote this note to the leader of the rival outfit:

"This is a good Indian. Give him a couple of steers."

Then he laughed and went on his way. But later—in Dodge City—he met the boss of the following herd.

"I got your note," drawled that individual, "and I did what you asked ... gave him three, in fact ... but they happened to be strays, Colonel, that I picked up out of your bunch."

BRAND
IKE T. PRYOR
RANCH

*There'll be fresh beef in camp tonight*

Photograph by W. D. Smithers

# Trails
# and
# Troubles

● Longhorns — From Texas on the hoof to the Platters of the World

TRAIL HERD CROSSING RED RIVER—AN EARLY PRINT.

O LD LAME DOCTOR
was a playful fellow.

In all the Osage Nation there was none who made greater effort to enjoy life while there was life to enjoy—and besides spring had come to the wooded hills on the northern rim of the Indian Territory.

And for Lame Doctor's renegade warriors, a band of Osages who for many moons had not honored a reservation with its presence, spring was a welcome season. It meant sport—for once again the longhorn herds were moving up the Chisholm Trail from Texas.

There were times when the renegade chieftain was less affable, but today—since his stomach was filled with beef purloined from a passing herd, and since he had no excuse for leading a mourning party on the hunt, he was just playful.

From the tips of his plaited pigtails . . . which stood out like hairy horns when he galloped into the face of the wind . . . to the toes of his moccasined feet, he was all savage. He lived on stolen meat, and on excitement. Whence he came no man knew, although there were some among the Indian agents who strongly suspected that the Doctor and his braves had been in the fight against the buffalo hunters at Adobe Walls in the summer of 1874.

They knew little else—except that the band was careful to avoid the reservation so generously provided by the Great White Chief at Washington, and that spring usually found it on the Salt Fork of the Arkansas, waiting for the herds from Texas . . .

In the early days of April in 1875 the Q-Bar outfit of a dozen riders had thrown their "hot-rolls" on the wagon in the south of Texas and had hit the trail for Kansas with 2,000 rangy steers strung between the point and drag.

The Q-Bar (that name will do as well as any other) had cut in on the main North Trail near Austin, headed north by way of Forth Worth, and had crossed the Red River near Spanish Fort, just above Nocona. The middle days of May had overtaken them on the Salt Fork.

On the evening of the arrival on the river, just as the hands . . . all but the night herders . . . were returning to the

wagon after settling the cattle on the bed-ground, a strange
rider approached the camp.

The 'punchers of the Q-Bar regarded the newcomer quizzi-
cally, and well they might.  He was a man of medium build,
rather inclined to heaviness, and he rode a big bay horse which
was equipped with a Mexican saddle and bridle, but that was
the least unusual thing about.him.  In the matter of dress his
like never had been seen before, at least not on Salt Fork.

He wore on his back a long-tailed coat, the tips of which
dangled down toward his boot tops, and on his head . . . most
remarkable of all . . . was a high plug hat!  The gentleman
appeared, in fact, to be a peculiar combination of Border horse
thief and circuit riding preacher, although the heavy piece of
artillery at his waist did much to shatter the latter illusion.

He was riding "kinder keerless" and the cook, as he scruti-
nized the visitor, remarked: "There's somethin' seldom about
that feller.  I've seen 'im summers afore this."

And the cook probably had, for as the man in the plug hat
rode up to the wagon the Q-Bar boss greeted him in a knowing way.

"Hi, Luke . . . git down and have some grub.  What you
doin' in these parts?"

### Notorious Luke wore Plug Hat as he worked cattle

The foreman knew the visitor well.  He had tossed many
a chip over the tables in the Red Dog Saloon at Dodge City
when Luke Short was the presiding elder in that temple of
chance, but that was before the dapper gambler had migrated
south to Fort Worth to engage in the business of faro, with
livestock on the side.  The foreman guessed that somewhere
down the river Short was holding a herd of steers, each brute
with the tip of the left horn sawed away, each carrying on
the left jaw the brand of the "Plug Hat."

The notorious Luke, who had adopted the plug hat as head

*Andy Murchison, trail boss, and his cowboys enjoying noonday meal, on way to Clayton, N. M., with herd of Texas Cattle, in 1907*

gear in studied defiance of roistering marksmen during his Dodge City days, commented that such was indeed the case; that he was holding several hundred head down the river a way, shaping up in anticipation of better prices at Caldwell or Dodge.

"I aim to move up in the summer," he said in his quiet way, adding: "The niggers are gettin' skeary . . . say they're afraid of the Osage mournin' parties."

The foreman of the Q-Bar grinned, for he had heard it said that the Fort Worth gambler would hire nothing but negroes to handle his cattle, and that he made with each employe a peculiar sort of contract containing two unusual features. First, every negro must, on all occasions, address him as "Mister" Short; and second, no man could quit his job under a certain specified time. Failing in either provision the employe would expect, under an added clause in the contract, to receive a bullet from "Mister" Short's Colt revolver.

And the dark-skinned cowboys knew he meant it; that he was capable of shooting them down as handily as he later would dispose of Mr. Jim Courtright, long-haired marshal of Fort Worth, on the day when the twain should meet and draw at the door of Mr. Short's Cowtown gaming hall.

But in that camp on the Salt Fork the gambler-cattleman, before he swung into his saddle to rejoin his outfit, did give the boss of the Q-Bar a word of warning.

"Old Lame Doctor's yellowbacks are on the prowl again," he said, "and if the devils jump you, you boys better tie your hats to the saddle and ride. He cut the last herd that went through, and he'll try cuttin' yours if his meat's played out."

The foreman said he would "keep an eye peeled," but when the outfit took the trail again in the morning he thought no more of the wily renegade.

Morning passed and afternoon came on . . . and the Q-Bar steers plodded on up the Chisholm. The dozen riders, their

264 CATTLE KINGS OF TEXAS

faces half-covered with bandannas that their lungs might escape the stifling dust, lolled easily in their saddles as they jogged along at strategic points beside the herd. They dreamed, perhaps, of the Lone Star Bar in Abilene, the rail terminal, where soon the Q-Bar steers would be loaded into cars of the Kansas Pacific en route to the platters of the world.

In Abilene there would be life and fun; and some boys, like as not, would "go a-gallin'." The riders of the Q-Bar dreamed of many things—but certainly not of Lame Doctor and his braves, even then lying in wait behind a grassy knoll ...

It all occurred in the twinkling of an eye. Before even the first of the Texans could jerk a Winchester from the saddle scabbard the Indians were in among the cattle, shouting, whooping, and creating in general a din which would have struck terror to the hearts of even less skittish beasts than moss-horn Texas steers.

Like a colorful segment from some hideous nightmare, the wild west leaped suddenly to life. Lame Doctor's men, their half-naked bodies ornamented with strips of otter skin, each scalplock crested with an eagle's feather, rode like painted devils. Tiny silver bells, plaited into the manes and tails of their ponies, jingled like music as the savage charge bore down upon the herd, but it was not music to the restless longhorns.

The Q-Bar foreman muttered something beneath his breath as he wrenched down on the lever of his rifle and shouldered up to let go a shot as one of the raiders broke through the herd near his station. He saw the Osage topple from his pony—to be caught under the pounding hoofs of the milling cattle as the bellowing mass of hides and horns started full tilt for nowhere.

Stampede! A sea of steers thundered over the prairie ... and Lame Doctor and his warriors (all save one) pulled free just in time, to make a stand on a far away knoll and watch the cursing cowboys bring order out of chaos.

The Doctor was well pleased with the afternoon's work. He had not wanted meat; he had plenty left from the last raid. He had wanted only sport, the pulse-quickening thrills of a mad stampede—for today, as I have pointed out, he was just a playful fellow.

But "there's always another verse," as one of the Q-Bar boys pointed out as he looked down on the mangled form of what had once been a man—the Indian the foreman's gun had winged. Later, Lame Doctor's men would return for him, and tomorrow an Osage mourning party would be starting on the hunt.

### The Mourning Parties were strange and terrible

It may be well to explain that among the old Osages it was a custom, when a brave died, to place with him in his grave a newly-lifted scalp—otherwise the dead warrior could not hope to enter the precincts of the Happy Hunting Ground. Hence, when death came to an Osage . . . whether in battle or in his lodge . . . a mourning party went on the rove to bring in the needed scalp, and it made no great difference whether it came from the head of a white man, negro, or enemy Indian. Luke Short's colored cowboys knew that.

"They're liable to catch hell now," observed the Q-Bar puncher as the cattle were started. "Either them or the next herd on the trail."

—And that's how, if you lived within the borders of civilization during the '70's, the beefsteak of the steer found its way to your table. It came up from Texas on the hoof . . . through heat and dust . . . through Comanche and Kiowa raiders . . . through those grim Osage mourning parties . . . red beef seared, one might say, by hell itself before it reached the Kansas rail terminals and found its way, eventually, to outer markets.

The great trail drives, the real boom period, really started in the late '60's when the Union Pacific and the Kansas Pacific began pushing their ribbons of steel across the Kansas plains.

The business, however, had its start in early years. James Ellison of Gonzales pioneered it in 1849 when he drove beef to the miners of California, but it was not until nine years later that the first trail went north from Texas—when Oliver Loving of Jack county drove to the Chicago market.

Loving followed up with more drives and became the real trail blazer. Leaving Palo Pinto county May 15, 1859, he drove north to the Arkansas and followed that river into Pueblo and Denver, establishing the first permanent route. Then a few years later, in company with Colonel Charles Goodnight, he blazed what is now known as the Goodnight-Loving trail, a route which led from Fort Griffin across West Texas to Horsehead Crossing on the Pecos, thence up the river over one corner of New Mexico, and on to Fort Sumner and Colorado.

In the south, about this same time, two routes were being well traveled in Louisiana—the "Shreveport" serving the lower Brazos and Colorado river sections, and the "Opelousas" serving the Gulf coast area.

Then came the others, most colorful and romantic of all— the Shawnee, the Chisholm, and the Dodge. Of these three, however, the Chisholm, much publicized in story and song, was the most famous. It apparently followed no well-defined and well-marked course, and in this account no attempt will be made to trace a definite trail, because for several years survivors of those early drives have been inclined to disagree on such questions as whether the "true" route followed to the east or to the west of a certain hill, or crossed certain rivers at this ford or that.

But, generally speaking, the southern terminus of a general Texas trail is supposed to have been at Austin, where the main trunk picked up feeder lines from the Matagorda, the Tres-

palacios, the Nueces, Victoria, Cottula, Encinal, and from all
the Brush Country between Corpus and the Rio Grande.

Extending northward from Austin, one branch of this general trail passed near Fort Worth (and sometimes through it),
and continued up through Wise and Montague counties to
make the water crossing at Red River Station near old Spanish

Photograph by W. D. Smithers

*Scenic Beauty*

Fort. From the Red River it ran to the Washita River, north
through the Territory to the Kansas line, where it branched
off to Abilene, Ellsworth, Hays, or whichever town the driver
was making.

This route in the Indian Territory took its name from Jesse
Chisholm, a part Cherokee trader. In 1865 Chisholm and
Black Beaver, a Delaware, acted as guides when Federal troops
were sent down from the Arkansas to take over posts on the
Washita, and the designation appears to have been dated from

This map shows the principal cattle trails, which between 1850 and the late '80's, carried millions of cattle from the breeding grounds of Texas to slaughter, and to the cattle ranges of the upper Great Plains. Principal trails on the map are indicated as follows: (1) Old Shawnee Trail, running from Preston, Texas, to Sedalia, Mo., and beyond.
(2) West Shawnee Trail, a westward extension to Abilene, Kan.; there was also an intermediate trail (not numbered on the map) leading to Kansas City.
(3) Chisholm Trail, l e a d i n g from Texas to Abilene and other Kansas shipping points; the main Red River crossing was at Red River Station, but there was also a crossing at Swell's Bend. (4) Dodge, or Western Trail, which crossed the Red River at Doan's Store, north of Vernon, Texas (5) Montana Trail, an extension of these extensions into Wyoming and Montana and even as far north as the Indian reservations across the Canadian border.
(6) Goodnight-Loving Trail, originating near Fort Belknap, near present Eliasville in Young County, Texas and extending westward to the Pecos, thence northward into New Mexico and Colorado. (7) Main California Trail. (8) Other trails leading to California over which some herds were driven. (9) Old Government Road, from Fort Washita on the Red to Little Rock, Ark. (10) Shreveport Trail leading from Blackland Prairies near Dallas to Shreveport and beyond. (11) Extensions of Shreveport Trail to Natchez and Vicksburg. (12) Atascosita Road and Opelousas Trail, an early

Courtesy T. C. Richardson and The Texas Geographic Magazine

that time, although there is no evidence that Chisholm ever traveled any other part of the route except that which traversed the country between the Arkansas and Arkansas City in Kansas.

In some quarters the belief still persists that the trail was named for John Chisum, the Jingle-Bob king, and in the south of Texas you still can find old-timers who refer to it as the "Chisum Trail," but Colonel Goodnight always insisted that John Chisum repeatedly told him that he never drove a trail north . . . only to New Mexico and Colorado.

Be this as it may, there are those who say that Chisum and Chisholm were remotely related, which is quite likely, since old John's family name originally was Chisholm, being changed later through error on army pension lists after the participation of John's father in the battle of New Orleans.

The Shawnee Trail started about the same time, but the Chisholm really received the big play. The Shawnee started on the general trail near San Antonio, touched near Fort Worth and Dallas but crossed the Red River near Preston in Grayson county above Sherman. It traversed Eastern Oklahoma and pushed into Southwest Missouri, but there the settlers took up arms to resist drives across their farms with the result that the trail soon was making its northern terminus at Baxter Springs in Southeastern Kansas. This point the Texans favored until 1866 when, through the suggestion of Joseph G. McCoy, a Kansas buyer, the Kansas Pacific rail facilities out of Abilene came under consideration. Then it was that the Chisholm Trail came into all its glory.

The Texas section also was known as the McCoy—in honor of the man who opened the markets.

Two hundred and sixty thousand cattle went into the cars at Abilene during that fall, but as they sold in the northern markets at prices which barely paid freight prices, the side-burned gentlemen who sat at the directors' table in the St. Louis headquarters of the Kansas Pacific openly scoffed at the whole project, called it the greatest joke in the report of the road's business for the year, and they felt justified in keeping up the spirit of jest when in 1867 the grand total fell to 35,000 head.

There happened to be young blood, however, on the directorate of the K. P. and in the face of much opposition they held to the idea that something could be done with the Abilene situation.  They were vindicated in this stand, for although only 75,000 were shipped in 1868 prices began improving in the north and in 1869 the great boom started, with 350,000 steers going into the cars.

### Beefsteak on the hoof, from the Rio Grande to Kansas

The Texans had discovered a bonanza, and the following year brought an equal number of cattle to the railroad, some from as far south as the Rio Grande.

The South Texans would start, usually, about the first of April with, as a rule, one man for every 200 head, and each man with two or three horses.  The outfits would drive slowly until noon, then stop for a meal, the chuck wagon having driven on ahead to prepare the victuals.  In the afternoon the pace would be quickened with no stop until night, when a bed-ground would be selected and the cattle huddled as closely as possible, with certain cowboys detailed to night herding.

The boys might take the trail merrily enough, but after a couple of weeks conversation would lag,  and the 'punchers would become silent, bored men ... driving, driving ... day in, day out ... for sometimes as long as two months.

Small wonder that the saddle-weary Texans sometimes were inclined to "cut loose" when Abilene or Dodge or any of the other rough-and-tumble Kansas mushroom towns marked the journey's end.  In these boarded towns on the plains the Texas cowboy was king.  He wore what he pleased ... he strutted to his pleasure, exhibiting a spirit of bravado and recklessness that is remembered, even to this day, in those parts.  He helped, to a large extent, in making jobs for certain gentlemen whose stories have been handed down through history merely because of their ability to handle six-guns fast and well—that roster of famed city marshals which includes the names of Bat Masterson, Wild Bill Hickok, Tom Smith, Wyatt Earp, and Bill Tilgham.

But Abilene was not destined for long to keep the goose which laid the golden egg. In 1871 the Texans outdid themselves, sending up to Abilene, Dodge, Wichita, and other points an almost unbelievable number of longhorns—600,000!

The market, naturally, was glutted, and prices dropped. There came a time, late in the season, when drivers were glad to get $2 a hundred, because feed was short and all the available range was crowded with cattle waiting for market. Prairie fires took many herds, and later the northers took heavy toll. The Texans, to put it mildly, took it on the chin.

Then another serious thing. Townsite promoters had drifted into Abilene, and with all and sundry trying to cut in on the profits of the lately-departed Great Boom, there followed a period of graft and blackmail so disgusting to the Texans that they determined to avoid Abilene in the future and turn their stock in Dodge, Winfield and Wichita; and most of them held to that policy.

So began the lean years, the period during which most of the larger Texas stockmen killed for hides and tallow. Only half as many steers passed through the Kansas terminals the following year. Then, after a flurry which brought 400,000 in '73, the drives began to steady, ranging from 150,000 to 375,000 up to 1880.

After the Abilene debacle most of the interest centered on the Dodge City or Fort Griffin Trail, a part of which also was known as the Western and as the Jones and Plummer. Starting as far south as Brownsville, it passed to the west of San Antonio, touched Fort Griffin in Shackleford county, and crossed the Red River at Doan's Store, in Wilbarger county just north of Vernon. It followed the western boundary of the Territory, pushed across the eastern end of the Territory Panhandle to Dodge.

An extension ran to Ogallala, Nebraska, near the Platte and on up into the Indian country of the Dakotas, Wyoming and Montana. This trail had feeders from the Texas Panhandle, notably one from Tascosa. This route, and the Goodnight Trail into Colorado and Montana, also were used by more southerly cattlemen in driving their stock to finishing pastures in the north, and the herds from the deep south often brought along epidemics of Texas fever, common in the warmer climes but unknown to the north.

### The Stockmen of Panhandle organize to fight fever

Of course, Panhandle cowmen did not care to have fever-infested herds cross their ranges, and since South Texans did not regard the fever as a serious bovine malady, trouble was inevitable.

In fact, it was the fever situation which led to the organization of the Panhandle Stockmen's Association at Mobeetie in 1881. Charles Goodnight of the JA was one of the leaders, and the membership included names well-konwn all over the high plains . . . Thomas Bugbee of the Quarter Circle T; Dick McNulty of the Turkey Track; Hank Cresswel of the Bar CC; W. E. Anderson of the Scissors; W. T. Munson of the T-Anchors; Evans of the Spade; the Matador; and to mention only a few others—the owners of the Shoe Bar, the Flying T, the Frying Pan, the Bar M, the 3-D, the Doll Baby, and the Quarter Circle Heart.

One of the association's first moves was to hire inspectors and send them to the Kansas terminals to check on incoming herds; and, according to the late O. H. Nelson, prominent Clarendon rancher at that time, it was not uncommon for these detectives to cut one-fourth of a herd for strays belonging to association members.

The Panhandlers gave their early attention to the fever problem. They warned the South Texans, gave them "hints" as to the best routes to take through the country, built water holes on designated routes that passing herds might have water, plowed a furrow through unoccupied country from the Caprock to the New Mexico line that it might be used as a guide, but still some of the southerners persisted in choosing their own routes of travel.

It was then that the Panhandlers originated the Winchester Quarantine. They put armed men on patrol with instructions to turn back trespassing herds.

Sometimes threats, sincere if thinly veiled, were made. In August of 1881, George T. Reynolds was on his way up the trail to Dodge and Colonel Goodnight heard that he was coming. Witness this letter which the Colonel sent Mr. Reynolds:

"Dear Sir: I send Mr. Smith to turn your cattle so they will not pass through our range. He will show you around and guide you until you strike the head of this stream and then you will have a road. The way he will show you is nearer and there are shorter drives to water than any route you can make. I hope you will take this advice as yourselves and I have always been good friends, but even friendship will not protect you in the drive through here, and should you attempt to pass through be kind enough to tell your men what they will have to face as I do not wish to hurt men that do not understand what they will be very sure to meet.

"I hope you will not treat this as idle talk, for I mean every word of this, and if you have any feeling for me as a friend or acquaintance, you will not put me to any desperate actions. I will not perhaps see you myself, but take this advice from one that is and always has been your friend. My cattle are now dying of fever contracted from cattle driven from Fort Worth, therefore do not have any hope that you can convince me that your cattle will not give mine the fever. This we will not speak of. I simply say that you will not pass through here in good health."

The cattleman retained his health, for later he sent the letter to the editor of the Fort Griffin *Echo* with this comment:

"Herewith I hand you a letter which is so plain it requires no explanation. I desire its publication that stockmen generally may know how overbearing prosperity can make a man.

                              Respectfully, George Reynolds."

The fear of Texas fever increased. In 1884 Southern Kansas ranchmen forbade Texans to take the Dodge Trail, but the Texans were not to be stopped so easily. Several owners armed their men and started up anyway, but they were met in Barber county by a large number of Kansas ranchers, just as efficiently armed. There was some palavering, and many hot words were passed, but finally the Texans turned their herds toward Colorado markets. Then Colorado and New Mexico passed quarantine laws, some requiring that all Texas cattle driven "north of 36" must be held in the Indian Territory for sixty days.

With hundreds of thousands of head on hand and no market, the Texans suffered before Secretary of the Interior Lamar—seeing in many of the laws the designing hand of Northern cattlemen seeking market protection—lifted quarantines and let the herds go through.

But even now more and more railroads were building into Texas and the day was at hand when the steers from the south would be taking the cars instead of the long and dusty trails which led into the North. Ties and rails were following the paths long marked by the cut of the hoof . . .

# Barb'd Wire
# and the
# Frying Pan

● **Sales from the profits of new-fangled 'Devil Rope' started ranch which caused the moving of an entire city**

**M**R. GLIDDEN was troubled. Here he was repairing fence behind a destructive herd of milk cows when he should be in his DeKalb workshop making eaves-troughs.

Orders were on file from all over that section of Illinois, but the cattle would give him time for little else but fence repairing. They seemed to take a bovine delight in the work. They smashed into the smooth wire strands and tore them from the posts as fast as Mr. Glidden could drive in new

275

staples. He had just about concluded that the successful business man ... especially an eaves-trough maker ... might do well to forego the pleasures of gentleman farming.

And then, even as he poised the hammer to drive a staple back into place, he saw it—the thing which was to doom the open range in the cattle country of the West.

The staple was hanging loose on the smooth wire, its points directed toward the eaves-trough maker of DeKalb. His hands, already raised to strike the blow, fell. Here was an idea ... foolish perhaps ... but still an idea, and great things have been accomplished with even less to go on.

Glidden considered. If all this smooth wire could be strung with sharp barbs at regular intervals, the troublesome cattle would take notice before they came up against the proposition a second time. The gentleman farmer went ahead with his work but he kept thinking of the thing, and before he went home that night he had decided on experiment.

Next morning he was in his shop early—tinkering with a strand of smooth wire and a coffee grinder equipped with a hand crank. Fastening one end of the wire to the grinder, he cut a series of two-point barbs and by use of a crude wrench began twisting them on the wire at regular intervals. Then, as he finished one section, he reeled it onto the coffee grinder and started another—repeating the process until the grinder spool would hold no more.

That day in the summer of 1873 marked a new era for the stock raisers of the world. Even Glidden suspected that he had stumbled onto something big and he lost no time in applying for a patent, which after some delay was recorded on November 24 of the next year.

Of course, the neighbors took an interest in the affair. They hoped that Mr. Glidden would make a lot of money, but privately they told one another that they wanted no stock in the project. People wouldn't want their cattle cut up by new fangled spikes twisted on a wire; there could be no sale for the stuff. That is, most neighbors said such things but I. L. Ellwood didn't.

He had watched with great interest the progress of Glidden's labor with the wire and coffee grinder, and now that the patent papers were on file he approached the latter with a proposition, which ended with Mr. Ellwood in possession of a half interest in the invention.

Together they succeeded in raking up sufficient money to build a plant and perfect a machine which would simplify the twisting of barbs. Thus the world's first barbed wire factory was opened—and no longer was J. S. Glidden known as the eaves-trough maker of DeKalb.

Factory beginnings were small. The partners started with a 150-foot strand which was coiled on a reel until a similar length could be added, and then another until the reel was full.

### A Horse-trader in a buggy brought first wire to Texas

Contrary to predictions of neighbors, the farmers of the north began buying the output, which in a few months had increased to about twenty reels a day. Both Glidden and Ellwood realized, however, that the market must be expanded if they were to make money from the venture, and so they began casting about for a salesman to put in the field.

"I think I know just the man we want," said Glidden. "You remember Henry, the young fellow who used to work for me? He's a likeable sort, and if anybody can sell wire he can. Trouble is, Sanborn is doing a lot of horse tradin' these days and might not be interested."

And Henry Sanborn wasn't vastly interested. When Glidden sent for him he came more out of friendship than anything else, and after hearing explanations he made it plain he didn't think much of the wire as a money-making proposition. He had, he said a good business . . . horse-trading . . . and he was making money shipping to the Denver market. Why should he forsake all to take up an uncertain thing?   Besides, he was rather inclined to agree with those who said the farmers would not buy through fear that stock might be damaged by the barbs.

"But Henry," argued Mr. Glidden, "isn't it logical that cattle, once they've come in contact with the wire, won't go up against it again? Does a burned child return to the fire?"

"There may be something in what you say," replied Sanborn, "but I'm still unconvinced."

Glidden and Ellwood presented new arguments; they cajoled and they pleaded, and at last they wore down the horse trader's resistance.

"All right," said Sanborn finally. "I'll try it, but only on condition that my partner goes with me. Jud Warner and I have been in business together for quite a spell now . . ."

So a contract was signed, and Henry Sanborn and Judson P. Warner set out in a buggy to carry the message of modern fencing to the hard-shell farmers.

The sucker citizens didn't fall over themselves getting to the buggy to buy barbed wire, and ere summer again appeared in the Middle West the former horse traders had disposed of few more reels than enough to pay expenses. But even if the majority of agriculturists had failed to recognize the merits of the product, others had. The Washburn and Moen Manufacturing Company of Worcester, Massachusetts, wanted a half interest in the plant, and Glidden and Ellwood let them have it.

It was about this time that Salesman Sanborn had a brilliant idea—an idea which was to bring barbed wire into its own and make a fortune for its manufacturers.

"Texas and the cattle country—that's the place to sell," he told his employers—and forthwith loaded a few reels in his buggy, climbed into the seat, whipped up the horses, and took the road south.

A few weeks later the redskins of the Indian Territory were

staring in blank amazement at the "devil rope" which a strange
white man was transporting in his carriage; and not many days
later, in September of 1875, that same "devil rope" was being
exhibited to the wondering citizens of Sherman, Texas.

Indeed, so much interest was evinced in the product that op-
timistic Henry, playing a horse trader's intuition, got a message
to his company ordering four carloads of wire—one car to each
of four cities—Sherman, Dallas, Austin and San Antonio. He
added, too, that the company had better send Warner down to
help him . . . all this without a single customer on the horizon.

But Sanborn wasn't long in finding one—a merchant in
Gainesville. The name of this gentleman, sadly enough has been
lost to history, but he took from Henry the first ten reels of
barbed wire to be stretched on Texas posts.

Business picked up immediately; and on a ten-day trip by
surrey—a journey which took in Decatur, Pilot Point and Denton—Sanborn sold fifty more reels. Then Jud Warner arrived.
He took over the east central area of the State, sold out the Dallas car in small lots, then hied himself to Austin to deal with
the consignment there.

He found many in the capitol city who already knew something about barbed wire. Back in 1857 an old Swiss iron foundry
worker by the name of Grenninger had carried on experiments
in a crude way. He had twisted spikes to a smooth strand and
nailed it to the top of a picket fence which inclosed his orchard
on the Colorado River, but the neighbors had feared for the
safety of their cattle and had raised so many objections that
Grenninger finally had been forced to tear down what probably
was the first barbed wire fence in America. But the iron master
had lost his rights when he failed to get a patent.

A dozen years can do much in overcoming prejudices and
Warner, upon arrival in Austin, found that the fame of the
newly patented wire had preceded him. Encouraged by the recent successes in North Texas, the salesman chose a prospect

and called. John A. Webb, Austin merchant, didn't even wait for a sales talk. He surprised Mr. Warner by purchasing the entire consignment—the first carload ever sold in Texas.

We next find Messrs. Sanborn and Warner in San Antonio preparing to branch out into the Matagorda and the Nueces area with a "high-powered" advertising campaign. John W. Gates, twenty-one-year-old salesman who had come down to join them, played a great part in that.

Young Gates knew the art of promotion. He went to the officials of the Alamo City and obtained permission to build a barbed wire corral in the Plaza, and when it was completed he penned therin twenty-five of the wildest longhorn steers he could find. Prominent South Texas cowmen, invited to witness the show, waited with eagerness. They knew the longhorn. This wire might hold eastern cattle, they said, but not the Texas breed.

And then Gates released his herd. Pell mell, the beasts charged the corral, but as the barbs ripped into their hides they turned back to the center of the ring. Then, like cavalry horses, they formed and charged again—but once more the "devil-rope" turned them back. After this second attempt they kept to the center, as far away from the wire as possible. It was an interesting demonstration, and it convinced many stockmen who otherwise might have stuck to board, rock and brush fencing.

### The Devil Rope met with disfavor in some quarters

But even then Sanborn and Warner didn't sell that San Antonio car of barbed wire outright; rather they scattered it in small lots all over the South Texas ranch country. They placed a few reels here, a few there . . . that all the stockmen might see and become barbed wire conscious. There was method in the procedure, for as soon as the samples were set the two former horse traders rushed back to DeKalb to obtain exclusive rights for the State of Texas.

They were back in a few months, only to discover that the

advertising campaign had gained enemies as well as friendly
buyers.   The lumbermen, who furnished much of the material
for the board fences then in vogue, were in bitter opposition,
and so were the railroads which hauled that lumber.

Even some of the cattlemen looked upon the innovation with
much disfavor. They still were afraid the barbs would slash the
cattle and bring on screw worms, those pests which attack fresh
cut wounds. At first even the great Shanghai Pierce was an
opponent, but some of his neighbors in the south began fencing.

Before the 'Seventies were out Bee county boasted twenty-
five miles of fence; a large pasture in San Patricio was enclosed;
*Shang's* close neighbor, Tom O'Connor, was stringing strands;
and the great King Ranch was preparing a program which in a
short time would call for 190,000 pounds of wire.

The same thing was occurring in the north and in the Pan-

Photograph by Erwin E. Smith
*Riding the line—winter drift fence.   Note the cow skull and the rider's*
*buffalo robe.*

handle, where a 175-mile drift fence was started in 1881 to halt cattle from the Territory. That same year Colonel Goodnight started digging post holes on the JA, and O. H. Nelson was similarly engaged on the Shoe-Bar.

All this caused trouble and the battle over the barbed wire issue reached into the State Legislature, where bills prohibiting its use were offered and argued one after another, with lobbies working on each side.

But those who already had strung their posts put up a determined fight, using witnesses and affidavits as ammunition to break the attack of those who charged animal injury. The bills, one by one, were defeated.

The wire was something which the salesman of today would call a "natural." The farmers and the squatters were beginning to slip over the borders of the West; and finally even the "die-hards" among the ranchers realized that the open range was doomed.

"Fencing bees" were held in many localities, and soon Sanborn and Warner were doing business at the rate of three-quarters of a million to a million dollars a year.

Then new troubles. Quite naturally, in a country where the range had been free and open, the arrival of wire wasn't greeted enthusiastically by many of the small cattlemen and farmers. They watched with rising concern and anger as the great cattle barons bought and leased land, hauled in posts and fenced in large tracts—sometimes including all the water for miles around.

They couldn't afford to buy for themselves, these small ranchers and farmers, but they could fight back. And they did . . . with the wire snippers and the pliers . . . with the result that a feud of major proportions was brought about in West Texas. Men banded together in secret societies, both to cut wire and to prevent cutting, and their acts inaugurated an era of gunplay which furnished countless grim meals for the prowling wolves of the *Llano Estacado*.

This fight, too, reached the legislature halls, and in one of the many legal contests based on fencing Colonel Charles Goodnight played the leading role.

Recognizing that the Panhandle rapidly was filling with new citizens and that barbed wire meant the end of the open arnge, the Legislature, in April of 1883, passed a law creating a State Land Office and providing for competitive leasing of alternate school sections at not less than four cents an acre. The cowmen, many of whom already had fenced in school lands, were supposed to make a tender of four cents on the acre, but the Land Office decided that eight cents would make a better price.

The larger cattlemen of the Panhandle rebelled; they said they wouldn't pay, and in December, '85, Attorney General John D. Templeton instructed W. H. Woodman, the Panhandle attorney, to bring charges against certain ranches for illegal inclosure.

Clarendon became a busy town.

Woodman called the grand jury, which had been drawn the previous summer, and which was made up of cowmen, with Colonel Goodnight as foreman. The evidence was considered and the first true bill found—against the jury foreman himself! Goodnight, boss of the great JA, was indicted for "unlawfully fencing and herding on public school lands."

Then the jury got down to real business. It found six more bills against its own foreman, and turned in a final batch totaling 76, most of which were divided up pretty well among the jurors themselves. Foreman Goodnight then delivered the bills to District Judge Willis, who discharged the jury, and then called the cases for trial.

But before the gavel falls let us look over the court ... Judge Frank Willis on the bench, the jurors taking their places in the box. They are men who wear high boots and carry high hats—

cattlemen. It seems evident, even now, how the cases will go.

The judge instructs the jury. The cowmen, he says, have admitted enclosure; the State has admitted that the cattlemen defendents have made legal tender bids of four cents an acre on the enclosures. The defense claims that such tender has been made yearly to the State Land Office—and if all these things are found to be true; the Judge said, then the jury should find a verdict of not guilty. And the jury did . . .

The twelve good men and true even tried several absent ranchmen who didn't know, until long after their acquittals, that they had been indicted!

This was the sort of judicial business which later caused Jim Hogg, succeeding attorney general (and later governor) to go before the Legislature with a plea for the impeachment of Judge Willis. Hogg termed as farcial a court which permitted a grand jury to indict its own members, and a trial jury made up of partisan cattlemen.

### Cattlemen take fortune up street in wheelbarrow

The Panhandle was a cattle country, friends of the judge replied, and where else could the court get qualified jurors? If the employes of the defendants were to be barred from the panel, they said, it would be impossible to muster a jury of twelve men in the district.  And, this argument was a factor in the acquittal of Judge Willis when the House finally did bring him to trial.

The Legislature later enacted a law definitely fixing four cents an acre as leasing price on school land, but Colonel Goodnight already had won a strange decision in behalf of those who objected to the eight cent rate.

Shortly after the Clarendon trials Goodnight was in Austin with two neighboring cowmen, W. T. Munson and Buck Walton of the T-Anchor. They were intent upon one thing—calling the hand of the land officials.

First, Goodnight went before the board with a written pro-

posal agreeing to take all school lands in his range at four cents
from the date of his own application in 1884—previous to the
enclosure act.

Then, with Munson and Walton, he went to an Austin bank
with a negro porter and a wheelbarrow. Goodnight drew
$72,000, the amount the JA would owe for leasing. Munson
drew enough to cover the amount owed by the T-Anchor,
slightly more than $25,000.

They loaded the cash on the wheelbarrow, put the negro at
the handles, and started him up Congress avenue to the Land
Office. There the money was tendered to Treasurer Lubbock,
who refused to accept it. However, the cattlemen did bluff him
into signing a paper showing that the money had been offered
at four cents an acre—which cowmen contended was the legal
rate. And after that the State couldn't do much about it.

Goodnight and the T-Anchor men took the money back to
the bank and paid $175 for its use.

The foregoing is only one incident among the troubles barbed
wire brought to the open range country, but through it all
Henry Sanborn profited. He made a comfortable fortune from
his state rights—quite enough to buy a good-sized ranch in
Grayson county, where he specialized in Percheron horses as
well as high-bred cattle. He fenced, of course, with the kind of
wire he sold, but in time this North Texas domain became too
small for a man with Henry's ambitions.

In 1881 he and Glidden had formed a partnership to buy 95
sections in the Panhandle counties of Potter and Randall—later
enlarging the private Kingdom by 125,000 acres. It was then
that the Panhandle began to find itself webbed with wire which
was to cause much trouble.

Fencing involved many difficulties then. Sanborn and Glidden hauled their wire 250 miles by wagon across the Plains,
freighted in cedar posts, and put up a four-strand fence at a cost
of $40,000. They stocked with a herd of 15,000 head, bring-

ing into existence one of the major ranches of the Plains—the Great Frying Pan.

For more than a decade it flourished and then, in 1894, the two partners sold the herd and part of the property to Mr. Ellwood, who died in 1910.

After the sale Sanborn and Glidden moved to Amarillo, the growing town which stood on the east boundary of the ranch. Sanborn, incidentally, always had displayed great interest in

Photograph by W. D. Smithers
*The wires are let down and the herd goes through.*

this little village. When he and Glidden established the ranch, Amarillo was a town of about 1,200 inhabitants squatting at the front gate of the Frying Pan.

The citizens, a civic-minded lot, had passed the hat to build a courthouse, but after the building had been completed the barbed-wire king objected to the location. He believed the site should have been about a mile farther west—on pasture land he owned—and so he decided to take a hand in affairs.

He built a new and stately hotel on his own property . . . then bought the town's original and only hotel and moved it to a spot near the new one. He built houses, drilled wells, and then—according to a story in one of the newspapers of that day—"he drove over to the old Amarillo, bought a store, put it on wheels, and hauled it to new Amarillo."

In this fashion Henry Sanborn modeled a city after his own design, and at last the old town found it possessed only a court building to mark its one-time place beneath the sun.

A new city arose from the Plains, and others about it—part and parcel of a once great cattle kingdom made possible because an Illinois eaves-trough maker once had trouble with his cows . . .

**BRAND**
**THE FRYING PAN**

*In the trans-Pecos—the wagon at the water tank*

Photograph by W. D. Smithers

# Hall Brothers— Empire Builders

"PINK" MURRAY, RANGE BOSS OF THE O R

● They bossed the Cimarron range and gathered the loose ends of the prairies to build their empire

COFFEE—COMING UP

AGUILA the Ute, wise in the wisdom bred into the countless generations of roving people, could drive a hard bargain. As he led his tribesmen and their hundreds of ponies into the green valley of the Cimarron none knew it better than he.

289

There, where the river snaked through the northeastern corner of New Mexico, the grass was better than in any other spot betwen the Carrizo and the Rio Purgatory up beyond the Colorado line ... better even than in the Neutral strip of the Indian Territory a few miles to the east; or in the Texas Panhandle a few hours ride to the south.

And Aguila, whom the white men called the Eagle, smiled to himself as his eyes took in the herd of fat steers sprinkled over the floor of the valley.

In the brain of the crafty Ute a scheme was hatching, had, in fact, already hatched. It awaited now only the appearance of one Bill Hall to bring it to the climax; and Bill Hall ... who with his brothers, Nathan and Jim, jealously guarded this cow Eden on the Cimarron ... would be along in a few days.

Of that Aguila of the Utes was certain as he loosed his ponies on the Cross L range. Hungry Indian ponies can cut the grass as rapidly as any bunch of longhorn steers and, true to prediction, Bill Hall was in the Eagle's camp before the setting of the second sun.

The cattleman was brief and to the point.

"Can't say I'm glad to see you, chief, because I ain't," said Hall, without preamble. "The grass in here is a little short for this season . . . just about enough for our own stock . . . and you'd better gather up your hosses and move out. There's range over to the west . . ."

The Eagle gazed with defiant eyes at the white man.

"You own this grass?" he asked in Spanish.

"Nope . . . but we've been here since '71. It's open range."

"Who put the grass here?" demanded Aguila. "You know?"

Bill was silent. He had not counted on dramatics.

"The Great Spirit put it here," said the Ute, answering his own question. "It was here for the Indian before the white man came."

Hall was no fool. He saw the point at once.

"Three hundred pounds of flour," he offered, "and 500 pounds of sugar."

"Too little," said the Indian. "What else you give?"

"All right, then . . . five beeves."

"And horses?" queried the savage racketeer. "You give no horses?"

The Cross L man was thoughtful. Flour, sugar and beef . . . he was willing to pay the price to save his grass, but horses were different. He knew, however, that the Ute could drive a hard bargain.

"Six," he said. "Six and no more."

The chief reflected for a moment, and then:

"There is one I want for my own," he said. "You will give the paint among the six?"

Photograph by Erwin E. Smith
*Three Block remuda*

Hall knew the animal, a fine saddler, and he was reluctant to surrender a stallion so promising, but at last he gave in. But—

"One thing more," said the Eagle. "The paint wears shoes, and you must take away the shoes."

This came near being the last straw with the boss of the Cross L but he swallowed his pride and overlooked the impertinent demand. Hall Brothers couldn't afford to have trouble with the Utes; there were too many fat steers on the Cimarron range . . . and when Aguila departed with his loot on the following morning the fine young saddler went along, without his shoes. Aguila could, indeed, drive a hard bargain . . .

### Cimarron was a cowman's Garden of Eden

But for the visits of occasional Ute serpents such as the Eagle and his lieutenant, Buckskin Charlie, the valley of the Cimarron was, in truth, a cowman's Garden of Eden.

The three Halls, who had left their native Tennessee in 1851 to take up residence in the Texas county of Caldwell, had first seen the valley back in 1868 while working with a herd trail en route from Texas to Colorado. They were taken with the favorable appearance of the spot and they unanimously agreed to claim it as a range as soon as a herd could be gathered to drive in.

Upon the return to Texas they pooled their resources, bought 2,500 head of cows at $7 each (calves thrown in) and started from Southwest Texas for New Mexico. They trailed up the Pecos, crossed at Horsehead, pushed north to the Canadian River and Carrizo Creek, and turned loose near the Black Mesa on the Colorado-New Mexico line.

That was in the fall of 1871, the year of the great panic at the Kansas trail terminals, but the Halls didn't worry. They appropriated land through taking up squatters' rights, built corrals and a ranch house, planted feed and, after turning the first year's calves at $14, bought more cattle to place under the brand of the Cross L. They had, in the first year, but one neighbor on the range—an Englishman named Jim Roberts, but he agreed to move out for 150 Texas steers.

Except for one serious fight in which two cowboys were killed, the Utes gave little trouble; and before the decade of the '70's had half run its course the Cross L range was sprinkled with many thousands of cattle. No one knew it yet, of course, but some of the largest Texas cattle empires were in the making . . . not one, but several.

One of the first drives from the valley was made by Bill Hall ... the younger brother ... and Bud Sumpter, one of the foremen, in 1873. They delivered 400 cows and calves to Apache Creek, thirty miles east of Denver, and turned them over to a rancher who had made the purchase. Then later in the year, the brothers trailed a herd up into Colorado and shipped them over the Kansas Pacific at Las Animas on the Arkansas River.

Photograph by Erwin E. Smith

*O R wagon and stray men throwin' in*

The Halls had the Cimarron Valley pretty much to themselves, their largest important neighbors being the Jones brothers ... Steve, Jim and Pate ... who had moved in below Las Animas to establish the JJ herd when the railroad reached that point in 1873. It would be four more years before the next large neighbor would move in—Stephen W. Dorsey, who in 1878 came to establish the Tringle-Dot at Chico Springs, fifty miles southwest of the Cross L range.

Meanwhile, with various drives to market, the Halls prospered. They began fusing Durham blood into their herds and developing a better type than rangy longhorns. How many cattle they held on the range at this period is problematical, but the extent of operations may be judged from the fact that they brought in 175 head of horses from Texas in 1877.

**A Puncher kills the cook and is given cook's job as punishment**

They brought in Texas cattle, too. Once, with only six men and a cook, the late George P. Robinson of Kansas City rode down to Tascosa and took over 2,600 T Heart steers purchased by the Halls for the Cimarron range. It was a small party for that many cattle, but Wagon Boss Robinson got in without any loss . . . except the negro cook.

One of the Cross L punchers, Windy by name, took a dislike to chuckwagon rations and at the end of an explosive argument killed the cook with a spade. Shorthanded as the outfit was at the start of the trail, this was a serious business and Robinson lost no time in dealing out justice according to his ideas on the subject.

"Unsaddle your hoss and get busy with those pans and ovens," he told the spade-swinging Windy, "and make sure the grub you fix is fit to eat. Next time you get a hankerin' to start a killin' pick a time when we're not so short-handed."

The Cross L, by 1879, had become one of the largest outfits in New Mexico. It was then that Jim Hall sold out his interest to his brothers and started back to Texas with $100,000 in his pocket. Jim had been thinking . . .

The high Panhandle of Texas had been filling with cattlemen. There was Colonel Charles Goodnight of the JA; Thomas Bugbee of the Quarter Circle T; Major George Littlefield of the LIT; the LX's; the T-Anchors; the Turkey Tracks, and others. Even the Cross L had branched out into the Panhandle, taking a range down near Buffalo Springs.

With barbed wire coming in, Jim looked ahead to the day when the open range would be no more, and he decided to find a site for a ranch all his own while land remained from which to choose. He set out for the south of Texas . . . one of his favorite employes, J. R. Beasley, going with him.

Next we find Messrs. Hall and Beasley in Refugio county buying coastal steers; and when a herd of 1,500 had been

completed they hired a few hands and took the trail for the
north, striking the Dodge City (or Western) Trail at Round
Rock and following it through to Fort Griffin. From there they
pushed on to Vernon, thence turning west up the Pease River
to turn loose near Caprock.

Then Jim made a business call on his brothers in New Mexico . . . to return to his Texas range with 800 cattle marked with
a new brand, which he chose to call the Spur. He consolidated
the South Texas and New Mexico herds, moved them down
into Dickens county and established headquarters on Red Mud

Photograph by Erwin E. Smith
*Spur Ranch headquarters*

Creek, a comfortable distance south of the Matadors, already
a thriving and going concern. Once settled, he adopted his road
brand, the Spur, as his permanent "coat-of-arms." Two new
cattle kingdoms, both among the greatest in the history of the
West, were about to be born—both on foundations laid by the
brothers Hall.

And they were brought about because the ranching fever,

heated by a period of prosperity in the business had been contracted by romantically minded capitalists in England and Scotland. It was a fever which swept the isles like a sudden epidemic.

The year 1881 found a group of gentlemen, some titled, gathered in Dowell's Rooms, 18 George Street, Edinburgh. Some of them, at one time or another, had been interested in the breeding of the shaggy West Highland cattle, and these spoke with seeming experience on the business in hand. The others listened and before adjournment Dowell's Rooms had become general headquarters for the Prairie Land and Cattle Company, Limited, a concern capitalized at 650,000 pounds sterling.

A few weeks later a branch office was opened in Kansas City under the name of Underwood, Clark and Company, and this firm was given unlimited power in the purchase of lands and cattle. The Scottish were going after things in a big way . . .

And not many weeks later a representative of the Kansas City office, Willard R. Green, dropped off the train at Trinidad, Colorado, where Bill and Nathan Hall, informed of his coming, were waiting with a hack.

Only a few days were required for Mr. Green to look over the stock and improvements in the Cimarron Valley, and then offer the Halls the sum of $450,000. The brothers accepted . . . and the Scotch syndicate had made its first move in a program which later led cattlemen to believe that "the Prairie was attempting to own all outdoors."

The Cross L's at this time must have numbered about 25,000 head, but the Scots weren't satisfied with that. They also bought Dorsey's Triangle-Dot brand, and then moved up into Colorado to take over 18,000 head from the JJ of the Jones brothers. This latter acquisition gave the Prairie an unbroken range through the northeastern corner of New Mexico far up into the Las Animas country of Colorado—but the syndicate wanted more.

The eyes of the Scots focused on Texas. Four miles from the rip-roaring cow town of Tascosa, on the banks of the Canadian, was the headquarters of the LIT, owned and managed by a Texan who still bore the scar of a wound received while a member of Hood's Brigade during the War between the States.

This gentleman had no thought of selling out, but when the Prairie offered him $248,000 for his 14,000 head of cattle, his 250 saddle horses, and his headquarters, Major George W. Littlefield gathered up his personal property, put the check in his pocket, and started south to take up a new profession, which was to lead to the presidency of the Austin National Bank.

Thus, before the year 1881 had closed, the Prairie Land and Cattle Company, Limited—or "Unlimited," as you choose—

Photograph by Erwin E. Smith
*A "Three Blocks" remuda—New Mexico*

owned approximately 100,000 head of cattle and many thousands of horses, with three brands in as many states. The first division was the JJ in Colorado, the second the Cross L in New Mexico, and the third the LIT in Texas. And before the next year was out the firm had bought up enough small land owners to give themselves an unbroken range from Tascosa up through

New Mexico to the Arkansas in Colorado . . . a strip more than 250 miles in length.

### The ranching fever became more intense in Britain

The Prairie had invested heavily, but in its first dividend the firm had paid more than 20 per cent . . . the money being raised, according to A. W. Thompson of Denver, an old employee, through the sale of some of the ranch's most valuable stock, including many young cows. Whatever the case, the dividend aggravated the ranching fever in the British Isles.

Let us now digress long enough to look into the fortunes of Jim Hall down in Dickens county. The Spur herd had grown; and it, too, was destined to fall into the hands of the British and take its place among the greater ranches of the *Llano Estacado*.

Jim, like his brothers, believed in taking profits while he could, and in 1882, when Stephens and Harris offered to buy, he sold the Spur. Within a few months the property changed hands again—this time being taken over by the newly-organized Espuela Cattle Company, which included among its directors A. M. Britton and S. W. Lomax, two men who helped Henry Campbell organize the *Matador*.

These gentlemen had just sold the *Matador* to a Scotch syndicate formed in Dundee; and Lomax, who had named the *Matador* out of his fondness for Spanish names, likewise gave the new company a Spanish title. *Espuela* means "the Spur."

The company was re-organized in 1884 as the Espuela Land and Cattle Company of Fort Worth, and it was at this time that Colonel Britton, thinking the time again ripe for profits, went to England to find a buyer.

He found the Scots and the Britons still suffering from the fever—the attack having been aggravated by the Prairie's recent dividend—and in April of 1885 the Spur's name became the Espuela Land and Cattle Company, Limited, of London, with Sir Charles Lewis the president of the corporation.

Thus the brothers Hall were originators of two of the larger

Southwestern ranches. If you care to put it that way . . . they broke the broncs from which the Britons and Scots would take a spill when they tried to sit in the saddles.  By "pulling leather" they held on for a while, these sirs from Surrey and baronets of bonnie Scotland, but soon they would be cursing the day they ever heard of Texas cattle.

In the first year of its operation the Prairie's manager, Gus Johnson, was killed by lightning while riding range. Willard Green then took over for Underwood and Clark, the American promoters of the project. He was succeeded by Richard H. Head, who reigned two years.

It was in the last days of his regime the Prairie suffered its first great loss—in the January blizzard of 1886.  The great storm, still remembered by old-timers, swept across Colorado, New Mexico and the Texas Panhandle killing cattle by thousands.

Some of the Prairie cattle tried to move south in the Panhandle but were halted by a forty-mile drift fence which ranchers below the Canadian had built on the north side of the river that they might keep up-country stock from their ranges.

A. W. Thompson, writing to *The Cattlemen* in 1934, quoted a fellow cowboy of the Prairie as saying:

"After the blizzard was over I rode south from camp some forty miles.  As I got nearer and nearer the drift fence I began to see piles of cattle that had frozen in the storm.  When two miles from the fence these piles grew larger.  Never have I seen such a sickening, pitiful sight.  I could truly have walked for miles on dead animals, stepping from one to another."

Needless to say, certain gentlemen overseas began wondering about their investment when the next dividend failed to materialize.

Then the Scots began sending over their own managers— men like W. J. Tod, Murdo Mackenzie, J. C. Johnson, and Howard Glazbrok—and with this native talent the Prairie was kept going a remarkably long while under the circumstances.

The outfit was a little too large and unwieldy to withstand the hard winters and low prices which followed. When the settlers and farmers began drifting into Colorado and New Mexico in the late '90's the Prairie began selling its vast ranges in small land parcels. In 1912 the company's interest consisted of little more than 200,000 acres in the northern Panhandle of Texas, which in turn went the way of properties in the other states. By 1916 the liquidation was complete, and another empire . . . one of the greatest of all . . . was shattered.

Murdo Mackenzie, who had left the company in the '90's was at this time boss of the *Matadors*, still owned by the Scots and now managed by his son.

As to the fate of the *Espuela*, or the Spur—the owners were not displeased in 1917 when a neighbor of the south sought to buy the property.

The Swenson, or the SMS, with ranges in Stonewall, Jones, Shackleford and Throckmorton counties, already was one of the larger ranches in the lower Panhandle country. The brand was from the initials of the founder—S. M. Swenson, a native of Sweden who in 1836 had settled at Richmond, Fort Bend county, after coming into the country aboard a trading boat. There he had established a store.

Richmond at that time was the head of navigation on the Brazos and as there were no railroads in the Republic the town had a large trade territory. Later S. M. Swenson moved to Austin to open a combination store and bank. During the regime of General Sam Houston as governor the Swedish merchant acted as financial agent for the Raven. Even at this early date Mr. Swenson realized that some day Texas lands would be valuable, and he began acquiring real estate in almost every section of the State . . . at one time holding deeds and patents in sixty-two counties.

### How the brand of the SMS came into West Texas

The lands in the lower Panhandle were patented by the merchant in 1859 on scrip which had been issued by the State in 1856 to the Buffalo Bayou and Gulf Colorado Railroad for railway construction—the scrip having been bought up by Mr. Swenson.

Taxes had become so burdensome by 1882 that it was considered imperative to provide some revenue from the lands until the country could be developed for farming purposes; and consequently two sons of the merchant—E. P. and S. A. Swenson—decided to fence the property and stock it with cattle in the hope of meeting tax expense. The elder Swenson had gone to New York, where, until his death, he remained in the banking business.

The two sons adopted the SMS as a brand, and in the following year, 1883, began buying registered Hereford bulls and heifers from Indiana— to establish a herd which for many years has been carrying away ribbons from the nation's major stock shows.

The Swensons added the *Espuela* to their already vast holdings through the purchase in 1907 and today the outfit—which still calls one of its divisions the Spur—remains one of the largest in the West.

The Company, now managed by A. J. Swenson, a nephew of the founder, always has proceeded on the theory that the cattle business was only a means of making the land carrry itself until such time when it would be needed for farming purposes. Thus the ranch has been a great factor in the development of West Texas as an agricultural country.

The Swensons were instrumental in bringing the railroad to Spur and into Stamford, the present headquarters, and in pushing forward the development of those two towns. During the past twenty-five years they have sold to more than 1,000 families and, to quote the present manager, "have never made a foreclosure."

The old Spur isn't of course, what it was in the olden days. Cattle types change, men come and go, and even the country takes on different aspects, but there still remain a few reminders of the time when the outfit carried the more lyrical name of *Espuela*.

*Applying the S M S brand*

At the time of the sale to the Swensons, when the last details were being cleared and the last accounts were being squared, the Spur bookkeeper found himself with a final puzzle. The financial sheets just wouldn't balance out as they should. The cash accounts held a surplus of hundreds of dollars.

The bookkeeper, after weary hours of checking and rechecking, let it be known to the loiterers without his door that he was having trouble. It was then that an old-timer of the outfit— who had been sitting on the office step waiting to learn whether he would be kept on by the new owners—ambled in and approached the desk of the pen-pusher.

He dipped down into a pocket and brought out a handful of checks . . . representing his monthly pay for the past year.

"Maybe," he suggested, "you ain't figured in these."

Jake Raines, who had worked with an *Espuela* wagon since 1885, stayed on with the Swensons. He is there now . . . as much of the outfit almost, as the iron of the SMS.

One of the best brand authorities in all the State of Texas, one of the best among the top hands of all the West is Jake Raines—but still he can't see anything romantic about his profession.

"There ain't nothin' to it," he will say, in his slow drawl. "It's about th' sorriest business in th' world."

But just the same you'll always find him at the non-professional rodeo which Bill Swenson, assistant manager, conducts each year at Stamford for the boys who make their living at the cattle punchers trade.

LIT
BRAND
THE PRAIRIE

BRAND
S. M. SWENSON
RANCH

BRAND
THE SPUR

*Grazing on the open range—in the land west of the Pecos*

Photograph by W. D. Smithers

# Protection

# Men

Ed Bomar

● Fast thinking, quick drawing, straight shooting—they were the nemesis of cattle thieves and an important factor in private law and order

"Pink" Higgins

U SUALLY he was a quiet sort of individual, oft-times small in stature and possessed with a certain shyness not wholly in keeping with the heavy Colt which dangled at one hip . . . and sometimes both.

There was nothing about him to suggest recklessness. He was as a rule, just one of the boys; a mild-mannered fellow who might give you, if he thought you needed it, the shirt from his back—but there was something in his eyes and general bearing which marked him apart from other men, something which seemed to command a certain respect and hint that here was a man with whom it would not be healthy to trifle.

Such was the "protection man" on the early ranches of the *Llano Estacado*. He was a factor just as important and necessary as the bronc buster and the herder, especially on those greater kingdoms whose ranges, stretching many lonely miles

Photograph by Erwin E. Smith

*Turning in*

into nowhere, furnished a happy hunting ground for the prowling cow thief.

The "protection man," or cattle detective, as he was sometimes called, carried his only authority in his holsters and during the term of his employment he had but one great mission in life—to patrol the ranges, find as many rustlers as he could, and kill them where he found them.

The Spur, like other great cattle kingdoms on the Plains, once had such a man . . .

Bill Standifer was born in Lampasas, and in the day and time—more than seventy years ago—the little town down in South-Central Texas was not a place that the Epworth League might choose as a convention city. Indeed, the social life of the community centered more behind the swinging doors of the Lampasas saloon than behind the portals of the First Methodist Church; and since the town's principal industry moved on the hoof it was not at all unusual to hear that business transactions involving several brands had been concluded with a sixshooter rather than with the more conventional pen.

In the mild atmosphere of this up-and-coming community Bill Standifer spent his early years. His mother died while he was yet a lad and his father married again, forming a connection with the famous Horrel family—which in the '70's was all but obliterated in a feud with the family and followers of one Pink Higgins.

There is nothing in the record to indicate that Bill had any active part in this feud, which originated over livestock matters, but it is no secret that his sympathies, as he watched from the side lines, were with the faction to which his step-mother belonged . . . a sentiment which later was to have an important bearing on Standifer's life.

Young Billy did not launch his colorful career until the summer of 1879, after going to Tom Green county to take employment on the ranch of Ike Mullins.

The small, dark-haired, brown-eyed kid from Lampasas had been working with Mr. Mullins but a few months when he became involved in an argument with John Mahan, a Gonzales gentleman who had journeyed into the Tom Green country to join in the general spring roundup.

Standifer was holding cattle in a pasture through which Mahan wanted to bring a few strays he had collected, and

Standifer refused to give way. Hot words passed between the two, and Mahan, seeing his way blocked by a mere youth . . . and a quiet and apparently shy youth at that—tried bluff.

"Kid," he said, "I'm a mind to get down and whip the daylights outa you. Think I will," he added, reaching for a heavy blacksnake whip he carried on his saddle.

"Then light, and git started," replied Bill, throwing himself from his own saddle and crooking his right elbow back until his fingers were within a few inches of his gun butt.

"Take it easy, kid," drawled another voice and Standifer turned to find himself gazing into the muzzle of a Winchester. The rifle was held in the hands of a companion of Mahan who, having heard the argument, had ridden up to see what the trouble was about. "Git down, John, and let him have it," said the gentleman. "I'll keep him covered."

### He quit his job because he had a man to kill

That whipping, carried out under the menace of the Winchester did somthing to Billy Standifer. He had to take it . . . take it or die . . . but as the whip snaked across his back, cutting long, bloody welts, he promised himself that there would be another verse.

When he recovered sufficient strength to mount his horse he rode home and told Mullins. "Ike," he said, "I'm quittin'. I gotta kill a man . . . an' I aint' aimin' to lose no time."

Mullins tried to dissuade him from such a course; warned him that he'd get himself into a mess of trouble but young Billy was determined.

"Trouble, hell!" he said. "You wouldn't talk that way if your back was sore as mine!"

And so Bill Standifer, mounted on a horse Mullins had given him, rode away to join the roundup, which was working just then through Tom Green and Runnels counties. Eight or nine outfits were in the field, gathering up strays and branding new calves, and the young man from Lampasas knew that Mahan, if he remained in the county, would be somewhere about.

He made a good guess, for within a week . . . scarcely before the welts on his back had healed . . . he found his man. The meeting was on Pony Creek and both men were mounted. Mahan, talking with a small group of punchers, failed to notice the approach of his enemy and was unaware of impending trouble until Bill reined in a few yards away.

Photograph by Erwin E. Smith
*Day herder in for lunch*

"Mahan," said Standifer, quietly, "Git ready . . . we're goin' to do a little shootin'."

Something in his voice told the Gonzales man what he was up against and as he wheeled his horse he drew and let go a snap shot. The lead went wild.

Bill fired as he brought the heavy Colt up from the holster, and he had more luck than his opponent . . . the bullet ripped an ugly hole through the wrist of Mahan's gun hand. It was a fluke shot, but it probably saved the life of the peeler who later was to become thief chaser for the Spurs.

Mahan was helpless now . . . as helpless as Billy had been under the muzzle of the Winchester . . . and as his revolver dropped from his numbed fingers he made one last bid for his life.

"You wouldn't shoot an unarmed man, would you?"

"You didn't show me any favors when you laid on the whip." replied Standifer. "But maybe you've forgotten that."

Again something in the younger man's voice warned Mahan. He flicked his bridle reins, kicked in his spurs, and turned to flee—but Standifer, anticipating such a move, was after him. Mahan made 600 yards before Bill got him. The first shot downed the horse, the second drilled through the fugitive's back. Mahan was dead before his body struck the ground.

Standifer left that night with a trail herd bound for Marfa, and his back felt better . . . much better . . . as he rode toward the Big Bend.

We next find him in a saloon near the frontier town of Fort Davis. He had gone there with some of his fellows for the purpose of making merry, but after two days of varied liquor absorption he had remembered that food sometimes becomes a necessary evil. He had just seated himself comfortably at the table when three negro troopers walked in.

"That's him," said one of the troopers. "He was in here raisin' hell last night. He's the man the Rangers want for that Runnels shootin'."

Standifer put aside his feeding tools and reached for his holster. He fired but two shots on his way out, but he left two negroes on the floor of the saloon. He vanished into the night and the trans-Pecos country saw him no more.

The Rangers finally caught Bill up in the lower Plains country. They took him down to Coleman and put him on trial for the murder of Mahan, but the jury, upon hearing that Mahan had fired the first shot, called it a clear-cut case of self-defense. Bill was acquitted, and since the two negro troopers had recovered, he was free to go.

When Standifer reached the lower Panhandle country, in the latter part of 1880, he found that his reputation as a gun slinger had preceded him. He worked a while with various cow outfits, killed a rustler near Estacado, and in time answered the call of the citizenry to become the sheriff of Crosby county.

Bill was small . . . he weighed less than one hundred and forty pounds . . . but he made one of the best sheriffs Crosby county ever had.

Take, for instance, the time the postoffice at Dockums, Dickens County, was looted by two thieves. Since Dickens was attached to Crosby for judicial purposes, Bill saddled a horse and started on the trail of the culprits. He thought he knew where to look and he headed toward New Mexico. With him went Charlie Quillen, a deputy.

### A gun fight in a dugout on the New Mexican Plains

In those days state or territorial lines did not matter as much as they do today, and Bill went across, made his arrests and started on the return trip to Texas. The prisoners were hard cases, two of the toughest appearing hombres Standifer and Quillen had ever seen, and Bill thought it might be wise to adopt his suggestion that the pair be shackled.

In the evening of the first day on the trail the four arrived at a dugout which a settler and his wife were occupying on the bleak New Mexican plains. The settler asked the officers to spend the night, and after supper, while Standifer and the settler were outside, the prisoners persuaded Quillen to remove the shackles "for a spell" that they might rest their cramped limbs. The irons were no sooner off than one of the men floored Quillen with a blow of his fist, then grabbed the deputy's rifle.

Quillen yelled and jumped to his feet—to get a Winchester slug through his body just above his heart. Seriously wounded though he was, the deputy went after the man, grappled with him and forced him to the floor. The settler's wife, who had been slightly wounded by the rifle ball, screamed.

Meanwhile the other prisoner had grabbed a double-barreled shotgun Standifer had left against the dugout wall. He pulled back the right hand hammer and was aiming for a pot shot at Quillen when Bill, hearing the commotion, pushed open the dugout door . . . to find himself looking into the barrels of his own weapon.

The range was much too short to miss, and Standifer, as he stood in the dugout door, set himself to take a charge of buckshot from a shell which he, himself, had loaded. The prisoner squeezed down on the trigger. The hammer fell, but . . . the gun missed fire!

"Well, I'll be damned!" excalimed Bill, as he wrenched the weapon from the man's hands and used it to knock him flat. "And I loaded those shells myself!"

There are men living today who knew Standifer well, and who often heard him tell of the incident, and they will tell you that Bill never ceased to marvel at that miracle in the dugout . . . that even if the fault saved his life, his inefficiency in loading the shell hurt his pride.

After subduing the prisoners Standifer and the settler gave their attention to the dressing of Quillen's wound, a small hole half an inch above the heart. They did the best they could, but as the deputy grew steadily weaker from loss of blood Standifer prepared to take the trail. He told the deputy he would hurry on with the prisoners, find a doctor as soon as possible and send him to the dugout. He rode away—the feet of the prisoners tied under the horses they were riding.

The sheriff reached Dickens county, sent aid to Quillen, and then discovered, much to his discomfiture, that his two captives were not the postoffice robbers at all. Those two gentlemen, the actual thieves, had been captured shortly after Standifer's departure for New Mexico, but—the men he brought home turnd out to be worse than the other two. They were wanted on half a dozen robbery counts in various places, and on two charges of murder. In that there was some consolation.

Quillen survived, and within a few weeks was back in Dickens.

"He often wore the coat with the bullet hole in the left breast," says Colonel R. P. Smyth of Plainview, "and when I was surveying in that country during the '80's I've looked across the table at that coat many a time...and I always wondered at Charlie being alive."

Standifer, while sheriff, made several trips to New Mexico. Once, while bringing back a prisoner whose feet were tied together under the horse he rode, Bill stopped at the lonely camp of a young cowboy in what is now Hockley county.

"It was on a stretch which later became a part of the old Spade Ranch," says J. Frank Norfleet of Hale Center. "I was just a young line-rider then and Billy wanted me to guard the prisoner while he got some sleep. I remember how the fellow cussed Standifer and called him a coward, and how Billy left his bed, came over to the prisoner, looked down at him, and said: 'So I'm a coward, am I? I suppose you're a brave man, because when I walked up to your dugout where you were hiding with four buckets of water and half a dozen guns, you came out when I told you to...and you came out with your hands up.' Bill Standifer was a brave man—as fearless as they came."

"And generous to a fault," adds Jim Standifer, a cousin

who still lives in Plainview. "He'd give you the shirt off his back if he thought you needed it."...Or a slug of lead if you stole a cow from the herd he was hired to protect. He could be generous about that, too, and that's why the Spur manager hired him off and on when cow thieves would cut in on the herds...off and on" because the thieves would lose no time in vacating the range of the Spurs when they heard that Billy Standifer was working. Thus Bill, more often than not, worked himself out of a job without ever "bustin' a cartridge".

### The Bartenders stocked up when the roundups began

At times when he wasn't working as a detective he usually found employment as a wagon-boss at spring round-ups, and during one of these periods a peculiar thing occurred—an incident which still is discussed in the cow camps of the Panhandle because it reveals one side of the cowboy's character which seldom reaches the outer world.

It was round-up time on the broad stretches of the *Llano Estacado*. Eight or nine outfits were working together, rounding up herds on the open range, each outfit cutting out and holding cattle in its own particular brand—taking, so to speak, the annual inventory.

The big spring get-together had started on the Conhco, had worked north to Colorado City, and then had moved on up to Snyder. At that time, 1883, Snyder, formerly a buffalo camp, could hardly be termed a city. It boasted two or three small houses and one saloon—the proprietor of which made mighty preparations when he heard that the 'punchers were headed north. He freighted in additional stocks of whisky and beer...for he knew that 150 tired and dusty cowboys could put away a sizeable amount of liquid refreshments. They always did.

But let Bill Meador, one of Captain Arrington's old rangers, tell the story. He was there that day with the JD outfit.

The wagon of Felix Franklin had been the first to arrive, it being closely followed by the outfits of Frank Cooksey and Bill Standifer.  Franklin, being a little more impatient . . . and thirsty . . . than his fellows, had hurried on to the oasis and had refreshed himself generously before the rest of the round-up crew reached the saloon.

Soon the hitching rail was full, making it necessary for late arrivals to twist their reins over the saddle horns of mounts already at the rack.  A good-sized "remuda" had been assembled in this fashion as Felix decided to desert the bar and seek the open air.  He came out whooping and as he reached the hitching rail, he jerked out his six-shooter and let go a volley under the hoofs of the horses.  A few of the animals, never too gentle, pulled loose and ran.

Bill Standifer, who had just slipped out of his saddle, was walking toward the saloon.

"Hey, Felix, stop it," he said.  "There ain't no call for all this cussin' an' raisin' hell.  There's some women . . . respectable women . . . in that house over there."

"Who are you to tell me what I can't do?" shouted Franklin, firing a couple more shots under the hoofs of the Standifer horses, and then reloading.

Standifer stopped.

"You're not as drunk as you make out," he said.  "Quiet down."

"You can't say that to me," said Franklin.

He started walking toward Bill, gun in hand.  The crowd grew tense, and there wasn't a man in all the round-up crew that didn't edge back a step or two.  But Standifer held his ground, his elbow slightly crooked.

"Felix," he said, as calm as a man in church, "don't you have a mother and sisters?"

"Yes."

"Then you *don't respect them* . . . if you don't respect the women in that house over there."

A hundred men stood waiting . . . and then Felix turned on his boot heel and walked away. But he did not re-enter the saloon; he walked toward his wagon.

"I went into the saloon with the rest of the JD boys," recalled Bill Meador, "but not a word was spoken. We lined up to the bar and had a round of drinks, and then we all walked out again to go to our own wagons. And there was no drinking in the bar that night. I don't think there was ever anything quite like it, before or since. There was something in what Billy Standifer said that went through that whole crowd . . . something that made them think of home . . . of when they were kids . . . and I'll tell you it was pretty lonesome out there on the Plains that night."

It was "pretty lonesome," too, for the bartender in Snyder's only saloon. He wore the face of a man who had suddenly encountered one of the more baffling mysteries of life; and his only comment was that "this is the damnedest round-up I ever heard tell of."

The late '80's and the '90's found Bill Standifer working "on and off" for the Spurs—on the payrolls for intervals long enough to put a scare into the hearts of those who looked with envious eyes upon another man's cows. His deeds in this particular phase of private law enforcement were never fully recorded, but there is evidence in the Spur records that he did his work well.

In the late '90's, during a particularly bad epidemic of cattle rustling, he had a partner—by a peculiar coincidence none other than Pink Higgins, late of Lampasas.

It was not in the cards that these two men, though their business interests were the same, should hit it off in perfect friendship. There was that old matter of the Horrel-Higgins feud, and it must be borne in mind that Standifer's sympathies

had been with the Horrel faction. Their differences, naturally, branched out into other channels, and there arrived a
time when it became obvious that one range would hardly be
enough for both men.

**"I regret to report a killing which took place on our range..."**

They began working separately, but it was inevitable that
they should meet at intervals; and at such time the words
which passed between them did not make phrases of brotherly
love. One day, in September, 1902, they met on a lonely
stretch of range—but let Fred Horsbrugh, manager of the
Spur at that time, complete the story. Following is the report
he mailed to the Spur's London office on October 6, 1902:

*I regret to report a killing that took place on our range
in Kent county some days ago. It resulted from an old grudge
existing between two men that I had watching cow thieves,
and they had so far been very successful in putting down
stealing. But they happened to have an old grudge between
them individually. When I found it out I made them both
understand that they were no good to me if they were not
friendly to each other, as their usefulness depended on their
relations one to the other. They fully promised to make it
all up and let by-gones be by-gones. Later it broke out again
and I turned them both off. Standifer, I turned off in August
and Higgins later. Higgins asked me to let him stay until
the end of September as he had some arrangements to make
about moving his family and children to a place where they
could attend school. I told him a month did not matter. I
was startled to get a message over the phone from Clairemont,
Kent county, last Saturday that Standifer had returned, and
he and Higgins had a meeting, and that Standifer was killed.
Later accounts show it to have been a premeditated (and mut-
tually arranged for) duel. They both had rifles and Higgins'
horse was killed the first shot. Standifer was shot twice, dy-*

*ing instantly. Higgins gave himself up to the sheriff at Clairemont, and I fancy will come clear on the plea of self-defense. I thought I had the whole thing settled quietly. But, of course, the returning of Standifer could have only one meaning for a jury. They were both fearless, determined men, and each had similar trouble before; and they were really the means of scaring out some of the worst cow-thieves we had.*

Pink Higgins lived awhile longer—to die of heart disease.

"Similar trouble before" . . . as Mr. Horsbrugh put it? Yes, there had been some little difficulties, but the record of Pink Higgins as to feudal enemies and cattle rustlers is just a bit vague in spots. Once, when I asked a son for enlightenment on the subject, this was the reply:

"Well . . . papa was indicted fourteen times, but I really think the count was nearer seventeen or eighteen."

# Ten
# in
# Texas

TEXAS STATE CAPITOL

AB BLOCKER

● The largest state capitol in the United States was built by the XIT ranch in exchange for 3,000,000 acres of land

IF railroad shipping clerks expressed surprise over the bill of lading for a certain big boxcar which traveled westward toward Kansas in the late 1880's they had a perfect right to do so—for the content listing was quite enough to shock the most hardened veteran of the transportation trade.

319

*Noon-time—with one of the old-time Panhandle outfits*

The car was billed to B. H. Campbell of the Texas town of Channing, and at every handling point between its place of origin in the East and the destination in the Panhandle of Texas, it had stirred unusual interest.

Everybody, at least those who lived nearest the Panhandle, knew that the XIT did things in a big way; but this time the manager of the great cattle kingdom had excelled himself. All up and down the country people wondered as they heard the story—that "Barbecue" Campbell had bought a carload of brown cigarette papers!

There were some who took out their pencils and tried to calculate just how long such a supply should last, but even for an enterprise as wide of range as the XIT the figures didn't seem to make sense, and the mathematicians had to put aside the problem.

The XIT, its three million acres stretching over a 200-mile range southward along the New Mexico line from the top of the high Panhandle, was a little hard to figure from any standpoint. But those brown cigarette papers—which "Barbecue" would freight down from the nearest rail point to scattered storehouses over the ranch's divisions—would last a long time even if the 111,000 cattle on company pastures could join the scores of 'punchers in "rolling their own." That many papers would last a long while even if the same privilege could be extended to the cattle empire's hundreds of horses, the animals which had humped their backs and kicked up their heels in protest against wearing blankets previously bought for them by Campbell—also in a carload lot.

All of which goes to show that the XIT was a rather sizeable place. It spread over Hockley, Cochran, Lamb, Bailey, Castro, Parmer, Deaf Smith, Oldham, Hartley and Dallam counties—"Ten in Texas;" and that is how, according to one legend, that the brand originated. The truth makes quite a different story.

Behind the building of the XIT were numerous personalities but the principal factor back of the ranch, which at one time boasted the largest acreage of any in the Southwest, was the State of Texas itself.

A great stone of red granite, eight tons in weight, lay atop the little hill which stands at the head of Congress Avenue in Austin. The day was March 2, 1885, the 49th anniversary of Texas independence, and an undercurrent of excitement could be sensed in the crowd which had collected on the spot.

Derricks groaned, cranes creaked, and the great red stone —which had been pulled fifteen miles to Burnet by ox power and then shipped over a specially constructed rail line to Austin—swung slowly into place. Workmen busied themselves with mortar and trowels, and the cornerstone of the new State Capitol building was laid. Something else, too ... the foundation for an enormous ranch, the 3,000,000-acre XIT.

The XIT built the Texas State house, second largest in the nation; the State of Texas built the XIT; they were, after a fashion, twins. In this may be found partial support for the well known poetical statement that *"other states were carved or born; Texas was made of hoof and horn."*

### Three million acres set aside to pay for new capitol

Back before the turn of the '80's the State had more land than she could use, especially in the semi-arid regions of the west. This area was populated only by a mere handful of hardy gentlemen who, like Lot and Abram, had wandered far afield in quest of sufficient elbow room to properly follow the pursuits of cattle raising ... men content to leave to the settler the more productive lands of the east.

There were among the inhabitants of the east, however, certain men who believed that the more arid portions of the commonwealth might be employed to public advantage—thus a legislative act in 1879 setting aside 5,000,000 acres of land as the Capitol Reservation, 3,000,000 to be used in the interest of a new capitol building.

The Statehouse at Austin in those days was a fair structure, as buildings of that type go, but it hardly seemed pretentious enough for the largest state in the union; and so, after the land had been set aside, a committee, headed by Governor O. M. Roberts began work on plans for a survey of the tract.

Under the legislative program, 50,000 additional acres were to be sold to pay for the survey, which was to be carried out under the direction of N. L. Norton of Salado, recently appointed capitol land commissioner. Contract for the work afield was awarded to J. T. Munson; and, the fifty thousand acres having been sold for fifty-five and one-half cents an acre, surveying was started in the fall of 1879.

It was not until the early days of 1881, however, that the state advertised for building plans, and after eleven firms had submitted blueprints drawn to state specifications, the batch was forwarded to N. LeBrun, a New York architect, whose decision would be final. He chose a set of plans entered by E. E. Myers of Detroit, and on May 7 Mr. Norton and Joseph Lee, another commissioner, approved the selection.

Then, in November of 1881, the old capitol building caught fire and burned, a catastrophe which spurred the State to immediate action. On New Year's Day, 1882, bids were asked for the construction of the new building, it being stipulated that the winning contractor should receive as payment for his work 3,000,000 acres out of the Capitol Reservation. Two bids were received, and less than a fortnight later the contract was awarded to Mattheas Schnell of Rock Island, Illinois.

Schnell posted a bond of $250,000, and within a few weeks had assigned a three-fourths interest in the project to a Chicago wholesale dry goods firm, Taylor, Babcock & Company. The directors of this company, Abner Taylor, John V. Farwell, A. C. Babcock and Charles B. Farwell, were a trusting lot.

They went into the enterprise without seeing the land, merely taking Commissioner Norton's word that they were getting a good deal.

But as Abner Taylor came, south to take active charge of preparatory work . . . to build a railroad to Burnet county quarries pending the arrival of granite experts from Scotland . . . Mr. Babcock landed in the Panhandle town of Tascosa in an ambulance hack which he had borrowed, along with a wagon and other equipment, from the army post at Fort Elliott.

In Tascosa, Mr. Babcock looked up W. S. Mabry, a surveyor, hired a few cowboys as escort, and in March of 1882 started a "tour of the prairies" to inspect his firm's newly acquired property.

The country was somewhat different from what he had expected, and since he soon discovered that in the absence of wood, cow-chips furnished the only fuel supply, the Chicagoan congratulated himself on his foresight in bringing along an ample store of canned goods . . . for he could not bring himself to relish food cooked with "prairie coal."

But when the journey came to an end on April 27 at the *Casas Amarillas* (Yellow Houses) in Hockley county, he could look back over 1,000 miles of travel and consider himself pleased with what he had seen. He made his report to Chicago—advising his fellow directors to fence the land and stock it with cattle.

This meant, of course, a great outlay of money, but John Farwell thought he knew where he could get it. In the early weeks of 1885, about the time the cornerstone was being laid for the building which would make merchants into cattle barons, John Farwell went to England to visit business acquaintances.

To shorten a lengthy story, the voyage resulted in the creation of the Capitol Freehold Land and Investment Company, Ltd., with capital of approximately 3,000,000 pound sterling.

It listed as its overseas directors a group of men caught by the fever of western ranching—the Earl of Aberdeen; the Scottish Marquis of Tweeddale, governor of the Commercial Bank of Scotland; Lord Thurlow; Quinton Hogg; Edward M. Denny, merchant; Henry Seton-Karr, M. P.; and Sir William Ewart of Belfast, Ireland. The American section of the board included the Farwells, Abner Taylor, and Walter Potter, a Boston banker.

John Farwell was made managing director; and since the capitol building was under way and part of the land had been deeded over, headquarters were established at Buffalo Springs in the north Panhandle, and preparations went forward for the stocking of the ranch—which still remained without a name.

Farwell at once began casting about for a suitable manager, a man who knew cattle, and at last he decided on Col. B. H. Campbell, more familiarly known as "Barbecue" Campbell because of his personal brand—the BQ. Campbell came down from his home in Wichita, Kansas, and took over.

When it became known in the cattle country to the south that Barbecue Campbell was in the market for range herds, and had plenty of money to make his purchases, the dust began rising all along the trails to the Panhandle.

The first herd came in July, 1885, from the Fort Concho country. It was brought in by a well known trail driver, Ab Blocker, and old timers say that it was he who first suggested the XIT brand—because it would be hard for the rustler to blot, and because it could be put on the hides with a single-bar iron.

Campbell, so the story goes, told Ab that he wanted a three-letter brand that could be applied with one bar; and Blocker after a moment's thought cut an XIT into the dirt with his boot heel. "Get to brandin'," Campbell told his men.

Other drivers followed Blocker—Rachell Brothers from Re-

fugio County;  A. G. Boyce, boss driver for Snyder Bros.;  Gus
O'Keefe, foreman for C. C. Slaughter's Lazy S;  and others.

### Gus O' Keefe was a man who could drive a bargain

William Ragland, an expert in his line, did the age classifying for Campbell, and it is recorded in Evetts Haley's vol-
uminous story of the XIT that Mr. Ragland found in Gus
O'Keefe a man who could drive a hard bargain.  Mr. O'Keefe,
who in later years built the Blackstone Hotel in Fort Worth
and whose name still remains above the door of one of "cow
town's" largest transfer companies,  strenuously objected  to
Ragland's habit of classifying as yearlings steers long since past
that age, with the result that frequent arguments delayed the
buying.  Cowboys were kept busy throwing dozens of steers

Photograph by Erwin E. Smith
*L S Strayman, Bert Killion, headed for the XIT*

in order that O'Keefe and Ragland could settle their differences by an examination of the animal's teeth.

By November of 1886  the herd on the XIT range was

estimated at nearly 111,000 head.  The same fall saw more than 700 miles of fence stretched across the 200-mile range, now divided into seven divisions, with a foreman working each division under the direction of a general manager.

Beginning in the north, near the top of the Panhandle, the divisions were:  Buffalo Springs, Middle Water, *Ojo Bravo*, *Rito Blanco*, *Escarbada*, Spring Lake, and *Las Casas Amarillas*. The latter (so named because certain cliffs in that region, when viewed from a distance,  took on the appearance of "yellow houses") was the more southerly division, its range to the west of the present city of Lubbock.

On each division Campbell put up barns, bunk houses, and store rooms—those same store rooms which housed for many, many years (among other things) "Barbecue's" enormous supply of brown cigarette papers.

Meanwhile, work on the capitol building at Austin had been progressing, and at intervals the State was deeding additional land to "the syndicate".  In 1887  the greater part of the three million-acre tract had been transferred over, but it was in that year that the owners and Barbecue Campbell came to a parting of the ways.

The complaints against Barbecue involved a great many angles—including, perhaps,  things like cigarette papers and horse blankets—and the syndicate suddenly decided to place A. L. Matlock, an attorney, in charge.  Matlock, a former legislator, went up to the ranch.  He "cleaned house", turning off dozens of men who had worked under Campbell.  A. G. Boyce was brought in as range foreman and he entered so enthusiastically into the house cleaning that some of the disgruntled former employes moved across the line to New Mexico and retaliated by raiding across the line to lift XIT steers from the Syndicate pastures.

Boyce, however, knew how to cope with the situation.  He hired many new men, some of whom could handle a gun with more skill than they could swing a rope. For instance, he made a former Texas Ranger, Ira Aten, foreman of the *Escarbada* division, and one of Mr. Aten's first official acts was to send for two former associates in the old Frontier Battalion, Wood Saunders, and Ed Connell, both known to be quick with the hammer thumb and the trigger finger.

A constant patrol was maintained on fence lines, and as the thieving from the westward side continued it became a custom among the riders to shoot first and then ask questions when anyone was seen on the New Mexico side of the XIT.

Photograph by Erwin E. Smith
*X I T puncher Davis calls the next night guard.*

The methods of Boyce differed in many ways from those of his predecessor. He required foremen and wagon bosses of the various divisions to make written records concerning every stranger who passed through or was seen near their ranges; and he required each foreman to keep his cattle within the

bounds of his own division and make monthly reports of the
condition of cattle, water and grass.

He made enemies, especially among the old hands he had
turned away, but he was careful to keep a gun always within
easy reach . . . and though firearms seldom were needed except
to frighten away prowlers he did as much as any man in the
Panhandle to discourage the promiscuous rustling of that day.

Boyce still sat in the saddle at the ranch when the capitol
building at Austin was completed by the Syndicate in April of
1888. The structure cost Taylor and the Farwells more than
they had estimated, $3,224,593.45 instead of a round $1,500,-
000, but they gave Texas a building 311 feet tall, 566 feet
long, and 280 feet wide. The Capitol Freehold Land and
Investment Company had its three million acres of land, well
stocked by this time with approximately 125,000 cattle . . .

And that is the story behind the building of America's
largest state capitol . . . and one of the largest ranches the
world has ever known. Today, however, the former is merely
a monument to the latter enterprise.

Through liquidation of bonds the English investment company finally passed from the picture, and in the late '90's,
when the agriculturists began drifting into the country in ever
increasing numbers, the XIT began selling off. The larger
tracts were disposed of during the first decade of the new century, and the cattle were sold. Boyce retired as manager after
the sell-off was started and was replaced by H. S. Boice, who
continued the work of gradual disposal.

Today the branding iron which once was coat-of-arms for
"ten counties in Texas" is a historic relic, nothing more. The
ranch has no cattle, and as for land Judge James D. Hamlin,
resident representative of the owners of the XIT for the past
thirty years, counts only 325,000 acres, of which about 175,-
000 lies adjacent to the far West Texas town of Farwell, and

150,000 acres near the town of Dalhart in the extreme north-western portion of the Panhandle.

"Ten in Texas" now is little better than a myth and the comparatively large grazing ranches which the XIT maintained in Montana in the time of Boyce have all but been forgotten.

But up in the Panhandle may be found men who remember

Photograph by Erwin E. Smith
*Harry Patton*

the days of the greater XIT, and they can furnish some idea of the vastness of that range in the period.

### How one XIT Puncher was elected to the legislature

Colonel R. P. Smyth of Plainview, who helped survey a part of the land and who once lived on the *Escarbada*, likes to tell of the time in 1896 when he was engaged in building dams and tanks for the XIT in the Canadian River valley near the New Mexico line, and his story furnishes an idea of how remote some corners of that giant cattle empire could be.

It was near Christmas time in '96 when a cowboy chanced to find Smyth working in the valley, and since Smyth had not seen a man for more than a month he was glad to welcome a visitor.

"Bet you didn't know that you've been elected to the legislature," said the puncher. "They'll be wantin' you to come out soon and go down to Austin."

Smyth, who later was to put through the Four-Sections Act permitting settlers to take up four sections of land instead of one, hadn't heard about it, although he was aware that he had won the nomination at Childress in the summer.

"No, I didn't know it," said the man who soon would be representing thirty-six counties in the building the Syndicate had constructed, "but what about the President . . . who was elected?"

The cowboy appeared perplexed. He studied hard for a moment as he tried to recall election returns, and then he gave his answer.

"The President?" he repeated. "The President? . . . damned if I didn't forget to look!"

And then, to cover his embarrassment, he rolled himself a cigarette—in one of "Barbecue's" brown papers.

*Action . . . . this little 'dogie' is due for a fall*

Photograph by W. D. Smithers

# D. Waggoner
# and Son

DANIEL WAGGONER

THOMAS WAGGONER

● "—A man who doesn't admire a good beef steer, a good horse, and a pretty woman... well, something is wrong with that man's head."—Tom Waggoner.

THE corn crop had been good that year, the best Wise County had known in many seasons. The leaves were thick and the stalks were tall, and for this the woman from the little house under Cactus Hill

333

was more than thankful as she lay in the edge of the field, her nervous hands clutching the stock of a heavy-bore rifle. The corn made an excellent place in which to hide.

Beside the woman lay a child, a very small boy who gazed in wakeful wonder at the yellow tassels which danced in the moonlight and flicked small shadows across his face.

Once a dog yelped in the clump of trees behind the house and the boy sat up to ask about the sound, but his mother's hand reached out to push him gently but firmly back to earth.

"Hush, Tom!" she whispered. "Hush . . . it is nothing but the dog. Go to sleep now."

She could have told him something else; something about the silent, slinking shadows which moved about the house, but she didn't . . . for she was aware that little Tom already knew. This was not the first time the Indians had come down in the light of the moon to prowl the settlements. The lad had slept in the corn rows before—at times when his father was away.

He wondered about his father now, wondered when he would be home; and then, as the tassels flicked new shadows across his face, he fell asleep. The woman spread a shawl across him, and again took up the rifle . . .

Dawn revealed that the slinking figures of the night had been something more than mere shadows. A mare was dead, and likewise the dog whose yelp had disturbed young Tom—both animals drilled through with the shaft of a Comanche arrow.

The mother, as she surveyed this loss, also wondered when her husband would return from the Indian trail he had been following to the west. She was tired of the corn field and the sleepless all-night vigils with the rifle in her hands.

Little Thomas Waggoner was scarcely more than a baby in those days, the late 1850's, but already he was certain of one thing—that his father was a very great man. Did he

not own more cattle than any man in the country? Did he not own more land than any among his few neigbors? Well...
15,000 acres was a sizeable tract for that section of frontier North Texas; and, considering the constant menace from marauding red-skins, he was a fortunate man who could keep intact a herd of 200 cattle. Dangerous days, but in the face of threats to life and property, Daniel Waggoner held on.

Born in Lincoln County, Tennessee, July 7, 1828, Daniel had migrated to Texas during his late 'teens with the family of his father, Solomon Waggoner, a farmer and stock raiser. The family first settled in Hopkins County, where Daniel helped his father farm until old Solomon's death in 1848. Then he met and married Miss Nancy Moore, and on August 31, 1852, the union was blessed with a son, who was given the name of William Thomas.

Meanwhile the young husband already had been looking toward the future. He had saved enough money to buy 242 head of longhorns and six horses and, with the help of a fifteen-year-old negro slave boy, he drove down into Wise County in search of a favorable ranch location. He halted his herd near the site of the present town of Decatur, in those days just a tiny frontier settlement. Then, after establishing his small family in a new home, he began considering the purchase of new land.

Two years later he was located on a 15,000-acre tract on the Trinity River near Cactus Hill, about eighteen miles west of Decatur... near the present site of Lake Bridgeport. To this place, which old-timers still call the "West Fork Pasture", Daniel Waggoner moved 200 additional head of cattle purchased from George Isabel... and it was this herd which helped form a nucleus for one of the greater ranch kingdoms, the *Zacaquiesta*.

### Dan Waggoner helped chase First Americans in Texas

A less courageous man than Dan Waggoner, tall and blue-eyed, might have abandoned the Cactus Hill place after the first half year, but as the Indians grew too bold he merely muttered beneath his full beard, saddled a horse and took the trail with his rifle.

In company with others he helped chase bands of "first Americans" all over North Texas, and once, while on an expedition into Parker County, he was at the Gilden Ranch home when it was attacked by sixteen Comanche braves. Seven men, Gilden, Waggoner, William Graham, Ben Blanton, Lansing Hunt, Bill Russell and George Buchanan, were in the house at the time, and as they rushed out to repel the attack in a brief skirmish Gilden and Buchanan were wounded by arrows. Waggoner played the role of doctor, and so expertly did he remove the arrows and dress the wounds that both men recovered.

It was from such skirmishes as this that he would return home to learn that his wife and young Tom had been forced to hide in the cornfield; and at last, fearing for their safety, he moved back to Denton Creek in Wise County.

But regardless of trouble from savage raiders the herd continued to grow until there came a time when it was possible to count in four figures the steers whose right hips wore the burn of the letter D, which stood for Dan.

William Thomas still was quite a small boy when his mother died. He went to live at the nearby home of his father's sister, Sarah, later Mrs. T. B. Yarbrough, but even with this change of residence he was with his father a great deal. A great understanding grew between the two. The father, sensing that he had become something of an idol in the eyes of his son, discussed with him all the problems of livestock and ranching, took him on short rides across the range, allowed him to help in the branding pen.

And so there is really nothing remarkable in the fact that the lad, by the time he had reached his fourteenth year, already had outlined in his own mind the future course of his ambition—"to run the best cow outfit, own the best horses, and do the most work of any man in the country."

In his own son, Daniel Waggoner was developing a greater cattleman than himself.

Just before the War between the States the elder Waggoner had taken a second wife—Miss Scylly Ann Halsell, daughter of a pioneer Wise County family— and he began making preparations to extend his domain.

The close of the war, however, had brought added troubles. Taking advantage of a frontier left virtually unprotected by reason of the civil conflict, the Indians became increasingly bolder in their raids on the settlements, and 1866 found Daniel Waggoner and his heavy rifle on many trails.

But this time he could ride forth without worrying over events at home. Young Tom was a man now, and could do a man's work—at fourteen.

The boy himself saw action for the first time at the age of seventeen, while the Waggoners and the Halsells were wintering and shaping up a herd on the Little Wichita. The Indians made a lightning raid in the night and Tom, standing guard over the restless longhorns, saw spurts of flame stab the darkness as rifles popped on the other side of the herd. When he could leave his post and ride around he found three of his companions bending over a mortally wounded man . . . his uncle, George Halsell.

It was this herd of cattle on the Little Wichita that laid the financial foundation for the great enterprise about to be born, for in the spring of the following year, 1870, Tom Waggoner and a few picked hands drove the steers up the trail to Kansas City, and came home with $55,000 in the saddle bags.

D. Waggoner & Son—the business was being operated under that title now—made good use of the money. The younger partner began buying more cattle, at $8 a head. The following

*Music by the campfire*

Photograph by Erwin E. Smith

spring he drove again to the northern market and sold, at $30 a head.

The profits made possible the acquisition of more land. The Waggoners started buying in Wilbarger, Foard, Wichita, Baylor, Archer and Knox counties. As new herds were fattened and sold and more property added to the private map of the cattleman, people began wondering if D. Waggoner & Son intended buying all the real estate in the north of Texas.

"No," the father once said in answer to a question, "I don't aim to buy it all ... just what joins me."

Anyhow the range spread outward into hundreds of thousands of acres. The herds grew ... five thousand, ten thousand, fifteen ... with the Waggoners traveling the country to buy and pay off from a pack horse loaded with gold.

But now, as the new cattle were purchased, the red-hot D iron was going onto each animal's hide three times, with the letter reversed. The single D had been too easy for thieves to burn into something entirely different.

Concerning the reversal of the letter there are different stories. Some say that it occurred when a blacksmith, in forging the iron, made the D backward by mistake and that Dan Waggoner adopted it because he considered it a distinctive mark—but the late Tom Yarbrough, former president of the First National Bank in Fort Worth, and a nephew of Dan, had a different version. The D, he said, was made backward not because of any mistake in forging the iron, but because the reversed letter is easier to see and recognize when looking at a cow from the front.

The '80's and the early '90's found the Three-D the best known cattle "coat-of-arms" in the northern section of the State. Headquarters were near Decatur, but the steers ... into which Hereford blood was being infused—were ranging over half a dozen counties, nibbling at the grass as far north as the present towns of Vernon and Electra.

Meanwhile, Tom Waggoner had married. One day in 1877 he had hitched to the buggy his two sorrel horses, Baldy and Charger, and had driven over to the home of Electious Halsell, where he had been a frequent visitor. He brought home as a bride one of the Halsell daughters, Miss Ella, a young sister of his stepmother.

*Draw one! Drinking wasn't permitted as a rule on the ranches, but sometimes in the slack seasons they brought a keg and some "factory ice" out from town.*

D. Waggoner & Son now began branching out on an even more extensive scale. They acquired an interest in the First National Bank of Decatur; and since their herds, by the middle '80's, made necessary the acquisition of more grass, they went into the Comanche-Kiowa country of the Indian Territory to lease from the Government and the tribes more than 600,000 acres of land.

### Jimmie Roberts carried his authority in his holsters

Those were troublesome days in the Territory. Other outfits, employing from a dozen to half a hundred men, were in

the Indian Territory on pastures ranging from 50,000 to 600,-
000 acres. The Waggoner wagons had as immediate neighbors
the outfits of Burk Burnett, Cal Sugg, and C. T. Herring,
and all were being victimized by cow thieves.

The Indians carried away a few head from time to time,
but the white rustlers did the great damage, and this was a
situation which called for the services of men who knew what
to do and how to do it.

D. Waggoner & Son had scores of men on the pay roll at
this time but none fitted better into the Territory situation
than a young and almost beardless gentleman who had ridden
up to Waggoner headquarters one day looking for work.

"A tow-headed kid of seventeen," said Mr. Yarbrough,
who heard the story many times from Dan Waggoner, "and
he was carrying a rifle on his saddle, two six-shooters at his
waist, and a shotgun in his hands. Uncle Dan asked him to
light and come in, and he did . . . but he brought his revolvers
and his shotgun with him. Mr. Waggoner said he had to do
a lot of talking to get him to put the shotgun aside . . . but
that day Jimmie Roberts became a Waggoner peeler, one of
the best hands the Three-D's ever had."

He was, according to Mr. Yarbrough, a small and almost
shy man whose quiet speech carried a slight lisp, but even so,
he could, when occasion demanded, match the more fiery
phrases of the King's English with anyone who spoke.

"I once heard Harry Halsell ask Roberts why he didn't
stop cussing," said Mr. Yarbrough, "and Jimmie explained
that before he learned to cuss he had had to shoot six or seven
men who had cussed him.

"But" added the banker, "he was really peace-loving and
a man of great honor, though he had one of the toughest
jobs—that of checking passing herds and cutting out steers
which carried the Three-D brand. Wandering thieves in the

Comanche country learned to respect Waggoner cows after
Roberts had shot one or two out of the saddle . . ."

The loyalty of top hands like Roberts went a long way in
helping Tom Waggoner realize his boyhood ambition of "running the best cow outfit in the country", and there are veterans
of those days who still remember what Jimmie said to W. T.
when the two were riding one day across the Comanche range,
expecting at any time to bump into a gang of thieves which
had been working on the herds.

"If we find 'em," said Roberts, "you stay back out of the
way . . . you have a family.  So just leave this business to me . . .
I'll get 'em all."

But the thieves, if they were abroad that day, did not appear.
Perhaps they knew who rode the range . . .

The "big pasture" in the Indian country couldn't last forever.  There came a day, at the turn of the century, when
new space was needed for the overflow population from the
civilized East.  The Government decided to open the Comanche country to settlers and homesteaders.  The cattlemen were
told to hitch their chuck and hoodlum wagons, saddle their
mounts, gather up their stock, and get out.

The Waggoners, the Burnetts, the Suggs, the Herrings and
others moved back across the Texas line, leaving hundreds of
miles of wire fence that had cost them many a good hard
dollar.

Tom Waggoner now was the leading light in a great cattle
enterprise which was running approximately 60,000 head, but
nothing on earth could have tempted him to make a change
in the wording carried on the firm's bank drafts—"D. Waggoner & Son".  The passing years had only served to increase
his worship of his father, whose age was forcing a less active
participation in the business.

The son already had realized the major part of his ambition.  He had one of the best cow outfits in the country, he

was doing as much work as any man, and he soon would be able to claim ownership of the best horses. Already he was acquiring thoroughbreds ... to build up his cow pony stock, to race on state tracks, and to enter in private contests with his cattleman neighbor, Burk Burnett of the Four Sixes.

Photograph by Erwin E. Smith

*Coming to dinner*

And then occurred a thing which any other man might have considered a favor direct from the gods. On the range near Electra, the town Tom Waggoner had founded and had named for his daughter, water was needed for cattle, and an experimental deep well was being put down. But the hole began filling with oil when at a depth of 2,000 feet. W. T. Waggoner was not pleased.

"Oil!" he said in disgust. "What do I want with oil? I'm looking for water. That's what the cattle need."

He finally had to admit, however, that the stuff, diluted to some extent, made fairly good "tick dip." And that is what ranchers from round about the country used it for during the next few years. They brought wagons to the well and hauled it away in barrels ... courtesy D. Waggoner & Son.

However, the disappointment over finding greasy petroleum rather than sparkling water was but a little thing compared with the grief which was about to overtake the boss of the Three-D's. In September of the following year, 1904, his father died in Colorado Springs, where he had gone in the hope of recovering his failing health.

**He admired a good steer, good horse, and a pretty woman**

The passing of Daniel Waggoner was a great blow to the son.  The younger partner was now 52 years of age, but in his love for his father he still was that small boy who sought safety from the Indians in the corn that grew near Cactus Hill.

Ask any old-timer ever connected with the Three-D's and he will tell you that no man ever worshipped a father more than W. T. Waggoner ... and in the town of Decatur they still like to tell a story illustrative of this sentiment.

Many years after the elder Waggoner's death, when it became necessary to issue new stock after a loss sustained by their bank,  the son went down into his pocket for all the $66,000 assessment on the stockholders—just because he wanted to keep the original stock, which carried his father's signature.  It was a high price to pay for sentiment, $40,000 more than his share,  but W. T. didn't mind at all.  Tom Waggoner himself is dead now, but the accounts of the estate in that bank still are carried as "D. Waggoner & Son," and the drafts still carry a signed picture of the father.

Perhaps it was the death of Daniel that caused the younger Waggoner to neglect development of that discovery oil well near Electra; perhaps it was because the motor age had not yet advanced far enough to bring on heavy demands for gasoline and lubricating oils, but he displayed no great interest for several years.

Even after he had leased a part of his holdings in the half dozen counties which made up his domain, and even after the Texas Company began developing on the *Zacaquiesta,* one of the major shallow oil fields of the world,  he could scarce reconcile himself to greasy derricks and rumbling trucks.

"They leave my gates open," he used to complain, thinking always of his stock ... now bald-faced Herefords.

Still later he went into the oil business himself, though somewhat reluctantly. He built refineries, tank cars and hundreds of filling stations, but on every piece of equipment he caused to be painted that coat-of-arms which (to him) looked a great deal better on a steer's hide than on a gas pump—the three reversed D's.

The "black gold" made his fortune one of the greatest in all the Southwest, but those many millions failed to change the son of Dan Waggoner from his original course ... for there was nothing in his ambition which even hinted at oil wells. Even in his later years he did not call himself an oil man; he preferred to be known as a cattleman and horseman ... a spirit always reflected in his own corner of the twenty-story office building he erected in Fort Worth.

The walls are covered with pictures of cattle and thoroughbred horses, and decorated with mounted steer and bull heads, but you will search in vain for one photo of a derrick or cluster of storage tanks. Once I heard him say:

"A man who doesn't admire a good beef steer, a good horse, and a pretty woman ... well, something is wrong with that man's head."

But that third, and seldom talked about, division of his business helped him to realize to the fullest one of the points of his boyhood ambition—"to own the best horses in the country."

In 1931 he staked $2,000,000 on a whim ... a sort of wager with himself that horse racing, outlawed in Texas since 1909, again would be legalized to encourage the breeding of better horses in the State. On his 3,000-acre farm midway between Dallas and Forth Worth he built *Arlington Downs*, one of the finest racing plants in the world, and he filled his own private stables with some of the best blooded horses he could buy.

He won that bet, at least temporarily, but on the morning

following the day in May, 1933, when Governor Miriam A. Ferguson signed a legislative bill approving race bets under the pari--mutuel system, the eighty-two-year-old master of the Downs suffered a stroke of paralysis.

He didn't see the first races, which brought his red, white and blue silks back to Texas tracks for the first time since 1909, but during the fall meet in 1934 he was often brought to the Downs in a long roadster which was parked in the infield near the finish line.

He could not see the horses in action, his illness having impaired his vision, but he could hear the pounding of the hoofs as they came thundering down the stretch, and that alone made him happy.

And quite often, during those fall days of 1934 he would have his chauffeur drive him to the stables for a visit with his thoroughbreds. The trainers would bring each horse to the cattleman's car and though he couldn't see he would caress each velvety nose and call each horse by name. And he knew them all—*Strideaway, Money Getter, Quatre Bras II, Chuck Wagon, Kerrio,* and even some of the yearlings.

### Every horse in the Three-D stable knew the Master

But once, while this ritual was taking place, there was a commotion at one end of the stable . . . a frantic neighing and a splintering of boards as heels drummed against the walls of a stall. It was *Cow Puncher,* the saddler which the Master of the Downs had used so often to ride about the plant in the days before his illness.

"I don't know what's the matter with that *Cow Puncher* horse," said one of the stable attendants. "Must be turnin' outlaw on us."

"No," said Dan Deering, chief stud groom for Three D stables, "I think I know what's wrong."

For answer Deering went to *Cow Puncher's* loose box and

unlatched the door. The old pony, once a fast one himself, stepped out. He hesitated but a moment, as though to get his bearings, and then dashed to the long, shiny roadster . . . to put his head through the open window and nuzzle his master affectionately.

And among those who watched as the Master called his favorite's name was one who said: "Don't tell me that a horse isn't something more than just a horse!"

*Cow Puncher* always knew when the big roadster was parked outside the stable, and he always demanded to be let out—but through the crisp days of December he waited in vain. The Master never came again.

On December 11, Tom Waggoner, one of the last of the great cattle kings, died from a second stroke and two days later he was buried within a stone's throw of one who remains a neighbor even in death, Burk Burnett.

But, of course, *Cow Puncher* couldn't be expected to know about such things . . . or could he?

The ranch goes on . . .

Thousands of Texas Herefords still wear the brand of the Three D's, and oil still flows from under the derricks which stud the acres of the vast cattle kingdom—but *Arlington Downs* the monument Tom Waggoner built to the thoroughbred, has passed into oblivion.

Early in June of 1937 a special session of the 45th Legislature passed a bill repealing the pari-mutuel betting law, striking a death blow at the $2,000,000 racing plant; and later in the month Guy and Paul Waggoner, sons of the cattleman, began selling off equipment and running stock, including the stars of the Three D stables.

And among the stockmen of North Texas there are some who believe that it is just as well that Tom Waggoner was not here to witness the finale, the shattering of his fondest dream.

—For Tom Waggoner was one whose love for horses was far greater than that of most men.

BRAND
W. T. WAGGONER
RANCH

# Burk Burnett
## of the
## Four Sixes

BURK BURNETT

QUANAH PARKER

● A friend of Chief Quanah Parker, he was king of the Kiowa and Comanche country

IT WAS in the early hours of morning that the yelling savages had descended on the bedding herd, and they struck with such suddenness that even the night riders were caught off guard.

Just a swift rush, a pounding of hoofs, a chorus of troubled nickering as the thud of more hoofs joined in the melee—and old Jerry Burnett of Denton Creek, Texas, could check on his loss sheet a remuda of horses as good as any that ever worked a herd along the trail to Kansas.

Those painted gentlemen of the north Indian Territory hills, the warriors of the Osage Nation, could count themselves the winners . . . by about twenty head.

Old Jerry Burnett was not there in person to appraise his loss in horseflesh that day in 1867, but he was well represented. He had put his son in charge of this trail outfit, made up of ten men and seventeen hundred head of longhorns, bound for the Abilene market.

Burk Burnett was only eighteen years of age at the time, but even then he could handle men and cattle like a veteran. Only the year before he had gone up the trail with Wiley Robin, receiving fifty dollars a month and furnishing his own horses, but this was his first experience as trail boss and he wanted to justify his father's trust.

Young Burk, after the lightning Osage raid had passed, took stock of the situation at once. Luckily the attack had been so swift that the longhorns had held on the bedground, and . . . more luck . . . enough horses were left to give each man a mount. This short horse situation could be regarded as serious, but—

"We'll move on," said the eighteen-year-old trail boss. "This herd is going through."

Move on they did, but throughout the remainder of that drive to Kansas the men walked during the day that the ponies might be saved for possible emergencies. The cattle did go through, and Burk returned to Texas with a good profit in his pocket. His father, well pleased, gave him as compensation, an interest in stock being held on Denton Creek.

Thus the beginning of a new cow kingdom in North Texas.

Samuel Burk Burnett had been in Texas since his tenth year. Born in Bates county, Missouri, January 1, 1849, he had few scholastic advantages in childhood days, but he learned thoroughly all the lessons of frontier life. His father was one of the farmer victims of the bloody Ruffian and Jayhawker raids in 1857 and 1858. After the family's home had been wrecked during the latter year, old Jerry decided to migrate. The early days of 1859 found the family jolting southward across the Indian Territory in a wagon. Denton Creek in Texas was the destination.

Here, on the open range, Jerry Burnett entered the cattle business with a small herd, which grew so rapidly during the next few years that he was in good position to take his profits when the trails were opened to the Kansas markets in the 'Sixties.

The first expansion began shortly after young Burk's return from the successful venture of 1867, and with the son taking the leading role. It was about this time that he acquired a small Denton county herd carrying a brand which remains, even to this day, the family coat-of-arms—the 6666.

In various parts of the cattle country may be heard a colorful story regarding the acquisition of that brand—some saying that Burk Burnett adopted it after winning a big stake with four sixes in a poker game—but this version appears to be just that, a story.

Anyhow, Burnett adopted the 6666 as his permanent brand, and it was on the hides of eleven hundred steers he drove to Wichita, Kansas, in 1873. He arrived at the rail terminal at an unfortunate time . . . during the market jam of that year . . . and he couldn't sell at even a fair price.

**Burnett killed buffalo that molested his cattle herd**

He stayed on a few weeks hoping that the market would improve, but since it didn't, and since "expenses were eating the heads off two or three steers a day," he dropped back to winter on the Osage reservation in the Territory. Then, in the Fall of 1874, with a year's weight on his stock, he sold in Wichita and went home with a profit of ten thousand dollars.

Photograph by W. D. Smithers
*That mournful bellow*

That winter Burnett bought thirteen hundred head in the Nueces and Rio Grande country and drove them north to the Little Wichita. Describing that move in later years he once wrote:

"I recollect as distinctly as if it were yesterday when I drove my first herd of cattle into that territory. My journey ended in the vicinity of the present location of Wichita Falls, and it would be hard to imagine a lonelier or more desolate place. At one time the buffaloes were so numerous and threatened so much injury to cattle that I actually had a Mexican employed to follow me around with a large seamless sack filled with cartridges . . . in order to do away with the buffalo more speedily. On one occasion we killed three hundred buffaloes before succeeding in driving them from our herd."

Owing to the defeat of the Quanah Parker Comanches that year by General R. S. Mackenzie in Tule Canyon, the country was becoming much safer; and Burnett began buying all-steer and fattening for the market. It was a new method for that part of the country, and it worked successfully, but the great drouth of 1881 forced the Four-Sixes up to Red River.

Meantime, Burnett bought land, which could be obtained then at prices as low as twenty-five cents an acre. He established headquarters near where Wichita Falls later would stand, and hauled the lumber for his house from Fort Worth, one hundred and twenty-five miles away. Meantime he had been married—to Miss Margaret Loyd, daughter of a Fort Worth banker.

The middle 'Eighties brought the great period of expansion to the 6666. With his neighbors, D. Waggoner & Son, he went into the Kiowa and Comanche reservation of the Territory to lease three hundred thousand acres of grazing land. Burnett's banker father-in-law, M. B. Loyd, was interested to some extent in this venture.

Burk Burnett took a leading part in this land leasing program. Being a friend of the hereditary chief, Quanah Parker, he acted as a sort of liasion agent between the cattlemen and the Indians, who gave him the Comanche name of *Mas-sa-suta* Burnett, meaning "Big Boss", or "He says so."

The cattlemen—usually the Waggoners, the Suggs, the Herrings, and others—would often meet and discuss leasing problems. Then Burnett, more often than not, would meet the

Comanche chief and close the deals. Leases were made from the head man through the tribal agencies and payments were made direct to the Indians themselves.

Tom Slack of Forth Worth accompanied Mr. Burnett on one of the annual pay-offs, and he describes the journey like this:

"I was working for Mr. Loyd in the California and Texas Bank at Fort Worth in the late 'Eighties, and I recall that when Burnett and I left Fort Worth we carried two satchels filled with currency . . . his share of the lease money. We traveled to Wichita Falls on the Fort Worth and Denver and met other cattlemen at Four-Sixes headquarters near the present town of Burkburnett. Next morning all the cattlemen belted on their six-shooters, took up their Winchesters and satchels of currency, boarded hacks and crossed the Red River, to be met on the Territory bank by an escort of cavalry from Fort Sill. Then we were escorted to the Indian agency at Anadarko.

"The Comanches and Kiowas were waiting, and for three days we passed ten dollar bills through the windows at the agency—ten dollars a head on presentation of the ration tickets the government issued to Indians in those days. Some of the Comanches opposed the leasing and were too proud to take the money and we came to the end of the payment with a good surplus on hand. The cattlemen turned this money over to the government to be credited to the tribes."

The handling of the Indians required a certain amount of tact and diplomacy and sometimes Tom Waggoner and Burk Burnett would bring their friend Quanah into Fort Worth for a cattlemen's convention, or to see the sights of the city—and one of these trips almost cost the Comanche chief the loss of his prestige in the tribe.

Another chief, Yellow Bear, accompanied him on this ill-fated junket, and when the two retired for the first night at the old Delaware Hotel, Yellow Bear, unaccustomed to the innovations of civilization, blew out the gas jet instead of turning the stop-cock. In the morning Yellow Bear was found dead, but physicians succeeded in bringing Quanah back from the borders of the Happy Hunting Ground.

### The Death of Yellow Bear was hard to explain

Yellow Bear was a great man in the tribe and when his body was returned to the reservation, Quanah, who accompanied it, was treated with a distinct coolness. The head man gave him to understand that his version of Yellow Bear's death just wouldn't go down—that they couldn't be asked to believe that a man could blow out a fire and then lie down and die. And it might have been an unhappy thing for Quanah's prestige had not some Fort Worth cattlemen carried to the reservation two big bottles of ammonia. These they placed under the noses of certain head men to prove that "bad air" could be a very real and terrible thing.

But all did not go peacefully among the cattlemen themselves on the Kiowa-Comanche wide ranges. Burnett and Cal Sugg, the dark-haired giant from the San Angelo country, were continually at loggerheads over  fence lines and lease boundaries. Although they often met in general lease discussions, each came in time to regard the other as Personal Enemy No. 1.

On one occasion, after a particlarly bitter quarrel, they met in the lobby of the Delaware Hotel and both men drew revolvers at the same time. Tom Waggoner, so the story goes, stepped between the two and averted what possibly might have been a tragedy . . . a tragedy which might have had far-reaching results, for both were great men in the Southwestern livestock industry.

Another incident showing the enmity between the two cattle outfits occurred in the First National Bank at Decatur, where a back room meeting was being held on lease matters. At one side of a table sat Daniel Waggoner, while across from him was Tom Yarbrough, late president of the First National Bank in Fort Worth.

A few minutes after these two gentlemen had seated themselves the other two conferees arrived—Burk Burnett and Ike Sugg, a brother and partner of Cal. They took seats across from each other, but not until each had shifted his six-shooter around to the front; and throughout the meeting they exchanged no word, each addressing his remarks to Dan Waggoner.

This was an important meeting, for at the turn of the century Washington had sent orders for the cattlemen to vacate their leases in the Kiowa-Comanche country in preparation for the government's plan to open the area to homesteaders. Since the orders were for immediate removal, the cattlemen saw themselves faced with almost unavoidable losses in the hasty removal of cows and young calves, and the meeting in Decatur was one of several which resulted in Burk Burnett's departure for Washington to put the case of the stockmen before the government.

Theodore Roosevelt had been president but a short time, and Burk Burnett went directly to him. With him went Senator Joe Bailey of Texas.

The President looked up from his desk as the two Texans entered his office at the White House and of course, knew Joe Bailey, but he wondered about the sandy-haired, blue-eyed man with the heavy mustache. Mr. Roosevelt recognized in the slight stoop of the visitor's shoulders and in the slight curvature of the legs, a type he had seen in the Northwest.

"Mr. President," said Senator Bailey, "I want you to meet a cattleman from Texas . . . Mr. Burk Burnett."

*T. R.* extended his hand.

"Glad to know you, Mr. Burnett," he said," "I'm a kind of cattleman myself."

"I'm glad to hear that, Mr. President," replied Burnett. "It's a cattleman I'm huntin'."

And then he sat down and told the President the whole story—explained the troubles the cattlemen would face if forced to move at once from the Kiowa-Comanche country. The President proved a good listener, and when the Texan had completed his recital he acted in characteristic fashion. According to the story Burnett told when he returned home, Roosevelt called Secretary of the Interior Hitchcock and said he wanted a change made in the order opening the Comanche country. Hitchcock, so the story goes, refused, whereupon Roosevelt told him that if the order wasn't changed he would change it himself. Anyhow, the Burnetts, the Waggoners and some of the other operators were granted a two-year stay.

At the end of that time the various outfits moved back across the Texas line. Both the 6666 and the Three-D's resumed operations on home ranges. And like his neighbor, Tom Waggoner, the Boss of the 6666 soon found himself with an oil field, which developed the boom town which took his name, Burkburnett, near the Red River line of Wichita county.

When the derricks began crowding the cattle, the Four-Sixes again expanded—branching out farther into Wichita county, and into King county to the west. Meanwhile, Mrs. Burnett and the cattleman were divorced and he had taken a second wife, Mary Couts Barradell of Weatherford.

**Brand of Four-Sixes still prominent on Texas steers**

The latter portion of Burk Burnett's life was spent in Fort Worth—where he built a mansion and an office building—but he made frequent trips between the city and headquarters of the 6666.

It was on one of these periodical journeys that he faced one of those experiences which often came to cattlemen. In the north country he had had difficulties regarding cattle with a stockman named Farley Sears, and on the ranges it was considered a foregone conclusion that gunplay would be inevitable should the two men meet.

And in 1916 at Paducah they did meet—in the wash room of the Paducah Hotel. Sears was washing his face as Burnett entered the door. He glanced up, recognized his enemy, and started for his gun—an automatic pistol carried in his right hand pants pocket—but his wet hands prevented a speedy draw.

Burk Burnett saw the move, and in the twinkling of an eye his own 45 Colt was out of the holster and in his right hand. Farley Sears died before he could complete his draw . . . and a few weeks later a jury turned in a verdict of self defense and justifiable homicide. Once before in his career Mr. Burnett had experienced similar trouble—in a shooting on one of his ranges—but that, too, in self defense.

Burk Burnett died in Fort Worth in June of 1922, and among his various bequests he left to the city—as a memorial to Burk, Jr., a son of the second marriage—a downtown park. A son of the first marriage, Tom Burnett, died in 1939 at Iowa Park; and, like his father, he was a cattleman.

Before he died Burk Burnett saw his ranch become one of the greatest in Texas; and under the Estate, which now is managed by John Burns, it remains, even now, one of the larger kingdoms. Present headquarters are at Guthrie in King county, but the four hundred thousand acre domain also extends into three other counties, Hutchinson, Wichita and Carson.

—And the brand of the Four-Sixes still is prominent on the Hereford hides which go to market.

BRAND
BuRK BURNETT

# Cowtowns

# and

# Cowboys

GOIN' TO TOWN

● How the range riders went
to town and of what trans-
pired when they arrived

OLD TASCOSA

**M**R. BILLIE BLEVINS,
late of the Texas Rangers, hummed a little cow camp melody
as he polished his "likker" glasses and pyramided them on
the shelf of the back bar in the Toyah Saloon.

Mr. Blevins was happy, for the "time of feast" was at hand —meaning that the great Spring roundup was moving up from the Barrilla Mountains to comb out the Trans-Pecos for mavericks which had escaped the branding irons in the previous year.

There would be merriment in the bar that night when the cattlemen ... perhaps two hundred of them, representing every brand within a radius of one hundred miles ... galloped into town, each with a sweaty shirt on his back and a long thirst in his throat.

These men would be taking "whisky with its hat off," none of the fancy mixed drinks such as those served in the White Elephant at Fort Worth, and that meant money in the till of Billie Blevins. Again he mentally checked his stock—a barrel of Old Crow, three kegs of Hill and Hill, and in addition to a varied assortment of bottled goods, two big barrels of Cedar Run.

Ah! There was the stuff to ease the troubles of hard-working round-up crews; and the saloon keeper of Toyah smiled a little pridefully as he glanced at the verse on the card over the back bar. It was something of his own composition, and it left no doubt of the proprietor's own choice among the wares he sold:

"Of all the whiskey beneath the sun,
We think the best is Cedar Run;
It'll make you laugh and make you shout,
And it'll send you to glory the shortest route.
And when you've reached the Golden Gate
Just tell old Peter you feel first rate;
For along your way you had lots of fun—
And laid it all to Cedar Run."

Toyah, thirty miles west of the meandering Pecos River, was a typical "cow town" of the eighties. It didn't have a

Chamber of Commerce, it didn't boast a Board of City Development—just one combination grocery and dry goods store— but it did have the Toyah Saloon. That saw-dust floored oasis with its long plank bar, its small and oft-replaced back mirror, and its two pool tables in the rear, was decidedly the center of things.

It was a rough and reckless group of men who tied their horses to the hitching rail before its doors in the time of the general roundup, but Billie Blevins, former member of Captain G. W. Arrington's company of Texas Rangers, (he died in Fort Worth in 1939) remembered with affection most of the boys who took liquor at his bar, and took it straight.

"They were rough," said he, "but as fine a bunch of men as you'll find anywhere. I remember that they used to come in tired, grimy and dirty from a day's hard ride, each man with his Stetson pulled down almost to his eyes. They would mumble out orders for a round of whiskey, and after the first those hats would be pushed back a little. With each following round, the hats would go back a little more, until after the third or fourth they would be resting on the backs of the owner's heads. Then they'd usually go to their wagons, clean up, put on their best clothes and come back for the night's fun."

#### They didn't get too rough, just did a lttle shooting

The night's fun, according to the former saloon keeper of Toyah, usually meant shooting the glasses off the back bar, the balls off the pool tables, and blasting out the coal oil lights with .45 slugs.

"But," added Mr. Blevins, "they seldom got too rough. It was all in fun, and they always paid for everything they shot up. I always took pride in the way I could pyramid my glasses on the back bar, but after every roundup visit I had to send for a new stock. I knew how to get along with the boys. For instance, when they'd start shootin' the balls off the pool tables I'd reach under the bar and get the old .45 I had carried in the Rangers and then say: 'Watch me get the fifteen ball.' And I always managed, too, to get one of the lights before the boys put 'em all out. But sometimes, after the roundup had passed on, I'd have to use a lot of putty on those pool tables. . . "

Such was Toyah in the good old days, and there were other municipalities of similar complexion—Tepee City, Mobeetie, Snyder, Colorado City, Clarendon, (sometimes called "the Saint's Roost") and old Tascosa (quite the opposite.)

Tepee City was even smaller than Toyah but Billy Meador of Plainview, likewise an old Arrington Ranger, believes it must have been the locale for one of the first West Texas stock "conventions."

"One day in 1882," says he, "I was one of twelve men with "Cap" Arrington on a ride across the Plains. Late in the afternoon down under the Caprock in Motley county . . . on the present Matador range . . . we came upon a little shack on the banks of Tepee Creek."

It was (held Meader) a queer sort of place . . . a sort of Tepee constructed of willow poles which had been plastered over with mud, and when the Rangers rode up a man put his head out of the shack for a squint at the visitors. "Cap" Arrington sized up this individual and then asked:

"What do you call this place . . . has it any name?"

"It has," replied the man of the teepee, and then with a show of dignity: "This, sir, is Teepee City."

The Rangers got down to "jaw" a bit and ease their saddles. They learned that their host's name was Cooper and that the teepee served not only as a small store but as postoffice for the boys who were working with the wagons of the cow outfits in the surrounding country. They learned something else, too—that a stockman's "convention" would be held there next day, and that in preparation for the event the storekeeper had freighted in an ample supply of beer and more lusty beverages.

Even then preparations were being made to put up two makeshift shacks, one to serve as a bunk house and the other as a restaurant . . . beef having been slaughtered to stock the latter. And so when the storekeeper suggested that "you fellers better stay over" "Cap" Arrington "allowed as how that might be a good idea."

The Captain had been thinking. He wondered, first, if Cooper "could be handled" for stocking liquor and selling it without a license, but since he wasn't sure of his ground on that score he decided to stay anyway, just in event his presence might be needed at the "convention."

"And that convention was a sight," recalls Billy Meador. "The wagons started rollin' in early in the morning, an' as far as I could see the main business those saddle warmers had to conduct concerned monte, stud poker and liquor. They was rarin' to go and by noon they was setting up the cups and plates in the restaurant and shootin' 'em off the table. I don't know how much ammunition they used, but they shot down one wall of that shack and then cut the bunks and bunk house to pieces with Colt slugs. They even took one fellow out and threw him in Teepee Creek. The man nearly drowned . . ."

But when the punchers decided to turn the attention of their revolvers on the Teepee itself, "Cap" Arrington put down his booted foot. That, held the Captain, was the postoffice and not the "convention" floor . . . and he went inside with a couple of six-shooters and defied the merry makers to fire one shot through the mud walls. They didn't, for the Captain was known for a man who could handle a wicked brace of guns.

And so the delegates diverted themselves by purchasing a barrel of sorghum molasses, rolling it down hill, and shooting it full of holes as it rolled—just to see the sorghum spew.

Playful fellows, these early riders of the range, but it should be remembered that their sports, such as they were, necessarily were home-made . . . like the game of stripping, for instance. Because of that Billy Meador, when he was riding with the cow outfits, once arrived in Colorado City in little more than his Stetson and his shop-made boots.

"Wildest roundup I ever saw, that one in '83," he recalls. "Eight or ten outfits in the bunch, and we was workin' in toward Colorado City. Just before we got there some of the boys started a strippin' game. I was ridin' point on a herd, with all the rest of the boys back behind, when suddenly a big 9R man loped up beside me with a grin on his face, reached over from his horse and jerked a sleeve off my shirt. I tried to keep away from him, but he rode up again, got me by the collar, and ripped the back outa that shirt. When we got into Colorado I was almost in my boots and hat, and most of the others were in the same fix."

But speaking of roundups one of the strangest, and most humorous in the annals of the *Llano Estacado* concerns an unidentified cowboy of the Indian days who went out to brand a few calves and was fired on by a Kiowa who had strayed down from the Territory reservation on business best known to himself.

When the bullet whizzed past his head the 'puncher didn't give the Indian time to reload, but jumped on his horse, spread a convenient loop, roped the redskin, and dragged him back to the branding fire. There he hog-tied his man, heated an iron and stamped it on the captive's right hip, then let him go with the comment: "Don't let anybody tell you you're a maverick . . . 'cause you'r carryin' the brand o' one o' the best outfits between here and the Mexico line."

The story goes that this cowboy, in later days, often made the boast that he had stock on the north side of Red River and "that if the market ever gets better in Kansas I may round him up sometime and trail him to Abilene."

It wasn't all range in those hectic times. There were a few cowtowns, sprawling villages in the sea of grass, but lively, rough-and-ready municipalities after the fashion of the day.

### Old Tascosa was lively place when the punchers came in

In 1880 a cattleman of the Indian Territory returned home from Texas after a month's absence and told his wife to pack the pots and kettles and gather up the kids—because "we're agoin' to move to Texas."

The good woman was not at all surprised that her lord and master had once again decided to migrate—for she was accustomed to sudden shifts of residence—but she was mildly curious about the social aspects of the new range. Might there be, she wanted to know, some town where the children could enjoy the benefits of culture and the polite refinements of civilization?

"Shore is," replied her spouse, "one of the most up-an'-comin' little towns in the west."

He was thinking of a sand-blown little village near the banks of the sluggish Canadian, the communtiy in which he had spent the major portion of his month abroad. He tried to describe the place . . . the rolling wind-troubled hills about it, the landscape which stretched into the sunset. . .

"Best town in those parts," said he. "They's a cuppla good stores, an' most o' the saloons seem right decent like."

This latter reference reminded his woman of one of the prime necessities of life.

"What about the water?" she asked. "Were it fitten to drink?"

The head of the household knit his brow in surprise. He appeared, for the moment, quite perplexed.

"Now ain't that hell!" he murmured. "I plumb forgot to taste it!"

He was speaking of Tascosa, one of the three cow capitols

of the Panhandle in the 'Eighties. Established in the late 'Seventies as the southern terminus of a freight line from Dodge City, Tascosa, in its prime, was a city of about five hundred souls . . . and, before long, many ghosts.

The civic life of the community centered in the five or six saloons grouped about the sun-baked plaza, and they all were well patronized by the boys who came in from the ranges to buy supplies and break, incidentally, the monotony of long days in the saddle.

Tascosa boasted a distinguished clientele at times. During that period when he was stealing Texas horses for use in the New Mexico cow theft trade the inimitable and none-too-gentle Billy the Kid often liquored at Tascosa's bars . . . and so did Pat Garrett, the man who later killed him. Bat Masterson came there and so did Billy Tilghman, a fellow buffalo hunter. Cape Willingham was another familiar figure on the streets, and in the cemetery above the town may be found, even to this day, proof of his prowess with a gun during the days when he wore the star as Tascosa's city marshal.

He was cock of the walk and ruler of the roost, the recognized arbiter of law and order around such business enterprises as the Last Chance, Wagon Yard, Jack Ryan's Saloon, the Jim East Saloon and the Martin Dunn Bar—and it was Cape's six-shooter which contributed the first customer to that grim plot of ground which was to earn the name of Boothill Cemetery.

The gentleman thus honored was a cowboy who came up the trail from South Texas with a herd bound for Dodge. It had been a long and thirsty ride and, quite naturally, this lad loosened up with a group of similar spirits, imbibed a little too freely, then started on a yelling, shooting ride through the town which—as the Tascosa *Pioneer* used to say—"was guiltless of church or Sunday school."

Cape Willingham, hearing the audible evidence of this afront to peace and dignity, came out of Ryan's Saloon to put things back into the proper groove. The cowboy went for his gun, but the city marshal was a shade too fast, with the result that the hapless cowboy was hauled in a buckboard out to the little sandhill overlooking the city.

Boothill made its start that day, and before it was to be left in peace it was to receive some thirty men, most of them with their boots and clothes on, just as they were shot down, and most of them sodded under without benefit of clergy.

"There wasn't a preacher nearer than two hundred miles,"

Photograph by Erwin E. Smith
*"Bury me not on the lone prairie"*

said Mrs. Mickey McCormick, an old settler who attended many of these rites, "and I doubt if there was a Bible or prayer book much closer . . . and since there wasn't a soul in Tascosa who could say a prayer we would just look as solemn as possible while they were being buried."

Boothill received its largest single day consignment on March 21, 1886—four men killed in a general ruckus in front of Jim East's Saloon. A woman caused it—a woman known as Sally Emory—and the motive, as nearly as ever determined, was unrequited love.

On the afternoon of March 21 four 'punchers from the LS Ranch rode into Tascosa seeking wine, women, song and trouble. Their names were Ed King, Fred Chilton, Frank Valley and John Long, and they were, even for this cow capital, a cocky bunch.

Long was just an ordinary cow hand, but the other three lately had been imported from Kansas to act as protection men for the LS, and since they had the backing a big outfit usually gives hired gunmen, they felt wild and wooly and strictly uncurried.

The first stop was at a saloon in the Hogtown suburb, where they "tanked up," insulted a few citizens, and then drifted on to other bars, at one of which they met Sally, the dance hall girl. And Sally was said to be beautiful—more beautiful even than Rocking-Chair Emma, Panhandle Ann, and Drowsy Dollie, others among the more eye-filling damsels of the community.

It appears that this Sally was in love—with Len Woodruff, who tended bar in the Dunn oasis—and that since her advances had been spurned by Mr. Woodruff, she wasn't exactly pleased about it. So Sally, sensing a golden opportunity with the arrival of the LS men, bantered King, more in jest than in earnest, to look up Woodruff and put a bullet hole through him.

King put away a few more drinks and announced that the idea was not without appeal, then set forth from the bar to attend to the matter. News of this sort, however, has a habit of traveling fast, and the LS gunman had scarcely started out before Len was informed that trouble was on the way.

Music and fun—and new graves on the slope of Boothill

He promptly closed bar and hid himself in a dark place between the saloon and an adobe house, and it was not long before King and John Long appeared. Finding the bar closed they started back, but in that moment Woodruff decided to act. Stepping out from his place of concealment, he opened with two guns. King fired one shot, which wounded Len in the left leg, then dropped dead.

Long had already taken to his heels, and a few seconds later he rushed into the bar where Chilton and Valley were drinking with the shout: "Woodruff's killed Ed!"

Valley and Chilton went into action immediately, dashing from the saloon with drawn guns, ready to pot Mr. Woodruff on sight. It was at this juncture that Jesse Sheets, the proprietor of the Dirty Shame Cafe, came out of his establishment in his nightshirt. He had heard the first shots and had arisen from his bed to investigate . . . but that was a fatal mistake. Frank Valley, in his hazy condition, mistook him in the darkness for Woodruff, and the proprietor of the Dirty Shame went down with a bullet through his heart.

Woodruff, meantime, had barricaded himself in the adobe house with two revolvers and a Winchester. At the approach of the enemy he began taking pot-shots into the dark. In their enthusiasm Chilton and Valley rushed the house, emptied their revolvers into the door, then retired to reload. Before they could do so Woodruff got their range. Taking careful aim he killed Chilton first; and then, as Valley turned to run, punctured him.

Using his Winchester as a crutch, Woodruff dragged himself away to take refuge in the ranch house of a friend, who protected him until the excitement had died away. Later he was tried and acquitted.

Thus ended one episode in the night life of old Tascosa—
with four new graves on Boothill.

But there was, at times, some semblance of law and order
in the town. Sometimes the Tascosa *Pioneer* would announce
in its columns: "District Court meets a week from Monday,
and we look for music and fun then."

*When cowmen published their brands
in the newspaper they used illustra-
tions like this to attract attention*

However, it wasn't all fun for the judge when he attempted
to draw jury panels.  Cowboys were drifters and seldom land
owners.  Once in 1884, when thirty men were charged with
cattle stealing, the judge had to ask the district attorney to
deed city lots to prospective jurors and put their names in the
deed book.  Then the questioning and qualifying of the panel
proceeded.

The judges and attorneys in those days traveled from court
to court in a hack.  Up in the Panhandle one may hear the
story of Judge Frank Willis and how the hack in which he
was riding once became bogged in quicksand on a crossing of
the Canadian.

The attorneys jumped out and swam ashore, but the judge
was fat and couldn't swim.  He stuck to the hack.  When the
others reached shore, they looked back and saw the court's

law books floating downstream. Immediately a shout went up for "somebody to save the law."

"To hell with the law!" yelled the judge. "Somebody save the court!"

The decline of Tascosa started in the '90's when the Rock Island railroad decided not to build through the town, a decision which drew from the *Pioneer's* editor the following comment:

"Truly, this is a world which has no regard for the established order of things, but knocks them sky west and crooked, and lo, the upstart (meaning Amarillo) hath the land and its fatness."

Contemporary with Tascosa were two other cow capitals in the Panhandle—Old Clarendon, a few miles from the present town of that name; and Mobeetie, the center of all things in Wheeler county to the east.

The former was known as "the Saint's Roost," because at the time of its colonization in 1878 by a group of farmers, the leading spirit had been a Methodist minister, the Rev. L. H. Carhart. But old Clarendon—named, they say, for the English lord of that title—could not long retain its sanctimony under the pressure of conflicting atmospheric conditions. It lost its place on the map when the Fort Worth and Denver railroad missed it by a few miles. Citizens moved over to the line and started a new town.

### A 'Bald-headed whisky town'—That was old Mobeetie

Mobeetie was ... well, Mobeetie; another "bald-headed whiskey" town where it was not at all uncommon for a cowboy to ride down the street with a bottle in one hand and a six-shooter in the other.

In its beginning, during the summer of 1875, it was known by the more simple but less lyrical name of Hidetown, because it was the Texas terminus of the Jones and Plummer Trail and

Old Mobeetie in the high Panhandle was a typical cowtown of the pioneer era. This picture made in the '80s shows a well in the street, but the cowboys found other places to slake their thirsts.

a place where freighters from Dodge City delivered goods and picked up buffalo hides to haul back to Dodge.

When the town took its first official name, it chose Sweetwater, after the creek on which it was located. Because of conflict with the Nolan county city of the same name, the Panhandle town later changed to *Mobeetie*, Indian for Sweetwater.

It had, like Tascosa, an ample supply of saloons, gambling halls and . . . as so many of the old-timers called them . . . fancy houses. The population, with the exception of the soldiers from nearby Fort Elliott, the sisterhood of Magdalena, and the transient trail-driving cowboys who drifted through on their way north, had much in common with the citizenry of any other small town of that era. The thirteen saloons— lucky or unlucky, as you will—made the difference.

Naturally it was the first place thought of when cow hands and ranchmen from the surrounding ranges decided to go to town—but there is little in the records to indicate that many of them stopped to refresh themselves at the well which stood in the center of upper Main street.

Sometimes, according to old-timers, the boys didn't even wait to dismount, but guided their horses right through the doors of the Exchange Saloon, ordered drinks, and took them in the saddle . . . and the townspeople thought nothing at all about it.

By these things, however, the cowboy of the early days should not be judged. Mrs. Temple Houston, who once lived in the city and saw many a cowboy ride whooping down the street, shooting a revolver with one hand and taking a drink from a bottle with the other, used to say that "they were harmless and did not mean to cause any trouble."

—Just a bunch of boys "loosening up" and breaking the spell of solitude after weeks and sometimes months of lonely riding on the range. There was not, in all reality, a better class of men to be found anywhere. They might have been

*Dodge City, Kansas, 1878, front street, the first hotel, the Dodge House, is shown in foreground.*

a little rough at times in earlier days but, as Colonel Charles Goodnight often said, "they were as brave and chivalrous as it is possible to be, and among them bullies and tyrants are almost unknown; and timid men were not known . . . the life did not fit."

The cowboy and the cattleman had no kinship with the hypocrite. He was direct and to the point and when he expressed his mind, either in writing or in speech, he seldom left doubt as to his meaning.

As an example of this directness witness the following letter, written by a Collingsworth county ranch manager to a grocery store:

"August 29, 1892.
Fore Brothers,
Memphis, Texas.
Gentlemen:

The 53 lbs. prunes you lately sent us were more worms than prunes: it is an outrage to try and put off such filthy stuff on us: we utterly refuse to receive and pay for such stuff & the said sack of prunes & worms has been left at Aberdeen in Mrs. J. J. Drew's care to be returned to you.

"We return you the bill & you will please strike out the prunes. It will save a great deal of trouble if you will bear in mind that we only receive & pay for articles that are good.

"Truly yours,
Rocking Chair Ranche, Lim'd,
by A. J. Marijoribanks."

And here is another, received by Manager Frank Hastings of the Swenson Ranch from one of his employes, a cowboy who had gone with a cattle train and had gotten into a wreck. It was posted from Caldwell, Kansas, on November 30, 1906:

"Dear Sir: 6:30 this morning in going to the stockyards to feed at this place another train run into my stock train. On an open switch & killed 2 cows & crippled 4, & the rest of the cows in that car is now all over town, so I got one car less & few cows in another car is feeling sore & some of them only got one horn left.

The crew of both train jumped off & myself, so it was no one hurt. It was not enough left of the engine & one stock car to tell the Fait. 8 or 10 of the Kansas cowboys is out all over Town picking up our Cattle—wish you could see them coming down the street driving one or two of them cows—I think they got about 10 of the cows in a Pen (down in town) & they heard of 5 cows in a cornfield just a little while ago, so I guess they will get most of them back today. I will leave here about 5 p. m. will make tomorrow market.

Yours truly, Dock.

P.S.—This R. R. ought to take charge of this whole shipment & pay for same.

P.S.—The Sheriff shot one cow on the street just a little while ago.

P.S.—The cows down in town is making the horses run off with buggys and running all the women out of town.

P.S.—I think this will cost the R. R. a good deal in this town.

P.S.—The Rail Road they give me a poor & sorry run.

P.S.—They run my cattle 40 hour before this happened without feed."

William Lyon Phelps of Yale, commenting on that letter, said: "There is one thing in which any professor of literature might imitate him—he leaves absolutely no doubt as to his meaning or intention."

There remain a few great ranches on the *Llano Estacado,* a few in the borders of the *Brasada* and the Matagorda, and still a few more in that country which stretches down toward the stream which the Mexicans call the *Rio Bravo del Norte,* but the day of the great cattle kings ... the beef barons who followed in the footsteps of Abraham and Lot, the cow kings of Jordan Valley ... is over.

But in the West of Texas, and in those more southerly areas which send beefsteaks to the platters of the world, still may be found a few men who can find the real meaning in that song of anonymous origin which goes:

"Under the star-studded canopy vast,
   Campfire coffee, and comfort at last;
   Bacon that sizzles and crisps in the pan,
   After the roundup smells good to a man.
   Tales of the ranchmen and rustlers retold,
   Over the pipes as the embers grow cold;
   These are the tunes that memories play,
   Make me a cowboy again for a day."

## THE END